Tyrant or Victim?

A HISTORY
of the
BRITISH
GOVERNESS

Tyrant or Victim?

A HISTORY
of the
BRITISH
GOVERNESS

Alice Renton

Weidenfeld and Nicolson
London

First published in Great Britain in 1991 by
George Weidenfeld and Nicolson Limited
91 Clapham High Street, London SW4 7TA

British Library Cataloguing-in-Publication Data
is available on request.
ISBN 0 297 81168 1

Photoset by Deltatype Ltd, Ellesmere Port
Printed and bound in Great Britain by
Butler and Tanner Ltd. Frome and London

Contents

Acknowledgements

I should like to thank all those who have advised and helped me in
different ways during the preparation of this book, and to mention
with particular gratitude the following:

The Hon. Lady Adams, The Hon. Mrs Susan Baring, Mrs Virginia
Barrington, Mr David Benson, Miss Ann Brooke, Mr Rodney
Castleden, Miss Hazel Chislett of Gabbitas, Truman and Thring, Miss
E. Coward, Lady Robert Crichton Stuart, Mrs A.M. Cunliffe,
ARMCM, The Lord Denman, The Hon. Lady Dundas, Mrs Scrope
Egerton, Mr Paul Eland of Gabbitas, Truman and Thring, Baroness
Elliot of Harewood, The Hon. Mrs Faber, Mrs Noel Fresson, Mr Cecil
Gould, Mrs J. F. Green of Collingham Tutors, The Dowager
Viscountess Hambleden, The Hon. Mrs Harries, Mr R. W. Hayward,
FRICS, Director of SGBI, Lady Heald, Lady Jane Howard, Lady
Susan Hussey, Mr Raymond Johnstone, Mrs Kay Knowles, Mrs
Penelope Loveday, Miss K. Matthews, Lady Alexandra Metcalfe, Mrs
Charlotte Mitchell, The Hon. Mrs Moris-Jones, Sir Jeremy Morse,
Miss Evelyn Northcroft, Miss Hilda Payne, Mrs Tim Raisin, Mr
Kenneth Rose, Miss V. A. Ross, Lady Stormonth-Darling, The
Viscount Scarsdale, Lady Daphne Straight, The Hon. Mrs Talbot,
Mrs Whale of SGBI, and Mr Clive Williams.

I am very fortunate to have had Mrs Hilary Laurie as my editor at
Weidenfeld & Nicolson. I am deeply appreciative, also, of the
assistance given to me by the staff of the London Library, of East Sussex
County Library, Lewes, of the Westminster Library, Maida Vale, of
the Mary Evans Picture Library, and of the Bridgeman Art Library.

Lastly, I acknowledge the debt of gratitude that I owe to Miss Helen
Evans and to Mlle Jeanne Le Gallen (Pipette), and I should like to
thank my family for their tolerance and unfailing encouragement.

Illustrations

For my husband

I would also, in reply to your correspondents' remarks, call the attention of the public to our city prison at Holloway, which for constructive arrangements and completeness of internal management I venture to say is not surpassed, if equalled, by any prison in this or any other country.

I am, Sir, your most obedient servant,
WM. A. ROSE, Member of the Court of Aldermen.
66, Upper Thames-street, Jan. 19.

WHITE SLAVERY.

TO THE EDITOR OF THE TIMES.

Sir,—Will you permit me, through the medium of your valuable paper, to make known one of the many cases of cruelty and insult to which governesses are exposed? I was one of about 50 ladies (most of whom were accomplished gentlewomen) who applied last week, in reply to an advertisement in *The Times*, for a situation as governess in a family in the neighbourhood of Kingsland. The applicants went from all parts of London and its environs; many were in consequence quite overcome with fatigue, having walked long distances to save expense. After having been kept standing in a cold draughty hall more than an hour, I at last obtained an interview with the lady, and learnt that the duties of the governess would consist in educating and taking the entire charge of the children, seven in number, two being quite babies; to perform for them all the menial offices of a nurse, make and mend their clothes; to teach at least three accomplishments, and "fill up the leisure hours of an evening by playing to company." For these combined duties the munificent sum of 10*l.* per annum was offered. I ascertained for a fact that the two domestic servants in the same family were paid respectively 12*l.* and 10*l.* Surely in a country like ours some employment besides that of teaching could be found for educated women, or at least better treatment might be expected for those to whom is intrusted the responsible duty of forming the minds and manners of the rising generation. As the best means of correcting this evil may I beg you, Sir, to wield your powerful pen in behalf of this much-abused class of individuals? A POOR GOVERNESS.

· INTRODUCTION ·

Elfgifu and after

A suitable companion or governess for a young girl, according to Saint Jerome, writing to a group of Christian matrons at the end of the fourth century AD, was not another cheerful young woman with whom she might whisper girlish secrets. An older person, who should ideally be *gravis, pallens, sordidata et subtristis* – severe, pale, sombre and melancholy – would be more likely to engender in her pupil a serious and devout frame of mind.[1] This description does not sound very encouraging for potential young charges, but it is prescient in describing members of a profession which came to have a particularly British association. For many people it still conjures up the image of the typical governess.

From earliest times a governess was a woman, usually a gentlewoman, who was down on her luck and who rarely had any qualification for the position, or any reason for taking it, except that she needed the money. Fifteen centuries after St Jerome, governesses were recruited from among women whom life had left in unfortunate circumstances, and it was not until the twentieth century that the profession became one in which a woman could take any pleasure or pride. Until then she was a helpless victim of the commonly held conviction that the education of girls was a matter of supreme unimportance. If the pupil was held not worthy of intellectual respect, there was no possibility of the teacher faring any better.

In 1846 Anna Jameson wrote,

Where we are to seek for the prototype of the governess in antique time I do not know, unless it be in Minerva herself, whose Olympian avocation it was to keep the Muses and Graces in order, and who taught the daughters of Pandarus to spin and weave; but we do not find that this celestial example served to give any dignity to governesship even in those times. Female arts were taught by females slaves: the liberal arts by men.[2]

Mrs Jameson conveniently disregarded the fact that Minerva was sometimes also portrayed as goddess of the liberal arts, but her evocation of that multi-faceted deity as the earliest of governesses is nevertheless apt on two counts: Minerva taught the daughters of Pandarus only those domestic accomplishments that would make them into good wives, and she herself remained forever celibate.

There are of course many honourable exceptions to the rule of neglect of the education of girls. Charlemagne is one of the first recorded Europeans who considered that his daughters should be well taught, and he decided that they might as well be educated at home rather than, as was the common practice, in a convent. He ensured that their literary education was conducted on the same lines as their brothers'; they were all taught, together with the sons and daughters of other members of the nobility, by Alcuin, an English monk and scholar who came from Archbishop Egbert's school of theology in York and entered the Emperor's service in 782 AD. The girls learnt to spin and weave wool as well – their serious studies did not excuse them from having to become proficient in the usual womanly household occupations.[3]

It is likely that the reputation of Alcuin and of this famous 'palace-school' was an influence in the late ninth century on the English king Alfred, who brought over scholars to teach his own people from the schools founded by Charlemagne. The ravages of the Danes had destroyed many monasteries, especially in the North of England, and Latin was in decline. Though there was some literature in the native Anglo Saxon tongue, Alfred was aware that for religious and general education a revival of Latin was important. The King himself was a late beginner, having been unable even to read at twelve, and starting Latin lessons only at the ripe age of thirty-eight. He undertook an important programme of educational reform, and set aside one sixth of his income to build schools.[4] Like Charlemagne, Alfred made sure his own daughters were properly taught, and the youngest, Aelfthryth, shared her brother Ethelweard's tutors and education, learning to love books and to repeat the Psalms and Saxon poetry by heart.[5] The shortage of books meant that a good memory was a valuable asset in the schoolroom. Six centuries had still to pass before the advent of printing and before books could be mass produced.

Alfred's successor, Edward the Elder, followed his father's example and established a schoolroom in his home in which his eight daughters were taught alongside his sons. (One of them became a nun at the age of three so she cannot have benefited much from this co-education.[6]) A well-born lady named Elfgifu became their governess, and she must have been a success, for she remained at court to care for the next generation as well.

We do not know what particular teaching methods Elfgifu preferred, but it is known that Aldhelm, Abbot of Malmesbury, was producing books in the late seventh century for young people to learn from. He is said to have originated the system of making the pupil memorize long lists of questions and their appropriate answers. It was still used by teachers in Victorian seminaries for young ladies ten centuries later, so probably also by Elfgifu. She may have relied on Aldhelm's textbooks as well. After he had become Bishop of Sherborne he agonized in a letter over the difficulties of writing textbooks for teaching the young:

> But what shall I say of arithmetic, whose long and intricate calculations are sufficient to overwhelm the mind and throw it into despair?[7]

These three fathers, Charlemagne, Alfred and Edward the Elder, at least by the standards of their times, took their daughters' education as seriously as that of their sons. There were not many parents so enlightened, even among the nobility. The concept that girls ought to be educated as thoroughly as boys was soon almost completely to disappear and by the beginning of the twelfth century the fashion for scholarship in women of noble families was gone. It was a sad decline in a country where, four hundred years earlier, the nuns had been the equals of the monks in learning, in theology as well as in the classics. They all copied manuscripts and corresponded in Latin, studying the same books. Education, for those who were in a position to acquire it, had known no sexual boundaries, and nunneries were in effect colleges of education run for successive groups of girls. Many men of note in Anglo-Saxon England had received their learning in settlements governed by women, and the uniquely valuable *Anglo Saxon Chronicle* had been drafted under the auspices of Saxon abbesses.[8]

The nunneries continued as centres of learning, but after the Conquest the nuns' influence as educators declined. Norman French became the vernacular among the nobility, and singing and the writing of verse in that language became the mode. The Latin in which the nuns had studied and taught slowly fell into disuse. The fashionable notions of chivalry that arrived with the Normans led to a marked divergence in the customs of education for boys and girls. Young men were expected to become proficient in archery, hawking, singing and writing verse, together with other knightly accomplishments. For girls there were other subjects to be studied, such as brewing and distilling, the use of herbs for healing, and all kinds of needlework, as well as the skills of running a household. The chatelaine of a castle would instruct the girls in her care in these arts. They also learnt some reading (though not always to write), and could be more advanced in this than many young men, 'who were trained to look on books as monkish and womanish, and not quite suited to a knight or a gentleman'.[9]

All this time the one constant in the education of girls was hand-work: spinning, weaving and embroidery. Without any doubt Elfgifu kept her young charges busy with their needles and spinning wheels. King Alfred's will describes his male heirs as the 'spear-side' of his family, and the females as the 'spindle-side'. While English men were learning to be brilliant craftsman and builders of magnificent cathedrals, the women at home and in the convent schools were learning the fine needlework whose fame spread beyond Britain's shores. Norman ladies arriving after the Conquest were as eager as latter-day tourists to acquire fine specimens of English work, and to learn the local skills.[10]

More and more time was spent by high-born young girls stitching away in the company of their ladies. Quantities of gold thread, silk, pearls and other materials were constantly delivered to their apartments. The chivalric concept, the new emphasis on love, beauty and romanticism that had arrived from southern Europe, turned girls' energies to another kind of learning as well. The social graces became important and much attention was given to deportment and table manners as well as to the art of conversation. The conventions were taught of how to greet a stranger or welcome a guest;[11] a girl must learn to sing and dance with grace and to strive for the ideal style of feminine beauty – a slim, supple body, a tiny mouth and beautiful, expressive hands. Her hair should be worn in a long, thick plait (golden, if she were lucky) and was sometimes dyed with saffron and padded with tow or wool if it were not as abundant as she might wish.[12] With all this to think about it is perhaps not surprising that most girls failed to develop their intellects. Nor, indeed, were they encouraged to do so. The concept that a girl's training was a direct preparation for early marriage was already widespread.

However, educational opportunities were available to the lucky few.

There were small schools in some nunneries where the daughters of fee-paying parents could still receive a serious education, but these were increasingly frowned upon by the bishops, who felt that such learning should be reserved for those taking the veil. Besides, they felt that contact with girls who were due to return to the outside world might be distracting for the nuns. But they were allowed to take some paying pupils if they were particularly short of cash. Throughout the countryside anchoresses, holy women, lived out their secluded lives, alone or with a single maidservant; they too were discouraged by the bishops from taking girl pupils, though this had long been their practice, largely with the same intention of making ends meet.[13]

The number of nunneries in England after the year 1200 remained at between 140 and 150 until the Reformation. Between them they housed some 3,300 inmates. When the Black Death ravaged the land in the middle of the fourteenth century this number dwindled to about 2000.[14] 'With the establishment of universities in the thirteenth century, in which girls had no part, the monasteries lost some of their prestige as centres of learning, and the educational standards of the nunneries fell even lower. In fact many medieval nuns could probably not write at all, even though they may have been able to read, and they spent their leisure time in sewing and embroidery, spinning and weaving.'[15] They could teach their pupils no more than they knew themselves, and these few subjects, allied to a degree of moral training, in time became the extent of what the nunneries could offer to any girl coming to them for an education. Women had become isolated from the mainstream of learning.

By the middle of the fourteenth century convents had lost their role as vocational retreats for devout females, and had mainly become places where unmarried women of high birth could live their lives with dignity. Some were placed there in youth by their fathers, for marriage dowries were a heavy burden on a man with several daughters. Though most nunneries expected a substantial payment before they would accept a girl, to pay their price could be a more economical way of dealing with her future than the alternative: a plain girl or one over twenty would need a large dowry to make her seem attractive, but once a girl had taken her vows, she lost her rights of inheritance, which reverted to the family. Medieval society was a sad place for spinsters.

From the time of the Conquest it became necessary for a well bred English girl to speak and write fluent French. It was the language of the Court and came to be regarded by the ordinary Englishman as a language of refinement and elegance. Though English was the every day language of most people, French came to be part of a well-bred girl's curriculum, both in the nunneries and in the home. Early in the fourteenth century guides to letter-writing in French, with correctly composed letters to copy, were available for the help of parents and governesses. Some were especially adapted for the needs of women – there were model letters from a Queen to a knight, from a knight in prison to his lady, from a lady to her lawyer, from an abbess to a lady, from a mother to her schoolboy son. Their content reflects the needs and life of the period, as a similar manual does today. Especially poignant is one from a girl advising her sister to submit to an unwelcome marriage urged upon her by her parents, a sample letter that might come in useful in any family.[16]

The role of the governess at this date was that of duenna rather than of teacher. By virtue of their having worked in the households of notable employers we know the names of some. Katherine Swynford, sister-in-law of Geoffrey Chaucer[17] and governess to John of Gaunt's daughters, was daughter of a Frenchman, a knight of Hainault. She became mistress to her employer, and eventually, at the age of forty-six, his third wife. Her four illegitimate children by John of Gaunt were far cleverer than his legitimate offspring, which may have caused some embarrassment; but Katherine probably smoothed things over, for she is reputed to have been exceptionally diplomatic, especially in her conduct of her complicated domestic role-change, managing to avoid making enemies among the ladies of the court.[18]

For a governess to become stepmother to her charges may have been out of the normal, but it was quite usual for governesses to fulfil the role of mothers and companions to children in royal families. This could often be the only stable relationship small princesses might know, used as they were as pawns in the political machinations that went on between different European states. In 1396, when Richard II married the eight-year-old French Princess Isabella as part of his peace negotiations with Charles VI of France, the little girl brought with her in her entourage her French governess, Lady de Coucy. King Richard, however, was keen to anglicize his small bride as quickly as possible, and the governess's fondness for an almost regal life style gave him the excuse he needed to dismiss her summarily and dispatch her back to France, her debts having been paid by his order. An English woman, Lady Mortimer, was then appointed governess to Isabella.[19]

In 1398 Mary Hervey, who was governess to the future Henry IV's small daughters Blanche and Phillipa, taught them to read from two of the A.B.C. books that were newly available. These cost 20d and comprised the Pater Noster, Ave, Credo, Ten Commandments and the Graces to be said before and after meals.[20] Philippa, the younger of the two girls, was still barely literate in English and Latin when she was sent away from her homeland at the age of eight, given as bride to Eric of Sweden, Norway and Denmark. An English governess, Dame Katherine Waterton, was appointed to accompany the little girl across the sea to her new life.[21]

The term 'governess' came into use in the fifteenth century, and at this time compares with the French *gouvernante*. It did not necessarily imply a teacher, but could simply mean one who was responsible for the well-being of children, usually those of a royal or noble household, and for directing their education. It later came also to denote a female teacher in a school and though from the nineteenth century it usually signified a private teacher in the family home, the older use persisted: in the 1930s the teachers at Mrs Fife's famous finishing school in Cambridge were still referred to as 'the governesses'.[22]

However, it is with the evolution of the private governess, the female teacher employed by a family to instruct girls, and occasionally young boys, in their own homes, that I am concerned. She is a mainly middle class phenomenon, an anomalous backwater in the mainstream of British education, but not an unimportant one. It was from their own experiences, bitter or inspiring, at the hands of their governess, that various nineteenth-century women drew the energy to make them leaders among the early reformers of woman's education.

Surprisingly, the nineteenth and early twentieth centuries, when movement was finally achieved towards parity in male and female education, also represented the hey-day of the British governess. Hey-day is perhaps too cheerful a word for the time when she existed in the greatest numbers, but the governess of this period is the main subject of my book. I hope to show that she came into being as a result of the attitude of parents throughout several hundred years to the education of their daughters, reflecting their attitudes towards women in general.

Nowadays, there are widely varying notions of the governess: she can be the down-trodden and victimised figure of fun, the brutal and hated tyrant, or the loved and respected member of an appreciative household. Each is a true image and, historically, one succeeded the other.

To understand how this came about it is helpful to give some attention first to the thinking, the battles and the development of the deeply rooted prejudices that delayed in Britain until the mid-nineteenth century the flowering of female education. Every attempt to improve it was subject to Socrates' dictum, 'Women are capable of learning anything that men are willing that they should know.'

[7]

· 1 ·

'Without any cherishing'

In the fifteenth century, private education for girls meant sending daughters into the homes of others so that they might be trained in household skills. This would be after their mother, sometimes with the help of a resident governess, had given them some elementary teaching, with tutors coming in by the day to teach the basics of music, French and dancing before they were 'boarded out'. Many of these children would have only rudimentary reading and writing skills when they were sent away at some stage between the ages of seven and twelve, usually into a household of higher social distinction than their own. It was done, of course, for their own good: the object was 'advancement', which meant the path towards a socially advantageous marriage as early as possible. At the age of about fourteen or fifteen suitable husbands would be found for them, often by their patron.

The system was the same for all, but the type of 'advancement' offered would vary according to the requirements of the girl's family, the depth of her father's purse, and the type of household accepting the boarder. Some girls from lowlier families went to acquire the skills of domestic service, often learning as well at the hands of their guardian the worst abuses that servants could suffer. Some learnt housewifery and needlecraft, the better to care for the home and family of potential husbands. A girl might be trained as a waiting maid in a relation's household, or a gentlewoman in service to a lady of title. The summit of ambition was to become one of the Queen's maids at Court, which could lead to dizzy marital heights.

Often the situation in which they found themselves was very unpleasant. Even in a private household comparable to her own, a girl might be beaten into submission by her foster parent. Life could be quite rough at home as well. There are instances in the well documented life of the Paston family: Elizabeth Paston, as a girl in their home in Norfolk, was made entirely miserable by her overbearing mother, so much so that a worried cousin in 1454 wrote to Elizabeth's brother for help, saying,

> . . . she was never in so great sorrow as she is nowadays, for she may speak with no man, whosoever come . . . nor with servants of her mother's . . . and she hath since Easter the most part been beaten once in the week or twice, and sometimes twice on a day, and her head broken in two or three places.[1]

Lady Paston was not an easy woman to live with and on another occasion is described as 'being set on great malice'.

In those days, when a sentimental view of children was not the norm, there were parents who preferred to employ governesses and supervise the beatings at home, or perhaps administer them themselves, rather than not know precisely what the chosen guardian/foster-parent might be doing to their young. This meant less risk, too, of the misappropriation of the funds they devoted to their offspring's advancement, particularly as it was quite usual to place the fortune, the potential dowry, of a girl in the hands of the guardians for their use during the period she was in their care. Litigation frequently ensued, with fathers charging foster-parents with receiving money for the children's upbringing and using it otherwise, or of withholding the promised education and treating their children simply as servants. Dorothie and Jane Parrott, together with their brother Thomas, were boarded out with a family called Stephynton. Their relation, Sir John Parrott, paid the agreed fees for four years and then stopped, accusing the guardians of having used the children 'as servants to do all the vilest business in their house'. The Stephyntons denied it, maintaining that the girls 'are brought uppe in writinge, redinge, sewinge, both white worke and blacke worke, and playenge of the lute and virginalls, as yonge gentlewomen and maydes of theire ages are accustomed . . .' and that all the children '. . . for their yeares do well come forewarde.'[2]

Some situations were happier and the parents were well pleased, but the girls' own wishes were not taken into account. They were treated entirely according to the whims and convenience of their families. Young

[9]

Anne Paston, sister of Elizabeth, was disposed of quite summarily when the cousin with whom she had been boarded out decided that her presence was becoming inconvenient. He found that the income he was receiving from his tenants was dwindling and decided to get rid of Anne. Lady Paston wrote to her son, 'He proposeth to lessen his household and to live straitlier, wherefore he desireth me to purvey for your sister Anne; he saith she waxeth high and it were time to purvey her a marriage . . . therefore do your part to help her forth.'[3]

Some parents found it more satisfactory to keep their daughters at home. But 'boarding out' was the fashion and it continued, with its abuses, into the seventeenth century, and paved the way for the eventual emergence of boarding schools.

In the last years before the Reformation, church rules discouraging nunneries from taking pupils were much relaxed, largely due to the urgent need of those insitutions for funds. Many parents took advantage of this. The competition that 'boarding out' provided meant that the abbesses were obliged to widen the scope of their intake and the daughters of yeomen and merchants were now accepted. Girls were taught reading and spelling, perhaps to play the harp, some Latin and certainly needlework, for skill in fine embroidery persisted in the fifteenth-century nunnery. No girl escaped the thrall of the needle, and 'nuns with their needles wrote histories also' said Thomas Fuller, the church historian, referring to embroidered hangings and altar cloths. However, the days of the nunneries were passing, and with them the dwindling habit of female scholarship, for there was nothing being created to take their place. After the dissolution of the monasteries in the sixteenth century some of the funds thus acquired by the crown were used to found grammar schools for boys, but none to do the same for girls. Endowments of nunneries that were closed down were transferred to men's colleges, a wrong that was not righted until late in the nineteenth century, when to some amendment was made.[4]* Thus the decline in female education was becoming all but irreversible.

There is evidence throughout the fifteenth century that books were still treasured by women, particularly in the North and in the Midlands, where the women of noble houses frequently left books to each other in their wills. When printing started (Caxton printed his first book in 1476), books slowly became more easily available, which increased women's chances of acquiring them. But the education of a girl in the middle or upper classes increasingly came to depend on whether her father believed that the female mind was capable of being

*St Radegund's nunnery at Cambridge, for instance, became Jesus College.[5]

educated for more than domestic duties and becoming accomplishments. As the sixteenth century dawned this question was much discussed.

Sir Thomas More (1478–1535) was an exceptional father who believed that learning could be appreciated by both sexes, and he had his motherless daughters taught accordingly and with every possible encouragement. Margaret, the eldest, excelled in Greek and Latin and was also instructed in philosophy, astronomy, arithmetic, logic, rhetoric, medicine and music. More was a strict father, who forbade all games in his household, but there is plenty of evidence of the loving relationship he had with his 'best beloved' children. In a much quoted letter he says of their studies in astronomy,

> I hear that you have proceeded so far in this science that you now know not only the polestar or dog, and such like of the common constellations, but also (which argueth an absolute and cunning astronomer) in the chief planets themselves you are able to discern the sun from the moon. Go forward therefore with this your new and admirable skill, by which you do thus climb up to the stars![6]

One wonders what More and his intelligent daughters thought of the attitude of the Spanish scholar Juan Luis Vives, proponent of the new learning of the Renaissance at Corpus Christi, Oxford, whom they welcomed into their home. Vives (1492–1540), a pupil and friend of Erasmus, regarded as an educational giant in his day, was keen to revive learning in women. Nevertheless he considered most women's intellects to be grossly inferior to men's, making them suitable only for domestic work. He advocated that no greater strain be put on them than the learning of reading and writing, and he made this opinion abundantly clear in his works. When he was asked in 1523 to plan the education of the Princess Mary, daughter of Henry VIII, he produced a reading list that included the works of Erasmus, Cicero, More, Seneca, Plutarch and Plato, and required her as well to read the Bible twice a day. The child was only seven years old at the time, and so it was a strange programme to be suggested by one who thought that 'a woman's mind is unstable and abideth not long in one place'.[7]

Vives advised that all except exceptionally intelligent girls should concentrate on domestic arts; cookery, he said, should be studied not to an extent to encourage gluttony, but enough to make her able to 'dress meat' for her parents and brothers before marriage and her husband and children thereafter. Women teachers he abhorred, since they were likely to understand wrongly what they had learned themselves and then to pass their misinformation on to others. A girl who felt inclined to learning could be allowed to indulge herself, but since marriage was her only goal he saw little point in it. He felt that boys should be taught with the regular help of the rod, and 'especially the daughters should be handled without any cherishing'; the girls should not be allowed to follow their own mistaken instinct in reading the romances beloved of their grandmothers. Erasmus (1466–1536), though a far kindlier man in the teaching methods he advocated, agreed with him in this: 'Amorous fables are violent poison for young maids.'

A translation was made in 1561 by Sir Thomas Hoby of a manual on courtly behaviour compiled by Count Baldassare Castiglione in 1528. From the elegant court of the Duke of Urbino, Castiglione moved through the royal courts of Europe to end his life in Spain, and was called 'one of the greatest gentlemen in the world'. Two centuries later his book was praised by Samuel Johnson as 'the best book that was ever written on good breeding'. Castiglione, this paragon who clearly knew what was what in polite society, said that though the ideal woman should not play games or 'bang a drum in an orchestra', she should be virtuous, literary and musical.[8] His book is considered to have had great influence on English manners in Elizabethan times.

Thomas Becon, the educational reformer who fled to France during the Marian persecutions in 1554, but never allowed his opinions to be silenced, deeply regretted the sweeping away of the nunneries as a source of women teachers. He called for the establishment of girls' schools with properly paid schoolmistresses, claiming that girls should be taught more than dancing and needlework; but his voice, too, was unheeded. Meanwhile, during the sixteenth century in the counties of Buckinghamshire, Hampshire, Kent, Lancashire, Norfolk, Somerset, Worcestershire and Yorkshire, in Bristol and in London, no boy lived more than twelve miles from a grammar school where he could obtain a free education.[9]

One of the problems confronting those who wished to set up the sort of girls' schools that Becon envisaged was that women teachers themselves suffered from the lack of anything beyond a very basic education, a foretaste of the difficulties encountered by the governesses and school-mistresses of the future. A vicious circle had been formed: the very fact that erudition was not required of women teachers or governesses meant that it was also virtually impossible for them to acquire it. There was no system whereby they could obtain formal qualifications; though schoolmasters were licensed by the church, such licences were not available to women teachers, and they were regarded as interlopers by those with teaching credentials.

A girl lucky enough to have been well taught at home by a good governess or an imaginative mother, or to have been boarded out successfully, might have attained rare skills in household management and music; but few were educated to any level comparable with that reached by their brothers, and in the latter half of the sixteenth century the fashion for practical teaching waned still further. It became less desirable for a young lady of breeding to have a knowledge of Greek or Latin than to be a model of modesty and temperance, and accomplished in music, dancing and poetry, with some knowledge of Italian, a language now becoming fashionable. Only in royal and aristocratic circles was ability in the classics still found among women, and here there were some notable women scholars. Henry VIII's sixth wife, Katherine Parr, had been brought up in the same tradition as the More daughters, and she helped to create an atmosphere in which the young Princesses Mary and Elizabeth could pursue their education. The Lady Jane Grey was also a member of her household, and her unhappy childhood had been made bearable by the care and good teaching of the kindly Roger Ascham; at an early age she reached a high level of proficiency in the classical languages which she spoke 'with as sweet fluency as if they had been natural and native to her'. She studied Plato and Aristotle with pleasure and understanding, and learnt French, Italian, Hebrew, Chaldee and Arabic.[10]

Princess Mary, too, was a good scholar and linguist, while the Princess Elizabeth was considered by Ascham to have a mind as able for learning as a man's. As Queen, she could converse with three foreign ambassadors at the same time, switching easily from Latin to French to Italian, the last two, it was said, with rather ugly accents.[11]

The object of any girl's training was to fit her for the role she would be called on to play in later life, but few were expected to be as proficient in languages and diplomacy as a royal princess. As a mere nobleman's daughter a girl could expect, by the time she was fourteen or fifteen, to be traded in marriage by her father with a neighbour, a friend or a stranger, for reasons of politics or of finance. Her own inclinations would rarely be taken into account, for well bred girls with decent dowries were valuable assets and must be used to the advantage of the family as a whole. She would, however, be expected to arrive in her new home not only looking decorative but fully trained in the management of a castle or large house: she must know how to order food from the surrounding countryside, and then to direct its storage and preparation; how to train and manage a number of servants and retainers; how to conduct and administer herbal remedies to the family and castle community; how to deal with the repair and maintenance of linen, tapestries and hangings; she must be able to keep accounts and generally manage the household finances. The new chatelaine must also have the confidence and presence to be able to entertain visitors with well planned banquets of good food, and to converse with her lord's guests with charm and courtesy; she must be able to play music with skill for their enjoyment.

In Ireland, as in mainland Britain, a newly married woman would be expected to bring with her the same formidable list of accomplishments. Eleanor, Countess of Desmond, 1534–1638, was brought up in Munster and scrupulously instructed by her parents in all this domestic detail. In addition, tutors were brought in to teach her to read and write fluently and to converse with ease in both English and in Irish, for which she was later very grateful. In time she became a prolific letter writer with a shrewd political brain.[12]

At a similar level of society, a valued private governess of this time was Mrs Hamblyn, who taught Grace Sherrington, afterwards Lady Mildmay, in the 1560s. Like many governesses then, she was a poor relation of no great learning, but was reputed to be a good letter writer, accountant and herbalist. She was remembered with gratitude by her pupil in later life, who appreciated her intelligence, her humour and her good judgement in everyday matters.

> She advised us to deal truly and faithfully in all things, both in small matters and in greate, to beware of all lyes and oathes and reporting of newes; to heare much and to speake little, seeming to be ignorant in some things rather than to boast of knowledge that we have not and thereby give occasion to be laughed att . . . I delighted soe much in her companye that I would sit with her all daye in her chamber and by my goodwill would never goe from her, embracing allwaies her rebukes and reproofs. . .

She also, it appears, had to embrace 'the rod', but her studies were so happy with Mrs Hamblyn that in later life she continued enthusiastically at the devotions she had learnt, and at practising the lute and composing settings of songs in five parts to its accompaniment; making and administering herbal remedies, and making her own designs for tapestry carpets and cushions.[13] Though she also learnt reading, writing and account-keeping from Mrs Hamblyn, Lady Mildmay had been content with a fairly unintellectual education. Other more ambitious girls sometimes were not so easily satisfied, and family relationships could be upset by their wishes, especially when their learning brought increased knowledge of the world that led to challenges to the parental right of decision on the question of suitable marriages. Even after marriage it could bring problems. A brilliant young woman, Elizabeth Tanfield, born in 1585 and later to become Lady Falkland, had a tiresome mother-in-law in Lady Carey, 'who loved very much to be humoured' and objected to the girl not wishing to pander to her in this. So 'she used her very hardly and confined her at last to her chamber; which seeing she little cared for but entertained herself with reading, Lady Carey took away all her books, with command to have no more brought to her. Then she set herself to make verses. . . '

Elizabeth went on to teach herself Latin and Hebrew, to translate many works and to write and publish a great deal of her verse.[14]

The writer Richard Mulcaster, (1530–1611), who was also a schoolmaster and had pratical experience in the teaching of girls, considered them to be quick-witted and as teachable as boys, though more easily tired by mental exertion. It should nevertheless be a matter of conscience, he said in about 1561, to have them well taught. He even hinted that if custom would allow they would benefit from being sent to grammar school. But, enlightened as he was, and far more generous in his thinking than many of his male contemporaries, he did not believe that women should be taught beyond the age of thirteen or fourteen, or that they could have any aptitude for geometry or mathematics. They were not suited, he said, to become lawyers, physicians, preachers or philosophers.[15]

Mulcaster's attitude was as positive as women of intellectual aspiration could hope to find at that time.

· 2 ·

'Kiss me, and be quiet'

The word 'governess' for the mass of girls still meant the woman who ran or taught in their school; only the royal family and the aristocracy would retain governesses privately in ther homes, as they would carpenters or medical advisors, for convenience sake. The gestation period of our governess is progessing, but she is still a long time from the universally known figure she will eventually become. Meanwhile, the stirrings of rebellion, indicating the start of the long fight to win better education for women, is her battle too, though she will be one of the last to benefit from it.

Throughout the seventeenth century women's own opinion of their needs was divided between those who genuinely distrusted their personal capacities and those who were convinced that the female intellect needed to be fed as much as did a man's. Men were unanimous in their attitude, and they were led from the top. Though after the accession in 1603 of James VI of Scotland to the throne of England some girls' schools were founded, they taught only the usual light-weight subjects, and the King himself had a very low opinion of the value of making women learned: it made them cunning, he maintained, as taming did to foxes. He held the common view that it was safer that they should be stitching away at their tapestries at home, as their ancestresses had before them. Most of his subjects, male and female, agreed.

The young Anne Harrison, born into a rich middle class

Hertfordshire family in 1625 (her father became Member of Parliament for the town of Lancaster), remembered in later life the subjects that her mother had had her carefully taught by her governess. '. . . working all sorts of fine works with my needle, and learning French, singing, lute, the virginals and dancing'. She also recalled, somewhat wistfully, that she would much have preferred to spend her days out of doors,

> . . . for I loved riding, in the first place, and running, and all active pastimes, and in fine I was what we graver people call 'a hoyting girl'. But to be just to myself, I never did a mischief to myself, or people, or one immodest action or word in my life; but skipping and activity were my delight.[1]

During the Commonwealth, from 1649 to 1660, there was little change, and the main subject for girls in the ordinary school curriculum was almost always needlework. Only in the schools designed for the upper classes were music, French and Italian taught as well.

Some women managed nevertheless to acquire a broader education, Lucy Apsley, daughter of the Lieutenant of the Tower of London, for instance. Intellectual activity came naturally to her and as 'for my needle, I absolutely hated it'.[2] She did not entirely manage to avoid sewing, but was lucky enough to have enlightened parents of some means, who engaged for her able tutors in other disciplines. She applied herself to her books to the point of making her mother anxious for her health, and, outstripping her school-trained brothers (as she boasted), she became a proficient Latin scholar. She married one of Charles I's judges, the austere and upright Colonel John Hutchinson, who was first attracted to her by her evident intelligence, thus disproving the popular belief that learning in women was unattractive to men.[3] With her husband she ensured that both their daughters as well as their sons learned languages and the sciences, and her daughters no doubt benefited from her having 'little understanding and less sympathy for feeble natures'.[4]

But this family was unusual: fashion in education had not changed and the men who dictated it preferred their women to be lovable and elegant rather than learned; a women who enjoyed learning for its own sake was considered odd and suspect. This was the Cavalier attitude; the Puritanical view was that enthusiasm for books in a woman was deleterious to her position as a Christian wife. To Richard Brathwait, writing in *The English Gentlewoman* in 1631, a respectable woman 'had rather bee approved by her living than learning . . . Some Bookes shee reads and those powerfull to stirree up devotion and fervour to prayer . . . She is no busie-body, nor was ever, unless it were about her family, needle or Sampler.[5] Sir Ralph Verney went further, adding insult to injury by stating that the actual difficulty of learning Latin might be relied on to keep a girl from 'that Vice, for soe I must esteeme it in a woeman . . . '.[6]

The Restoration of the monarchy in 1660 brought little change of heart. The atmosphere of liberality and revelry which soon came to pervade Court, theatre and social life was not conducive to the encouragement of intellectual development in women, and although fashionable boarding schools for the upper classes continued to come into being in London and the provinces, they were no more dedicated than before to serious study. In Mrs de la Mare's boarding school in St Marylebone, as in the private schoolroom, a disproportionate amount of time was still spent wielding the needle, doing 'cut work' and embroidery in gold and silver thread, and making tinsel laces. The spinette and the guitar were becoming fashionable, and at Mr Papillon's school in Charles Street, St James, 'designing' of needlework was also offered.[7]

A well qualified governess, in a school or in a private home, would also be able to teach drawing, the art of working in straw, of wax-work, rock-work, moss-work, shell-work, cabinet work, 'beugle'-work and japanning – the sort of list that inspired the complaint that girls' time could be better spent than 'in making Flowers of Coloured Straw and building Houses of stained paper'.

The standard of music taught was sometimes high, and the embroidery fine. Cookery, accountancy, calligraphy and housewifery were included in the prospectus at Mrs Perwich's vastly successful school flourishing in 1643 in Hackney. French dances were learned under the guidance of Mr Hazard, a celebrated dancing master, but nothing was taught that would enable a girl to do more than embellish the home of her future husband. Fees ranged from £11 to £25 per year, depending on the location or the range of subjects offered and how many 'extras' were taken, such as lessons with a scrivener or a music teacher.

Hannah Woolley, born in 1623, and determinedly self-educated, published in 1675 *The Gentlewoman's Companion: Or a Guide to the Female Sex, for the guidance of mothers and governesses*. She gave good advice on how governesses should treat the children in their care:

> Let them be lovingly and quietly governed: not with perpetual Chiding and Brawling, but treat with them mildly and gently; unless you find them Refractory to your Commands; if so, then some Austere language must be used.

Then, in rather defeatist strain:

> if by ill-Fate (after all this care) you should have a rebellious and refractory child, your frequent prayers to Almighty God will be the only way to reclaim them.[8]

She had been a governess from the age of seventeen, and from her experience had developed strong views on how others should conduct themselves in this 'difficult employ'. She had a common-sense approach to teaching and recommended that a governess should study the pupils' dispositions and suit her teaching to their capacity. She said that girls should get plenty of exercise – 'If the season be dry walk them in the fields . . .' – and that over-harsh punishment could only be counter-productive.

She was an intelligent and humorous woman, who had had ample opportunity to observe attitudes to female education, for she had also run a small school and married a free school usher. 'Most in this depraved later Age', she said, 'think a Woman learned and wise enough if she can distinguish her Husband's bed from another's.' She complained that lack of reading of serious books 'hath made so many Country Gentlewomen stand like so many Mutes or Statues when they have hapned (*sic*) into the company of the ingenious; their quaint expressions have seem'd to them Arabian sentences and have stared like so many distracted persons in that they should hear the sound of English and yet understand but here and there a word of their own language.'[9] She suggested that if women were taught as were men, they would 'find our brains as fruitful as our bodies' and condemned 'the great negligence of parents, in letting the fertile ground of their Daughters lie fallow, yet send the barren Noddles of their sons to University, where they stay for no other purpose than to fill their empty Sconces with idle Notions to make a noise in the Countrey.'[10]

It was indeed a time when the educational system for boys and young men was in difficulties. Both the grammar schools and the universities were being criticised for falling standards, which meant that there was little hope that calls for improving the teaching of mere girls would be heeded.[11] Yet the calls persisted. Meanwhile, girls' schools proliferated. Anyone could set one up, and it was a favourite way for a widow or a spinster to make a living. No qualifications were needed – only male teachers were required to hold licenses. All a woman had to do was open her doors, advertise, and charge a fee. In a smart locality she would hire visiting dancing and music masters to come in by the day; the rest of the teaching she and perhaps an assistant governess could manage themselves. The pupils poured in to the 'Dame schools', which became a feature of village and small town life for the following two hundred years.

Bathsua Makin, daughter of a Sussex rector and governess for eight years to Elizabeth, daughter of Charles I, was another experienced woman teacher demanding better education for women. She taught the princess to read and write, and then went on to instruct her in French, Italian, Hebrew and the classics. A year after the young girl's death in 1650 she opened a school in Tottenham and published an *Essay to revive the Ancient Education of Gentlewomen*. In this she set out first the qualifications that had determined the King's selection of herself as governess to his daughter, and then claimed that to give girls as good an education as they had had in earlier times would not only benefit them but also their families and the entire nation.

> Were a competent number of Schools erected to Educate Ladys ingenuously, methinks I see how asham'd men would be of their ignorance, and how industrious the next Generation would be to wipe off their Reproach.[12]

She saw no limit to the subjects that women had the ability to study, but in opening the doors of her school she did not dare to break totally with current fashion, and half of the curriculum was devoted to the usual subjects – dancing, singing, music, sewing, writing, keeping accounts – for without them she would have found it hard to find a complement of pupils. However, the rest of the day was to be spent in learning Latin and French, and 'those that please may learn Greek and Hebrew, the Italian and Spanish in all which this gentlewoman hath a complete knowledge', according to her school advertisement. (Those who wished to know more could enquire at Mr Mason's coffee-house in Cornhill.)[13]

Alas, neither the next generation nor the one after that were to emulate Bathsua Makin. Her school, with its sensible balance of domestic knowledge and serious learning, was not taken as a pattern for others.

Daniel Defoe, prolific author (*The Life and Strange Surprizing Adventures of Robinson Crusoe* was published in 1719) and espouser of many worthy causes, added his voice to the argument in 1698. In *An Essay on Projects* he said that it was 'barbarous' that women were not allowed to acquire real learning.

> The greatest distinguishing difference, which is seen in the world between men and women is in their education . . . and herein it is that I take upon me to make such a bold assertion, that all the world are mistaken in their practice about women.

He pointed out that in cases where women had achieved comparable education their wit was equal to men's 'which upbraids us with injustice, and looks as if we denied women the advantages of education for fear that they should *vie* with the men in their improvements'.

Women, he said, should be taught by teachers who were themselves academics; '. . .they should be brought to read books, especially history, and so to read them to make them understand the world, and be able to know and judge of things when they hear of them. To such whose genius would lead them to it I would deny no sort of learning.'

This last sentence was revolutionary in concept, and far ahead of its time, ahead even of what women were yet asking for themselves. Defoe further risked alienating his readers by boldly discussing women's rights of possession, anticipating the first Married Women's Property Act by nearly 200 years. It was explosive talk at that period.

Such support coming from a man was of great value to the women's argument. The great problem for the women who were writing in defence of their own right to education was that, in doing so, they were justifying the fears of those who wished to keep the *status quo* and who argued that to give women too much learning made them pedantic and intractable. Any attempt by women at intellectual argument provoked cries of 'We told you so.' As Montaigne said, a little learning was a dangerous weapon in women's hands and simply made them 'trouble-some . . . affected . . . ridiculous', in their demands for more. Moreover, the same voices that ridiculed women for being ignorant expressed loathing for the 'Female Virtuoso'. Even those men who felt that women were hard done by set firm limits on the extent of the knowledge they should be allowed to acquire.

Lady Masham, patroness and friend of the philosopher John Locke, (1632–1674), wrote that 'a lady knowing and singular' would be lucky to escape calumny and derision, and a gentleman who respected her for her prudent conduct and management of her affairs 'could not yet chuse but be afraid for her, lest too much learning might in Time make her mad'.[14]

It is small wonder, then, that Mary Astell, the well educated daughter of a merchant in Newcastle-upon-Tyne, felt obliged to publish her arguments anonymously, for fear that her thoughts be lost in the stream of male abuse and witticism that invariably followed when a woman acknowledged authorship. Anonymity was a device that many women felt obliged to use, usually under the pseudonym 'A Lady', until as late as the 1850s, if they were tackling any subject more controversial than hints on household management. Anonymity was Mary Astell's only way of ensuring her own freedom of speech, and indeed enabled her most important work, *A Serious Proposal to the Ladies for the Advancement of their True and Greatest Interest*, to be read and noted. It made a valuable addition to the weight of opinion against the frivolity of girls' schooling and subsequent lives.

It was probably Mary Astell who wrote '*An Essay in Defence of the Female Sex*' which was published anonymously in 1697, though it was commonly supposed to be the work of a Mrs Drake. Not being ignorant, she said in her preface, of the outcry there would be against her, she had resolved:

> to keep 'em in Ignorance of my name, and if they have a mind to find me out, let 'em catch me (if they can) as Children at Blind-man's Buff do one another, Hoodwinkt; and I am of Opinion I have room enough to put 'em out of Breath before they come near me.

The writer went on with wit and eloquence to defend women's brain-power and ability to learn, pointing out that male and female monkeys are equally teachable, and that bitches can be trained just as well as dogs. She maintained that 'Nature has not been so niggardly' as men suggested in the mental endowment of women, and that men forced them to fly against the face of that nature in not allowing them to use their capacities. She contrasted the ignorance of English women with the learning of their Dutch counterparts, who were capable of running a business as ably as their menfolk and so were not left helpless if they were widowed. She made the acerbic comment that 'a man ought no more to value himself upon being wiser than a woman if he owes his Advantage to a better Education, and greater means of Information, than he ought to boast of his Courage, for beating a Man, when his hands were bound'.

Mary Astell spent most of her life in London, where she tried in vain to find funding for a college of higher education for ladies. She herself had been encouraged by an uncle to study philosophy, mathematics and logic, and she had taught herself Latin. Her great desire was to raise the level of women's self respect, to make them see that they were capable of more than the pursuit of 'butterflies and trifles'. She felt that they were held back by an inbred conviction that they were 'incapable of great attainments', but the evidence of history, she maintained, should give them encouragement. Women in the past who had had access to books and learning had become great scholars, and they could do so again.

Mary Astell saw the need for well trained women teachers, and she had visionary and ambitious plans for her college which would be run on monastic lines: prayer, charitable works and study would go hand in hand, and the women would be properly taught and could learn to teach others. She received promises of support, mainly from other women, but in the end they came to nothing. Dean Atterbury, who lived near her in Chelsea and knew her well, commented that she could be too direct and tactless in her method of approach, which lessened the chances of her plan succeeding.

The beautiful and eccentric Lady Mary Wortley Montagu (1689–1762) was a friend of Mary Astell. This remarkable woman, described by a contemporary as 'one who neither thinks, speaks, acts nor dresses like anybody else', led a highly unconventional life. Her education was by her own account 'the worst in the world'. She had what she described generously as 'a good homespun governess' but was in fact an elderly and incompetent woman who had been Lady Mary's mother's nurse, and had no greater claim to being a teacher than that she had a wide knowledge of ghostly stories and superstitions. Lady Mary survived her ministrations and managed to educate herself by constant reading. As a young woman she determined to learn Latin.

> I used to study five or six hours a day for two years in my father's library, and so got that language whilst everyone else thought I was reading nothing but novels and romances.

When she was twenty-one she wrote to the Bishop of Salisbury, sending for his approval her translation of Epictetus, and apologising for any mistakes resulting from her imperfect knowledge of Latin, explaining,

> My sex is usually forbidden studies of this nature . . . we are permitted no books but such as tend to the weakening and effeminating of the mind . . . There is hardly a character more despicable in the world, or more liable to universal ridicule, than that of a learned woman.

Lady Mary lived abroad for many years, in Turkey, where her husband was Ambassador, and in Italy and France, after leaving him in 1739. She came to the conclusion that only in England did fashion make it necessary for women's knowledge to be concealed 'and be as useless to the world as gold in the mine'. She was an avid letter writer, corresponding with many friends, and wrote regularly and entertainingly to her estranged husband and to her daughter, the Countess of Bute, who was bringing up her eleven surviving children on the Isle of Arran. In the 1750s, she wrote to her 'Dear Child' advising her (though this advice was not always well received) on the education of her eldest daughter, also called Mary. The girl was already a good arithmetician, to her grandmother's great pleasure.

> Learning, if she has a real taste for it, will not only make her contented, but happy in it. No entertainment is so cheap as reading, nor any pleasure so lasting . . .

She suggested that young Mary be encouraged to learn other languages, but that she should remember that a knowledge of Latin and Greek did not make a person learned, for languages were only 'vehicles of learning, and not learning itself'.

However, she warned that if the girl should excel at any serious subject she must

> conceal whatever learning she attains with as much solicitude as she would hide crookedness or lameness. The parade of it can only serve to draw on her the envy, and consequently the most inveterate hatred, of all he and she fools, which will certainly be at least three parts in four of all her aquaintance.[15]

Lady Mary wrote all her life, well and wittily, in poetry and in prose, parodying and ridiculing many of the foolishnesses of the day, both written and performed. In 1734, the first Lord Lyttelton, another prolific versifier, wrote a lengthy poem entitled 'Advice to Belinda, or to a Lady'. It was full of no doubt well-meant advice on how to become the perfect woman, who devotes all her energies to her husband's care. It contained such lines as,

> The household sceptre if he bids you bear,
> Make it your pride his servant to appear.

Such provocation was irresistible to Lady Mary, who wrote her shortest poem in reply:

A SUMMARY

of Lord Lyttelton's advice to a lady

> Be plain in dress, and sober in your diet;
> In short, my deary, kiss me! and be quiet.[16]

· 3 ·

'The custom of knowing nothing'

The debate about educating girls was pursued throughout the eighteenth century to no conclusion, with the result that, for a hundred years, in schools and in private homes, education beyond the most elementary was not available to the average middle class female. (This, of course, was the stratum of society from which private governesses were traditionally drawn.) It was a period of argument rather then of action. There was no lack of thought, or indeed of those willing to put pen to paper on the subject of women's education; but the diverse and often totally opposing views expressed and argued had the effect of creating an extraordinary degree of ambivalence in the attitude of ordinary people, male and female, as to the desirability of women being given the same educational opportunities as men. It was this ambivalence that would for many years to come impede the progress of private governesses and other female teachers towards acceptance as professionals or a decent standard of living.

In earlier centuries a good example had been set by the Court in the matter of educating daughters. But at this period the royal family was not in the habit of trying to give the nation a lead in either moral or intellectual affairs. George II, a finicky man in matters of daily routine, of no great brain and a lout in his behaviour towards his wife, could not be accused of taking his daughters' schooldays very seriously. In the 1730s he installed as governess to the Princesses Mary and Louisa, his two youngest daughters, Lady Deloraine, 'one of the vainest as well as one of the simplest women that ever lived: but to this wretched head was certainly joined one of the prettiest faces that ever was formed.' She was a widow, in her mid-thirties, who had agreed that as a condition of becoming the royal governess she would remain unmarried. She soon broke this agreement, but her remarriage in 1734 did not prevent her from meeting the King every evening in the elder princesses' apartments where he liked to 'talk a little bawdy' with her. Even before she was known as his mistress the King bragged that he had 'lain' with Lady Deloraine to Sir Robert Walpole, who repeated it to Lord Hervey. The latter, who faithfully recorded all gossip in his journal, concluded that if it were true this must also have occurred in the princesses' rooms, for the King and the governess never met anywhere else. Lady Deloraine made the unfortunate Princess Caroline her confidante in the progress of the affair, asking her advice on how to control the urgency of her father's passion. She even asked the poor girl to act as her messenger to express her embarrassment as a wife to her own cuckolded husband, pretending that she was ashamed to do it herself. Walpole said to Hervey that he wished the King had chosen a mistress less mischievous than 'that lying bitch'.[1]

Clearly Lady Deloraine had not been selected as governess for any particular educational abilities that might be beneficial to the young Princesses, but this was in keeping with prevailing fashion.

British opinion on female education was echoed on the other side of the Channel. In France too there were two schools of thought. One is exemplified by the attitude taken by La Bruyère, who was at one time tutor to Mademoiselle de Nantes, an illegitimate daughter of Louis XIV. in his *Caractères*, which appeared in 1688, he had said that men should not be blamed for women's lack of learning:

> There are no laws to prevent their opening their eyes and reading, retaining what they read and using it in their conversation and life. The problem is that they are firmly set in the custom of knowing nothing, either from feebleness of body, laziness of mind, too much care for their looks, or some volatility that makes them incapable of prolonged study – or perhaps they are constitutionally only suited to work with their hands, or find household cares too distractng, or have a natural distaste for serious matters, or a lack of need for intellectual satisfaction, or possibly just a preference for anything except using their memories.[2]

Whatever the reason, men, he concludes, are quite happy that women who dominate them in so many other ways should at least not have over them the advantage of learning. He considered that an exceptional woman – *une femme savante* – is like a beautifully forged weapon, finely decorated and polished; she is a *pièce de cabinet*, to show to the connoisseur and not for use, just as a horse trained in *haute école* is no use for hunting or on the battle field.

A contempory of La Bruyère at the Court of Versailles, Madame de Maintenon, who rose to eminence as *gouvernante* to other natural children of the Sun King, might have taken him to task on this. As a child she had been in the charge of a governess so ignorant that she had been obliged to teach herself to read and write. But, according to Saint-Simon, it was her skill in writing letters that first overcame the King's aversion to her.[3] She was not just a letter writer: during her time as royal governess, she became a glowing member of a brilliant literary circle, which included Madame de Sevigné.

In 1674 the philosopher Malebranche offered a precise explanation for the difference he saw between male and female brain power in his *La Recherche de la Verité*. It may have been his own deformity and constitutional feebleness that made him look for physical weakness in others: in any case, he concluded that it was the greater delicacy of the fibres in women's brains that made them intellectually inferior to men.[4] In Britain, too, it was held that there was a physical difference in the structure of women's brains which made them unalterably and permanently of lower mental capacity than the male sex. This assumption, though backed by no scientific research, was widely accepted. Through ignorance, very sweeping statements were made by intelligent people: Jonathan Swift (1667–1745) wrote advising young women about the dangers of losing 'credit' through becoming conceited about their knowledge, adding deprecatingly, 'But there is an easy remedy for this, if you consider, that, after all the pains you may be at, you can never arrive, in point of learning, to the perfection of a schoolboy.'[5]

This stigma was to prove hard to throw off. As late as 1855, the Council of Bedford College in London considered, with regard to the awarding of scholarships, that the physical difference between male and female mental capacity and stamina was such that the element of competition involved was positively dangerous to the health of girls. Even in the 1860s, as was related in an 1895 Royal Commission report, 'it was seriously doubted whether a girl's brains were able to grapple with the difficulties of vulgar fractions, and [when] it was generally considered that her physical and moral delicacy was so frail, that both would be injured by a written examination to be looked over by a strange man'.

By 1894 Frances Power Cobbe, journalist and author, could laugh at such ideas, but proved that they were still current when she commented:

It is always amusing for me to read the complacent arguments of despisers of women when they think to prove the inevitable mental inferiority of my sex by specifying the smaller circumference of our heads. On this line of logic an elephant should be twice as wise as a man. But in my case, as it happens, their argument leans the wrong way, for my head is larger than most of my countrymen, – Doctors included, as measured by a skilled phrenologist with proper instruments . . . On the other hand dear Mrs Somerville's* little head, which held three times as much as mine has ever done, was below the average of that of women. So much for that argument!

But now in the eighteenth century many women still believed these myths, and many more believed that too much cerebral activity in females was not just physically risky but was even slightly indecent. Lady Bradshaigh, a correspondent of the novelist Samuel Richardson (1689–1761), wrote ingratiatingly to him,

> I hate to hear Latin out of a woman's mouth. There is something in it, to me, masculine . . . I should be ashamed of having more learning than my husband. A very uncomfortable life do I see between an ignorant husband and a learned wife. Not that I would have it thought unnecessary for a woman to read, to spell, or speak English . . .[6]

This kind of thinking meant that in the rare cases where the services of an educated woman were available in a governess they were unlikely to be appreciated. Elizabeth Elstob (1683–1756) is an example of a good brain wasted as a governess in private service. She was born in Newcastle-upon-Tyne and lived under the guardianship of her uncle, a prebendary of Canterbury Cathedral. He tried to quell her determination to study, believing that 'one tongue is enough for a woman'. Despite this discouragement, in time she managed to master eight languages. She was the first woman known to have pursued 'the frightful study of Anglo-Saxon', and she became a considerable Anglo-Saxon scholar, renowned even in her own day. In 1709 she translated Abbot Aelfric of Eynsham's *English Saxon Homily on the birth of St. Greogory*, and in 1715 produced *Rudiments of Grammar for the English Saxon tongue*. But she could not make a living out of such an esoteric subject, and at the age of thirty one, after the death of her brother William, on whom she was financially dependent, Elizabeth Elstob became destitute. She tried at first to live by giving reading and writing lessons to poor children in Evesham, and friends and admirers who deplored her penury made efforts to set her up as mistress of a charity school.

*The eminent scientist

This she refused, feeling unqualified for the job, since she had no capability for teaching the necessary spinning and knitting. The concluding fourteen years of her life were spent as governess to the children of the Duke of Portland at a salary of £30 a year. Despite her known erudition, her duties were to teach her pupils only the basics of reading and writing with the principles of religion. Though reasonably comfortable and secure, with a room of her own where she could work, she had little time for herself. Her position of servitude was only made bearable by her fondness for her charges. She continued to study, but wrote sadly to a friend of the atmosphere that surrounded her in the Portland household and of 'open and vehement exclamation against learned Women, and those Women who read much themselves'.

One enlighened mother advised her daughters in 1761 to learn the first four rules of arithmetic, but 'more, you can never have occasion for and the mind should not be burthened with needless Application'.[7]

It is not surprising that handwork and sewing occupied so much of the time that a governess spent with her pupils. and long were the hours they spent bending over their cloth-work, crape-work, chenille work, ribbon-work, and wafer-work. Years later Maria Edgeworth mourned that so many of the results of her forebears' years of toil were afterwards 'consigned to the garret' when fashion changed. She spoke of the 'truly substantial ten-stitch chairs and carpets, the huge needlework pictures' of Solomon meeting the Queen of Sheba and similar bibical scenes, which excited wonder at the 'strange patience and miserable destiny of former generations'.[8] She might also have considered the good fortune of Victorian girls, at least partly released from the tyranny of the needle.

Many well-meaning parents genuinely felt that an open show of learning in their daughters could render them unmarriageable, believing that no man wished his wife to be his equal intellectually. Dr Gregory, a Presbyterian minister and a loving father to his daughters, whose greatest desire was that they should find good husbands, told them that only a few men were 'superior to this meanness',[9] and advised them to conceal any learning they acquired. Without encouraging them to be in any way frail, he warned them of the danger of seeming otherwise:

> We so naturally associate the idea of female softness and delicacy with a corresponding delicacy of constitution, that when a woman speaks of her great strength, her ability to bear excessive fatigue, we recoil at the description in a way she is little aware of.[10]

A girl who wanted to get on in the world must always appear just a little weak in mind as in body.

The people who thought like this formed an important section of the school of reactionary thought; another was composed of those who felt with great conviction that women should not be over-educated because it would make them unsuited, and indeed unwilling, for that position in life that God had ordained for them. It was the same argument that was used for denying education beyond a certain level to the poor.

A lecturer in a girl's school at this time said, 'The respective employment of the Male and Female Sex being different, a different mode of education is consequently required . . . the Female Sex . . . must evidently be instructed in a manner suitable to their destination and to the tasks that they will have to perform . . .' Girls must be trained to be 'obedient daughters, faithful Wives and prudent Mothers.'[11] As late as 1808 a young lawyer, John Bowdler, was speaking in the same tones: he suggested patronisingly that women with a higher education than they needed might be tempted to try to insinuate themselves into professions more exalted 'than the order of the world will permit them to engage in'.

William Law, in 1728, in his much lauded, *A Serious Call to a devout and Holy Life* appeared to take a more enlightened attitude when he complained that parents educated their daughters in the wrong way and for mistaken motives. 'They are not indeed suffered to dispute with us the proud prizes of arts and sciences, of learning and eloquences, in which I have much suspicion they would often prove our superiors; but we turn them over to the study of beauty and dress, and the whole world conspires to make them think of nothing else. Fathers and mothers, friends and relations, seem to have no other wish towards the little girl but that she may have a fair skin, a fine shape, dress well, and dance to admiration.' In educating them 'not only in pride, but in the silliest and most contemptible part of it', a precious resource was being wasted. Nevertheless, despite apparently being aware of women's intellectual potential, he stresses that the perfect mother (he calls his prototype Eusebia) 'brings them up to all kinds of labour that are proper for women, as sowing, [sic] knitting, spinning and all other parts of housewifery; not for their own amusement, but that they may be serviceable to themselves and others and be saved from those temptations which attend an idle life.'[12] The same school lecturer I referred to earlier said that it was 'an illiberal prejudice to say that Women should be kept in ignorance, in order to render them more docile in the management of domestic concerns', for 'a certain degree of knowledge is both ornamental and useful', which only shows that the prejudice was held by not a few people.

With French candour, the philosopher Jean-Jacques Rousseau (1712–1778) was much more open in expounding this theme, making it quite clear that one of the dangers of educating women was that it would lessen their subservience to men, which was a part of the natural order of things. Girls, he said, should be taught early to put up with discomfort and constraint (*la gène*) since this is to be their lot in life, from which they will never escape. They must restrain their imaginations, so that they may be more prepared to submit themselves to the will of others, and to this end he suggested that girls who wish always to be at work should be forced periodically to be totally idle. They should not be allowed to do anything, even play games, with too much enthusiasm, and they should be made accustomed to having their pleasures abruptly curtailed without making any protest.

This perpetual constraint applied from a young age would produce an ingrained docility which would be useful to them all their lives, since they would be required to submit themselves to the will and judgement of men who, he admitted, are imperfect, often full of vice and always full of faults. So a girl must learn early to suffer wrong and injustice at her husband's hands without complaint, since to do otherwise would only make her the more unfortunate.

Had irony and humour featured in Rousseau's make-up one might suspect them here, but he suggests all this in a genuine spirit of kindness and common sense, and with the intention of lessening women's distress in their marriages. He was not deliberately unkind in what he advocated for others. He considered that a girl should be taught arithmetic even before reading, as nothing would be more important in her life than keeping accurate accounts, and he advocates a psychological approach to such teaching. There is a charming passage in *Emile, ou De l'Education*; in a section advising on the upbringing of the perfect wife Rousseau recommends bribery by cherry: '*Si la petite n'avait les cerises de son gouté que par une opération d'arithmétique, je vous réponds qu'elle saurait bientot calculer.*'[13]

His strictures on training children sound a little strange in view of his own home life. Having found his very simple wife ineducable, he is reputed to have treated her with callous indifference. He never laid eyes on any children she may have had by him. (It has been suggested that she and her mother invented these children, as a form of blackmail, and even that he may have invented them himself.) He seems in any case to have been happy to accept that they had been handed over to a foundling hospital. Whatever the facts, the story came back to embarrass him when he was a celebrated writer on domestic matters.

Rousseau's theories on the education of children generally had enormous influence on other educationalists well into the next century. His ideas about girls, which were based on a very shallow understanding of women's needs and motivations and on an idealised vision of their sex as a comfortable complement to his own, struck a chord that rang true to many people. They were recognised as conforming to a view widely held of the world as it should be, of man as the toiler and protector and of woman as the helpmeet and raiser of children. Sixty years later, parents who took their daughters' education seriously were still studying his work and, if not always following his advice in detail, were at least adhering to the principle.

If the arguments of the secular voices were not enough to convince parents that it was a mistake to over-educate their daughters, the churches were more than ready to recommend abstinence for females in learning as in most other pleasurable occupations: their studies should be confined to contemplation of the Holy Mysteries. Dr James Fordyce was a popular Scottish Presbyterian preacher whose eloquence and polished style filled his church in Monkwell Street, near St Paul's, week after week in the 1760s. In his *Sermons to Young Women* he effused glutinously, 'Never, perhaps, does a fine woman strike more deeply than when, composed into pious recollection, . . . the beauties of holiness seem to radiate about her and the bystanders are almost induced to fancy her already worshipping among her kindred angels.'[14]

A fashionable girls' school flourished in Queen's Square, Bloomsbury, in the 1790s. It was a well run establishment. The girls learnt English – Mrs Devis, the governess, had published 'a very good little English Grammar' for the express use of her pupils – some geography and history, and also learned to speak French 'with a very good accent'. Harpsichord lessons were part of the normal curriculum. But the main subject, and in Mrs Devis' eyes apparently the most important one – 'the very rudiments of feminine knowledge' – was decorum.

> In Queen Square, nothing that was not decorous was for a moment admitted. Every moment of the body in entering or quitting a room, in taking a seat or rising from it, was duly criticised. There was kept, in the back premises, a carriage taken off the wheels, and propped up *en permanence*, for the purpose of enabling the young ladies to practise ascending and descending with calmness and grace, and without any unnecessary display of their ankles. Every girl was dressed in the full fashion of the day. My mother, like all her companions, wore hair powder and rouge on her cheeks when she entered the school a blooming girl of fifteen.

The girls were also instructed 'in the art of properly paying and receiving visits, of saluting acquaintances in the street and drawing-room; and of writing letters of compliment.'[15]

Mrs Devis's school embodied everything that was most despised by those people who considered women to be worthy of education; and yet Frances Power Cobbe, campaigner for women's rights, whose mother attended the school and whose description of it I have quoted above, defended it. She maintained that the teaching of girls deteriorated still further, and that such schools represented a standard of excellence that was to disappear and not to be seen again until far into the next century.

A similar and successful establishment was run in Streatham by a Miss Eveleigh with the help of her two nieces, Miss Fry and Miss Kay. Charlotte Albert, who joined as a boarding pupil in 1773, remembered all three ladies as 'remarkably well bred, well informed and of surprising height'. The good breeding would certainly have counted with Charlotte's parents in their choice of school, for they were attached to the household of George III, but they were also evidently concerned for her happiness. She recounted how her father, of whom she was very fond, took the trouble to travel from Kew on the second day of her stay at Miss Eveleigh's to make sure that she was settling in. She was very touched by this gesture and pleased with the 'white leather shoes with stone buckles' he brought her for her dancing lessons with Monsieur Villeneuve.

Miss Eveleigh's school was a happy place – Charlotte called her 'my kind governess' – and if the curriculum was typically narrow, it seems to have been well taught. Music and singing lessons were taken:

> by Mr Knyvett, a well known musician, Mr Mirlan, also known, for Latin and English . . . Every kind of needlework, both useful and ornamental, was taught in the schoolroom, embroidery in coloured silks being taught in the first line of perfection by that angelic soul, Miss Fry . . . Miss Kay superintended in one room the music, drawing and geography, the latter taught inimitably clear by Mr Povoleri, who was also for Italian, a language at that time rarely studied, and only to enable a person to read the words of an Italian song.

There was some practical preparation for life as well; the girls who were old enough were taught to repair their own linen, and 'when the stores were given out the young people of a certain age were called to assist, and by this means an insight into the mysteries of housekeeping was obtained'.

There were eighty girls, among them 'Miss Chaworth, the illegitimate daughter of a Mr Chaworth who had been killed in a duel with

Lord Byron, and many others of note'. But not all went on to the beneficial marriages for which their schooling was to groom them. For one girl at least a very different prospect was ahead; Charlotte tells the sad story:

> In the autumn of 1778 an occurrence took place that made an impression on us all. Miss Vaughan was to leave school to be introduced at a ball on the evening of the Lord Mayor's Day, by dancing a minuet, in imitation of the evenings of the King's and Queen's birthdays, when the young nobility were introduced in the same manner. Her mother, Mrs Vaughan, arrived at Streatham, not, as we expected, to fetch her for this event, but on a very different mission. It was to tell her daughter that Mr Vaughan, who was a wholesale haberdasher, had failed, and so lamentable was their condition that they were no longer at home, but in the house of a friend. Miss Vaughan, with the presence of mind of a good heart and a strong family affection, said, 'I thank you, dear mother, for my liberal education, which I hope now to turn to account for your comfort.'

This model of filial perfection announced that she would become a governess, but Charlotte's description of her makes one wonder whether any children would enjoy learning from her.

> She had always been assiduous, and very eager to improve, but she had no taste for the ornamental. She learnt music, but it could never interest anyone to listen to the extreme accuracy of her performance, with a coldness and seeming want of mind that was unaccountable. For drawing and needlework she has more feeling, but books particularly took hold of her attention. She had excellent understanding and a good disposition, but as she never associated with her companions in the usual pursuits of the young, nor in any way cultivated a friendly intercourse, she was not generally beloved. She was at this time seventeen, and was highly respected and looked up to as a superior being, and in her trouble was greatly commiserated.

With her fashionable education, gained from Miss Eveleigh's school, however cold in spirit Miss Vaughan might be, she would not find it hard to get a suitable governess post. As Charlotte noted,

> When the French emigrated in shoals to this country at the time of the Revolution, the nature of education was changed. It became the fashion for people to have governesses in their homes instead of sending their daughters to schools, which had been supported to accommodate every rank in society.

[34]

Charlotte's father and husband both held fairly minor places in the royal household, and when she said 'people' she meant people of their milieu, doctors, musicians, court painters, professional people who till now had been accustomed to sending their daughters to boarding or day schools.

Down at Kew Palace there were, of course, governors for the young princes, and governesses for their sisters. Though the court was generally more sober than in George II's reign, little had changed in attitudes to the girls' education. George III and Queen Charlotte had appointed Lady Charlotte Finch as the royal governess. Charlotte Albert commented acidly that, though Lady Charlotte had the authority to recommend individuals for service in the royal nursery, she was inclined to 'assume the power to herself to make her own appointments', implying that suitability for the job was not necessarily what she looked for in promoting her friends. Lady Charlotte had under her in 1772 a Miss Coultsworth who 'retired from age, and Miss Goldworthy, sister of the Queen's first equerry, was received in her stead; a lady of private fortune, and of general endowments that in every respect qualified her for the situation of sub-governess.' A hint of irony can be detected.

The hand of Lady Charlotte can be seen again in Charlotte Albert's account of what happened when Miss Planta, the sub-governess who taught the young princesses English, 'died of an accidental illness'. She was replaced by her younger sister, Miss Peggy Planta, whose 'manner was much more brilliant than that of her sister; her disposition was more flexible, and her whole deportment more suitable to a Court; yet I should say a decided loss was sustained in the death of the former. No doubt but that Miss Peggy was equally well informed, yet as the instructive part of the education of the Princesses devolved on the English teacher, the quiet, patient, plodding and persevering disposition of the late Miss Planta was more adapted to that arduous business. Miss Peggy was, however, well received, and much approved, and the schoolroom now was one of gaiety and cheerfulness.'[16]

Though the King's daughters may have had more fun under the younger Miss Planta, who had previously been a teacher at Miss Eveleigh's, even they received only a basic education. Still, the practices of the court were slavishly followed by aspiring middle class families, and a governess was a status symbol within the financial reach of a substantial section of society. So, like the coachman, the footman and the boot-boy, the governess would soon become an essential member of the household of every family of a certain income level and social status. How she was used depended often on the educational attainments of the parents who employed her: mothers who themselves had learnt little at school had no wish to be put to shame by their governesses or by their daughters. Thus teaching skills were not necessarily the attributes that a governess needed to offer.

The private governess, in the form that we are accustomed to think of her, was now beginning to take shape.

· 4 ·

'This phrenzy of accomplishments'

As I have already said, there was no shortage in the eighteenth century of powerful voices advocating proper teaching for girls, though few of them yet went so far as to say that they should receive an equal level of teaching with boys. Women themselves became bolder, and some even dared to publish under their own names. One of the most effective in putting her case was Maria Edgeworth (1768–1849), who became popular as a writer of fiction, in particular of children's stories with a strong moral message. In *Essays on Practical Education*, written in conjunction with her father and published in 1798, she urged that girls be taught accurately, and in depth, even if only a narrow range of serious subjects were tackled; she made the sensible point that ancient literature could be studied in translation – that it was not essential to 'pay too much in time and leisure for this classic pleasure'. This attitude could of course bring it within the range of the ordinary governess in the schoolroom.

On the subject of women teaching, she went as far as to suggest that in order to produce a breed of effective governesses it was important to pay them properly, since they had as much right to security in old age as anyone else; she mentioned the exorbitant figure of £300 a year, which at a time when a middle class family would expect to pay not more than £15 to £20, must have come as a startling suggestion and, as it turned out, an unacceptable one. She inveighed against the stuffing of girls with what were known as 'accomplishments' – music, singing, dancing, ornamental needlework and smatterings of French and Italian – with the sole end that they might catch a 'prize in the matrimonial field'. Miss Edgeworth summed up with great clarity the dilemma faced by women of the period. 'Sentiment and ridicule have conspired to represent reason, knowledge, and science as unsuitable and dangerous to women; yet, at the same time, wit and superficial acquirements in literature have been the object of admiration in society; so that this dangerous inference has been drawn, almost without our perceiving its fallacy, that superficial knowledge is more desirable in women than accurate knowledge.'[1]

Fénelon, (1651–1715) whose educational works were introduced into Britain in 1704 by Dr George Hickes (1642–1715), had stressed the importance of the good training of teachers for girls. He urged parents to choose as a governess for their daughter a person of 'tolerable good sense' and a 'tractable humour', and to make sure of her proficiency. 'Endeavour to form her betimes for this Employment, and keep her some time near you to try her before you trust her with so precious a treasure.' This advice, too, must have read strangely in a society where the governess was looked on as just another servant in the household, underpaid and held in as little esteem.* More importantly, Fénelon recognised that good governesses would by their teaching produce others, and that they must be encouraged to proliferate: 'But Five or Six Governesses form'd after this Manner would be capable of forming in a little time a great number of others. There would be perhaps disappointment in some of them; but out of this Number there would be always enough to make amends; and we should not be put to that extream Perplexity as we generally are nowadays.'[2]

Jonathan Swift, ever critical, wrote that 'Out of fifteen thousand families of lords and estated gentlemen, one in thirty is tolerably educated.' The daughters of 'great and rich families' were taught either by ignorant mothers, in boarding schools or at the hands of English or French governesses 'generally the worst that can be gotten for money'. Both men and women, he said, took such a languid interest in their daughters' education that, as a result, most educated members of the gentry 'must either remain single or perforce marry women for whom they can possibly have no esteem'.[3] Charles Darwin (1731–1802) was

---

*In 1731 was published anonymously the intriguingly titled 'Chicken feed Capons: or a Dissertation on the Pertness of our Youth in General, especially those trained up at Tea-tables . . . not forgetting the Insolence and Scorn with which the generality of young Persons treat their Elders and Betters' in which the author declared that children 'have no respect for their teachers, and this is not to be wondered at for in great families they are put contemptuously on a footing with the servants'.

another who complained that those people who taught girls, at home or in school, seldom had an adequate education themselves – a criticism that governesses were long to suffer, but that no one was yet prepared to do anything about.

Mary Wollstonecraft, the writer, worked as a governess for nine years from the age of nineteen. In her first position, from 1778, she looked after the daughters of Lord and Lady Kingsborough in Dublin and in Bristol, and is said to have been dismissed only because the children were showing signs of loving the governess better than their mother. Her experiences in the Kingsborough household had taught her that even in well-to-do circles, where books and instruction were readily available, education took a lower place in the scale of priorities than the study of fashion. 'A mere fine lady' was how she described Lady Kingsborough, and she had been appalled to find that upper class women who had the opportunity of improving themselves failed to take advantage of their position to do so.

Mary Wollstonecraft, herself a handsome, impulsive woman with great charm of person and manner, was a passionate believer that women could and should be educated to the same level as men, and felt that far too much emphasis was placed on the learning of 'accomplishments'. In her book *Thoughts on the Education of daughters*, published in 1787, she devoted a chapter to 'Exterior accomplishments', which begins:

> Under this head may be ranked all those accomplishments which merely render the person attractive, and those half learnt ones which do not improve the mind . . . Girls learn something of music, drawing and geography; but they do not know enough to engage their attention, and render it an employment for the mind. If they can play over a few tunes to their acquaintance, and have a drawing or two (half done by the master) to hang up in their rooms they imagine themselves artists for the rest of their lives.

In her more important work *A Vindication of the Rights of Women*, published in 1792, she sets out to demolish some of the more ludicrous assumptions made about women in the writings of the most respected of male educationalists. With great clarity and common sense she shoots down Rousseau's much studied arguments on the teaching of girls, not flinching from describing some of his remarks as 'nonsense'. As she points out, 'I have, probably, had the opportunity of observing more girls in their infancy than J. J. Rousseau – and I have looked steadily around me.' She condemns him with other writers for having 'contributed to render women more artificial, weak characters than they would otherwise have been, and consequently more useless members of society'. Women had been persuaded, she claims, to model themselves on idealised beings created by the male imagination: They must now do something to help themselves to achieve intellectual respectability by resigning the 'arbitrary power of beauty' which men have accorded them and return to 'nature and equality'. By using flirtation rather then brain power to achieve their ends they 'will prove that they have less mind than man'.

Mary Wollstonecraft says that some of Rousseau's remarks about girls 'are so puerile as not to merit a serious refutation' and regrets that his thinking is echoed by so many other writers. One of these, 'the worthy Doctor Gregory', he who advised his daughters to 'feign delicacy' for fear of putting off would-be suitors, also gets the rough side of her tongue:

> In the name of truth and common sense, why should not one woman acknowledge that she can take more exercise than another? Or, in other words, that she has a sound constitution?[4]

Her robust views earned her the wrath of Horace Walpole, who called her 'a hyena in petticoats' and 'a philosophising serpent'.

Mary Wollstonecraft also attacked the 'learning by rote' which was widely practised by governesses and in schools, often covering the ignorance of teachers who took refuge in the simple device of making their pupils learn and repeat pages of information by heart.

> I have known children who repeat things in the order they learnt them, that were quite at a loss when put off the beaten track. If the understanding is not exercised, the memory will be employed to little purpose.

Mary Fairfax, 1782–1875, (later Mary Somerville) described her lessons at Miss Primrose's fashionable boarding school in Mussleborough, near Edinburgh, where she went at the age of ten and where she was 'perpetually in tears'. She had been made to 'learn by heart a page of Johnson's dictionary, not only to spell the words, give their parts of speech and meaning, but as an exercise of memory to remember their order of succession . . . The method of teaching was extremely tedious and inefficient.' She rose above it eventually, but when she left school, aged eleven, she was unable to compose even a short answer to a neighbour's letter, so poor were her writing and spelling. Miss Primrose's fees had not been slight, and the child was reproached by her family for having wasted their money. Mary was not at fault, however. Her formal education over, and with positive discouragement from her mother, she studied clandestinely, burning candles late at night in her room till the servants complained. She taught herself Greek, geometry, algebra and astonomy, became a competent botanist and a very able landscape painter in the studio of Alexander Nasmyth, who described her as 'the cleverest young lady he ever taught'. Despite a first husband who, she said, 'possessed in full the prejudice against learned women that was common at the time,' she continued to study, and with full support of her second husband became a renowned astronomer and physicist.[5]

Many others deplored the system of force feeding children with facts and figures, but it was to be used for another hundred years before it died out. 'Precocity and display were what parents demanded,' wrote Alice Zimmern, 'and schools and governesses contrived to supply the requirements.'

One of the most vehement in attacking the cramming of girls with accomplishments was the redoubtable Hannah More (1745–1833), one of the original 'Bluestockings'. This name was adopted in the 1750s by a group of intelligent people, male and female, who gathered regularly in the house of Elizabeth Montagu in Hill Street, Mayfair, for the purpose of enjoying conversation more intellectual in tone than the usual gossip and flirtation common in London assemblies. Mrs Montagu's parties were attended by Samuel Johnson, the actor David Garrick and other notable people, and her female friends wore blue stockings as a badge of their informal society.* Hannah More, whose portraits show a firm, thin lipped mouth and a determined chin, was a woman of strong views and expressions; she called Mary Wollstonecraft 'a disgusting and unnatural character', believing mistakenly that her call for equal rights in education was a demand for equality of the sexes. She also held strong prejudices, not least against the French, both before and after the Revolution. The fashion that was spreading for all things French distressed her, and she devoted most of a chapter of her *Strictures on the Education of Women*, published in 1799, to the subject of French governesses being preferred to English.

---

*A story is told of the first meeting of Hannah More with Dr Johnson: 'She was most desirous to have an interview with him, and at last obtained a promise that he would receive her at his house in town. Thither, then, she repaired with a friend, and was shown into his library to await his convenience, where seeing a big leather chair, she cast herself into it, saying, "This is doubtless the great man's chair! I will try to gain from it a few sparks of his genius." On his entering the room, she told him what she had done, when in his quiet, dry manner, he answered, "Unfortunately, I never sit in that chair. I should be afraid of its gloomy inspirations." '[6]

Under the just impression of the evils that we are sustaining from the principles and practices of *modern* France, we are apt to lose sight of those deep and lasting mischiefs which so long, so regularly, and so systematically, we have been importing from the same country, though in another form and under another government . . . This is not the place to descant on that levity of manners, that contempt of the Sabbath, that fatal familiarity with loose principles, and those relaxed notions of conjugal fidelity, which have often been transplanted into this country by women of fashion as a too common effect of a long residence in that [country] . . .

Because what she really wants to get on to is a condemnation of 'the risks that have been run, and the sacrifices that have been made, in order to furnish our young ladies with the means of acquiring the French language in the greatest possible purity'.

She is talking, of course, of the risks taken by parents who employ French governesses who, by definition, will practise all the evils she has listed, parents who have ventured to 'entrust their daughters to foreigners, of whose principles they know nothing, except that they were Roman Catholics'.

Hannah More must have been accustomed to seeing parents reel before this kind of attack. Their usual response, she says, is that 'they had taken care that . . . the question of religion should never be agitated between teacher and pupil'. She sweeps it aside: To ban religion from the schoolroom

is like starving to death to avoid being poisoned . . . Surely it would not be exacting too much to suggest at least that an attention no less scrupulous should be exerted to insure the character of our children's instructor . . . than is thought necessary to ascertain that she has nothing *patois* in her dialect.

She ends with a flourish of sarcasm:

I would not offer up principle to sounds and accents. And the matter is now made more easy; for whatever disgrace it might once have brought on an English lady to have had it suspected from her accent that she had the misfortune not to be born in a neighbouring country; some recent events [she is talking, here, of 'The Terror' which followed the Revolution] may serve to reconcile her to the suspicion of having been bred in her own.

Vehement though Hannah More could be when roused, in gentler mood she could offer a pleasant, almost lyrically expressed argument for proper female education.

Since then there is a season when the youthful must cease to be young, and the beautiful to excite admiration; to grow old gracefully is perhaps one of the rarest and most valuable arts which can be taught to woman. It is for this sober season of life that education should lay up its rich resources. However disregarded they may hitherto have been, they will be wanted now . . . when admirers fall away and flatterers become mute.

But this leads into an attack on 'this phrenzy of accomplishments' which fashion demanded instead of education and which

unhappily, is no longer restricted within the usual limits of rank and fortune; the middle orders have caught the contagion, and it rages downward with increasing violence, from the elegantly dressed but slenderly portioned curate's daughter, to the equally fashionable daughter of the little tradesman, and of the more opulent, but not more judicious farmer.

She returns to her main theme:

A young lady may excel in speaking French and Italian, may repeat a few passages from a volume of extracts; play like a professor, and sing like a syren; have her dressing-room decorated with her own drawings, tables, stands, screens, and cabinets; nay, she may dance like Sempronia herself, and yet may have been very badly educated.'[7]

But the passionate diatribes of Hannah More, pleading for an end to fashionable frivolity and for a sound religious base to girls' education, made little impression on the average parent of the day. Perhaps like Mary Astell she cared too much, and failed to carry her listeners by reason of her very vehemence. But similar views on girls' education were expressed far more gently, if less entertainingly, by Vicesimus Knox, Master of Tonbridge School, in 1789:

There are many prejudices entertained against the character of a learned lady, and perhaps, if all ladies were profoundly educated, some inconveniences might arise from it; but I must own it does not appear to me, that a woman will be rendered less acceptable in the world, or worse qualified to perform any part of her duty in it, by having employed the time from six to sixteen, in the cultivation of her mind.

Such mildness of view and expression could offend no one, but it had equally little effect on educational fashion and the opinion that dictated it.

A paradox becomes evident during the late eighteenth century because of the discrepancy between the way girls were viewed physically and the way they were treated physically. The widely held belief that women's brains were frail and that care had to be taken never to overload them with knowledge has already been illustrated. That their bodies and constitutions were considered equally delicate is apparent from the concern shown by different writers. These, too, should be carefully treated, for were not 'their whole frames incessantly deranged by the most trivial shocks, such as a banging door, a violent gust of wind or the appearance of a frog or a mouse'?[8]

In view of this recognition of the physical frailty of gentlewomen, it is surprising to discover how violent and often how painful were the methods that a governess or a schoolteacher would use, with the approval of the parents, to improve their daughters' posture, and to reshape the frames of those weakly girls into the form that fashion demanded. A little girl would be compelled to drink 'tar water' if she was considered to have weak eyes,[9] and she might be obliged to do all her daily lessons in the schoolroom standing with her feet held in 'stocks' to ensure well turned out toes, with an iron collar round her neck to hold it erect and a board strapped to her shoulders to force them back. In 1790, when little Mary Fairfax went to Miss Primrose's school, although by her own account she was 'perfectly straight and well made', she was forced to wear an apparatus that makes the 'bearing reins' suffered by Black Beauty sound quite comfortable.

> I was enclosed in stiff stays with a steel busk in front, while, above my frock, bands drew my shoulders back till the shoulder-blades met. Then a steel rod, with a semi-circle which went under the chin, was clasped to the steel busk in my stays. In this constrained state I, and most of the younger girls, had to prepare our lessons.[10]

Even the recommended exercise of dancing was often performed in a collar that forced a girl's head into the position thought to be most elegant. Her shoes were weighted with lead to strengthen her leg muscles, and she could be made to 'swing by her chin' for a period each day to increase the length of her neck. Maria Edgeworth was one of those who was made to swing like this from her head, to lengthen her spine and make her grow, but she stubbornly remained short and dumpy.

Swinging by the arms from a bar had long been considered a valuable way of stretching the muscles. It is recorded that in 1637 it was considered as 'being good to exercize the body of children in growing'. A young girl called Alice Wandesforde, while doing her daily exercise of hanging from a rail, was pushed too hard by a rough French page so that her hands slipped and she fell and broke her chin bone.[11]

Mary Wollstonecraft abhorred the petty and excessive disciplines that were imposed on children by governesses and schoolteachers. She saw that they led to no physical advantage and simply curbed normal and healthy development in young bodies and minds. Every girl, she claimed, was by nature 'a romp', and should in youth be allowed to indulge herself.

> With what disgust I have heard sensible women ... speak of the wearisome confinement which they endured at school. Not allowed, perhaps, to step out of one broad walk in a superb garden, and obliged to pace with steady deportment stupidly backwards and forwards, holding up their heads and turning out their toes, with shoulders braced back, instead of bounding, as nature directs to complete her own design, in the various attitudes so conducive to health.[12]

As for her figure, the practice was current of lacing up young woman's stays until she might even faint from the constriction. In Frances Power Cobbe's nursery in Ireland in the 1820s she remembered a beam across the ceiling in which a large iron staple was still firmly fixed from which had once dangled a hand-swing. Her great-aunts had used it to hang from by their arms so that their maids could lace their stays up as tight as possible. Strait-lacing it was called; it had been much attacked by John Locke, who compared mothers who allowed the practice with monkeys who killed their young by holding them too tightly. William Law, castigating the type of mother that he most deplores, one who ruins her daughters in her determination that they should be fashionable, described in his *Serious Call to a Devout and Holy Life* a horrific situation. A daughter, having been starved and 'physicked' into pale slimness and her spirit broken, died in her twentieth year.

> When her body was opened, it appeared that her ribs had grown into her liver, and that her other entrails were much hurt, by being crush'd together with her stays, which her mother had order'd to be twitch'd so strait, that it often brought tears into her eyes, whilst the maid was dressing her.

As a result, her younger sister wisely ran away with a gambling man.

It has to be assumed that such a description, however fanciful, would horrify parents who read it, but those who practised the idiocies of fashion probably were not the type that would read Law's book.

It is only fair to see this pursuit of perfection in the female form in the context of the day. To be in fashion was all, if the attainment of a good marriage was the object, and fashion, as it always has, dictated that the female shape should not be as nature intended. 'Correct' deportment was essential, and the torture inflicted on young bodies was done, however mistakenly, out of love by parents and out of duty by the governess.

Skill in dancing was a prerequisite in society, so the dancing masters had to be engaged and obeyed. The governess handed over her pupils into their care for many hours each week. Hannah More said sarcastically that the teaching of dancing 'cannot in any degree of safety be confided to one instructor; a whole train of successive masters are considered as absolutely essential to its perfection.' There had to be a professor for the Scottish steps, another for the French ones, both working with a finishing master, and each receiving 'a stipend which would make the pious curate rich and happy'. Girls were kept so busy at their dancing that 'a delighted mother has been heard to declare that her girls had not a moment's interval to look at a book.'[13]

Mrs Papandiek remembered with pleasure her youthful prowess in dancing the minuet:

> Noverre was a most excellent master, and was much pleased with me. I had a correct ear for music, and taste with *naïveté* in dancing. Minuet time is three fourths, or crotchets, in a bar, and two bars are required for the four steps. Instead of making a dead stop on the first step, I filled up the time by raising and sinking the instep, so as to glide into the second step, with which Noverre, being a Frenchman, professed himself *enchanté*. He was also particularly pleased with my manner of giving and withdrawing the hand. In the minuet de la Cour I was renowned for my finish of the different movements, the jump being accomplished without brusqueness. In those days, dancing was considered quite an important part of the education, and the grace shown in the various movements was very different to the rough style of the present day [she was writing in 1833], proving at a glance if a young lady were refined and had received an elegant education.

For a ball at the mayor's house in Streatham, where Charlotte was to shine as a prize pupil,

> Noverre ordered my white kid shoes from the opera-shoe maker. He also would have the sleeve of my gown made to his order, that my arm might be observed; and the train was to be thrown back, so that it might not impede my 'beautiful' steps![14]

Maria Edgeworth, too, had something to say on dancing. She

considered it an agreeable exercise, conducive to health and advantageous in that it conferred a certain degree of ease and grace. But she questioned the importance attached to the teaching of it and its relevance as training for life:

Nobody comes into a room regularly as their dancing master taught them to make their entrance; we should think a strict adherence to his lessons ridiculous and awkward in well-bred company![15]

Mary Somerville has left us a delightful description of Strange, an Edinburgh dancing master who taught her and other fashionable young ladies of the town in the 1790s.

Strange himself was exactly like a figure on the stage; tall and thin, he wore a powdered wig, with cannons at the ears, and a pigtail. Ruffles at the breast and wrists, white waistcoat, black silk or velvet shorts, white silk stockings, large silver buckles, and a pale blue coat completed his costume. He had a little fiddle on which he played, called a kit. My first lesson was how to walk and make a curtsey. 'Young lady, if you visit the queen you must make three curtsies, lower and lower and lower as you approach her. So – o – o,' leading me on and making me curtsey. 'Now, if the queen were to ask you to eat a bit of mutton with her, what would you say?'[16]

Alas, the correct reply that a young visitor should give to such an invitation is not recorded. Daisy Ashford would surely have known.

· 5 ·

Lessons with the governess

Education in the private home in the early nineteenth century was in effect the same as that offered in the fashionable schools of the time, usually with an extra emphasis on moral training: this was a subject at which governesses excelled, for many of them had a rectory background.

Apart from acting as a companion to her charges, and teaching them the accomplishments that would enable them to compete effectively in society, a governess had also to train them in deportment and to inculcate enough general knowledge that they should 'know what people were talking about', as Charlotte M. Yonge put it. The required 'accomplishments' were still one or two languages, preferably French and Italian, music, dancing, drawing and needlework. If the governess could not teach them all, tutors would be called in to help with any deficiencies. The eventual aim was the best possible marriage, as no parent was ashamed to admit.

Fathers, mothers and daughters alike were in agreement that early marriage was an enormously desirable goal. Though in most families there were bonds of affection that would mean sorrow as well as pride on the day that the daughter left home, there were pressures on all members of the family which made them long for this day to arrive. It meant for the father the handing over of financial responsibility for his daughter to another man, and it meant that she would then be cared for, in all likelihood, for life.

For the mother it was socially advantageous to marry daughters as young as possible, and a matter for shame to have a daughter left on the shelf. Jane Austen's novels reflect the middle class attitude of the time: In *Pride and Prejudice*, published in 1813, Mrs Bennet takes to her bed for two weeks at the news of her youngest daughter's elopement. But her misery is swiftly converted to rapture on hearing that Captain Wickham, the girl's seducer, has been perusaded to marry her:

> My dear, dear Lydia! this is delightful indeed! . . . She will be married at sixteen! . . . Well, I am so happy. In a short time I shall have a daughter married. Mrs Wickham! How well it sounds! And she was only sixteen last June![1]

To the daughter at a time when the parental word was law, when discipline in the home was highly restrictive, becoming increasingly so as the century wore on, marriage represented freedom, a chance at last for a young woman to make decisions in a home of her own. The plain Charlotte Lucas in the same book welcomes the intolerable Mr Collins' proposal of marriage with alacrity, and makes no hesitation in naming an early date for her wedding day. 'Miss Lucas, who accepted him solely from the pure and disinterested desire of an establishment, cared not how soon that establishment were gained.'[2] A married woman carried a dignity and an authority that a single one could never hope to match, as Lydia Bennet takes pleasure in demonstrating on her return home with her new husband. 'Ah Jane', she says to her eldest sister, as they go in to dinner, 'I must take your place now, and you must go lower, because I am a married woman.'[3] The first of a family to go to the altar could be as patronising and condescending as she wished to her unmarried sisters.

The smaller the dowry available, the more important looks and accomplishments became, and the governess would play her part in improving these. For a girl to dress well was of course also important. She must be taught not only what to wear but how to move gracefully in her garments. The high waist lines, the straight loose skirts and raised hemlines of the regency period, when for a while women were permitted to move and breathe freely, gave way to new fashions. Tiny waists in the normal place were set off by vast skirts supported by innumerable layers of flannel, muslin and cotton petticoats, sweeping to the ground. One of the practical problems in the administration of the Crystal Palace during the Great Exhibition of 1851 was solved: the floor, it was claimed, was kept clean by the skirts of the lady visitors.[4]

The crinoline became instantly popular, when it appeared in the 1850s, since it provided the same outline with far less weight and heat.

The resulting gain in manoevrability was however soon lost, as the fashion-mongers took over and the size of the crinoline increased until the immense area covered by a fully dressed female made her the butt of jokes and cartoons.

> Lady, to sentinel on duty, 'Can I pass, soldier?'
> Sentinel, 'Well, I really can't say, Ma'am, but there was a waggon-load of hay went through five minutes since.'

Tight lacing was again in vogue, and once again whales died to give their bones and little seamstresses slaved away in garrets stitching them into the corsets and stays that were needed to squeeze fashionable women into shape.

In vain did doctors preach, warning of deformed ribs and crushed livers, cancer, consumption and ruined spines. One writer tried another tactic:

> There would be no tight lacing if girls could be made to understand this simple fact, that men dread the thought of marrying a woman who has fits of irritable temper, bad headaches and other ailments, all of which are the first products of compression of the waist.

But to no avail. It would take a major war to release women from their rigid bodices.

With so much emphasis placed on early marriage, a governess who was capable of teaching more than the usual subjects was generally little valued. If she had a particular talent for teaching, this would only be appreciated if she had the good fortune to have been found by an unusually enlightened family, for well brought up young women throughout the century were still being advised to disguise any learning they might have managed to acquire, on the grounds that 'the men won't like it'. Little had changed in this respect since Lady Mary Wortley Montagu's indignant outburst in 1752.

Thomas Broadhurst, who ran with his wife a girls' school in Bath, published in 1808 his *Advice to Young Ladies on the Improvement of the Mind*, in which he congratulated them on living in an enlightened age when education was available to them, but he warned them against 'any display of literary attainments; since of all objects that are disagreeable to the other sex, a pedantic female is, I believe, the most confessedly so.'[5] Facts were to be absorbed, but constructive or analytical thought was discouraged.

Broadhurst was not unusual in his views. There were any number of articles and essays, often published by that prolific author 'A Lady', to discourage girls from overdoing their studies. A particular 'Lady' wrote,

> Of one thing a clever woman who wants to be a man's favourite must always be careful – to keep that half step in the rear which alone reconciles men to the superiority of her wit. She must not shine so much by her own light as by contact with theirs and her most brilliant sallies ought to convey the impression of being struck out by them rather than being elaborated by herself alone.[6]

Another proclaimed in an essay on the subject of science: it was 'not necessary that you should sacrifice any portion of your feminine delicacy by diving too deep or approaching too near the professor's chair. A slight knowledge of science in general is all that is here recommended.' One of the advantages derived by women from a general knowledge of science was that it rendered them 'more companionable' to men.

> If they are solicitous to charm the nobler sex by their appearance of dress and manners, surely it is of more importance to interest them by their conversation, yet how is this possible without some understanding of the subjects which chiefly accupy the minds of men? Most kindly, however, has it been accorded by man to his feeble sister, that it should not be necessary to *talk much* even on his favourite topics, in order to obtain his favour. An attentive listener is generally all that he requires; but in order to listen attentively, and with real interest, it is highly important that we should have a considerable understanding of the subject discussed; for the interruption of a single foolish or irreverent question, the evidence of a wandering thought . . . or the rapid response that conveys no proof of having received an idea, are each sufficient to break the charm and destroy the satisfaction which most men feel in conversing with really intelligent women.[7]

It was deeply depressing for the really intelligent women who were fighting to obtain proper education for women to read this kind of comment written by those of their own sex. They were constantly and irritatingly told that erudition, literary ability and skill in political argument were all very fine and, if they gave pleasure, let women by all means acquire them. But let them keep quiet about it, for these were male preserves, and not only did men hate women encroaching upon them, but females had other duties in their own province to attend to. Too many women were taking to writing, for instance, and far too many were doing it successfully.

Does it never strike these delightful creatures that their little fingers were meant to be kissed, not to be inked? Women's proper sphere of activity is elsewhere. Are there not husbands, brothers, friends, lovers to coddle and console? Are there no stockings to darn, no purses to make, no braces to embroider? *My* idea of a perfect woman is one who can write, but won't.[8]

These arguments were certainly agreeable to many women who were happy in their marriages and had no particular ambition to change their position in life or to crusade for the rights of others. Even those who might find the phraseology objectionable might not find the conclusions far from their instinctive feeling that woman's natural role was one of subjection on intellectual as well as physical matters. For those who found the arguments frivolous or simplistic, the church continued to provide others equally persuasive. There were ample sermons and tracts to be read that advised women, as part of their Christian duty, against acquiring too much knowledge beyond the knowledge of their creator by study of the scriptures.

The pupil of the average governess was, however, in little danger of absorbing any unattractive excess learning. Governesses, not having any of the advantages of 'teacher training', relied heavily on 'learning by heart' as a teaching aid, and the mind-stopping boredom of this method, so criticised in the 1780s by Mary Wollstonecraft, ensured that most pupils were left suitably ignorant. At best they would acquire a smattering of superifical knowledge in a huge variety of subjects. Fénelon, that wise man who knew that children would only learn if they enjoyed their lessons, had advised a century before against making children learn by heart. 'These repetitions . . . torture children, and take away from them all the pleasure they would otherwise find . . . ' The writer Mary Russell Mitford (1787–1855) told of how she was taught by a woman of whom she was very fond,

> getting by rote . . . sundry tedious abridgements of heraldry, botany, biography, mineralogy, mythology and at least half a dozen ologies more, compiled for my express edification. I gave her fair warning that I should forget all these wise things in no time, and kept my word; but there was no escaping the previous formality of learning them. Oh! dear me! I groan in spirit at the very recollection.[9]

Mary Russell Mitford was unusually lucky to have a teacher who compiled her own lists of facts. Most teachers and governesses at that time relied heavily on printed books of facts in 'Question and Answer' form which were to be memorized by pupils. This tedious system of teaching had been in use in the seventh century and was still considered a good, or at least a convenient one, twelve centuries later. One of the most popular textbooks in this form was published in 1800, Miss Richmal Mangnall's *Historical and Miscellaneous Questions for the Use of Young People*, and incredibly it was still in use and in print in 1909, successive publishers having had it altered and added to as the years went by. 'Miscellaneous' the questions were indeed, and leading with a sometimes fairly tenuous connection from one to another. To the modern eye they resemble a long-winded 'Christmas Quiz' in a newspaper rather than a serious book of instruction.

Q. What is whalebone?
A. A sort of gristle found inside the whale in long, flat pieces three or four yards long; it supplies the place of teeth.
  Q. Are there not four hundred or five hundred of them in one whale?
A. Yes; they stick to the upper jaw and form a kind of strainer to keep in sea snails and other small creatures on which whales live.
Q. What is whalebone used for?
A. To stiffen stays, umbrellas and whips.
Q. Are not umbrellas of great antiquity?
A. Yes; the Greeks, Romans and all eastern nations used them to keep off the sun; *ombrello*, in Italian, signifies a little shade.
Q. Did not the use of this article travel from Italy into the other countries of Europe?
A. Yes, but very slowly, for they have scarcely been used in England above eighty years.

The next question is about whips, stays being perhaps too personal a subject to tackle.

One can imagine the delight of a young woman who had learnt her questions with care, at being able, on hearing the word 'maple' mentioned, to impress the company by informing them that 'The maple is a low tree, common in woods and hedges, so much valued by the Romans that they gave an extravagant price for it for their tables.'

Opportunities for pious instuction were not missed. On the subject of leopards:

Q. Is it not a mark of the kindness of the Creator that these savage beasts go in search of prey during the night?
A. Yes, for in the day when man is abroad they usually sleep in their dens.[10]

Miss Mangnall, 1769–1820, ran her own school, The Academy for Girls at Crofton, near Wakefield in Yorkshire. She had been educated there herself as a child, staying on as a teacher, eventually taking over as head mistress and not leaving until she died. It has been said in defence of Miss Mangnall's book that she never intended her 'Questions' to be used as more than a pointer to education, and that it was not intended as an instruction manual. This may be so, but she certainly knew the problems and dangers for a teacher practising without such aids. One of her pupils recalled,

> Our class of geography was two hours looking for the Emperor of Persia's name. My governess [Miss Mangnall] said it was Mahommet.[11]

Miss Mangnall's *Questions*, and her compendium of geography, were so popular as teaching aids for many ignorant or lazy school teachers and governesses that they spawned other similar manuals. *The Children's Guide to Knowledge, 262 Questions and Answers,* by a Lady (the pseudonym on this occasion concealed Fanny Ward) was published in 1825 and was still in use in 1899 when Agatha Christie as a nine year old child learnt its pages by heart. To the end of her days she remembered certain questions and answers: 'What are the three diseases of wheat? Rust, mildew and soot.' 'What is the principle manufacture in the town of Redditch? Needles.' She does not record whether she ever found an opportunity to use this information. [12]

The Revd. Dr Ebenezer Cobham Brewer published another very popular series of elementary textbooks on astronomy, Grecian history, science, reading and spelling and other subjects, which were widely used by governesses. *My First Book of History of England* and *My First Book of Geography* were published in 1864 and were also based on the 'Question and Answer' principle, to be memorised by the pupils.

Q. Who was Henry VIII?
A. Son of Henry VII.
Q. What was his character?
A. As a young man, he was bluff, generous, right royal and very handsome.
Q. How was he when he grew older?
A. He was bloated, vain, cruel, and selfish.

The counties of England were to be learned in groups, and the pain of learning them can be imagined from this short extract of text:

> How many form the Eastern group? Nine.
> Name those that face the sea: Lincoln, Norfolk, Suffolk and Essex.
> Name the five inland counties of the Eastern group: Cambridge, Huntingdon, Bedford, Hertford and Middlesex.

A music lesson in the 17th century.

'Servante Walker, I pray you that you will out of the money you receive of my fathers lett my sisters olde governess Mrs Anne Mantell have the summe of twentie poundes which is dew unto her for her wages my father gives her. if you possibly may I pray you doe this and you shall doe me a greate pleasure. and so farewell this 20th of Februarie 1526. Youre lovinge frende, Philippe Sidney.'

The Minuet.

The Dancing Lesson___ P.t 2.

The Sailors Hornpipe

The Dancing Lesson P.t 4

'The Dancing Lesson', from a series by George Cruikshank, 1824 and 1825.

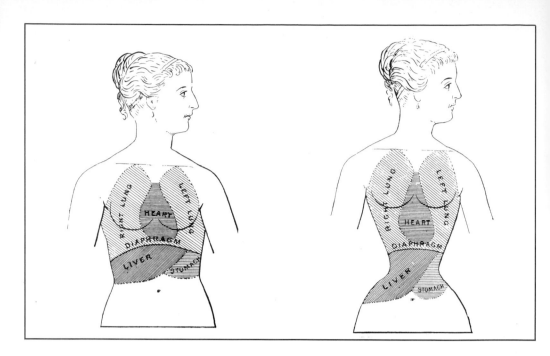

Tight Lacing: doctors warned
of deformed ribs and crushed
livers.

The Victorian girl,
demonstrating the 'phrenzy of
accomplishments'.

Richmal Mangnall, author of 'Historical and Miscellaneous Questions for the Use of Young People'.

Mrs Sarah Trimmer, the first person to act as an agent for governesses.

'They might as well have said their lessons to the armchair as to her.'

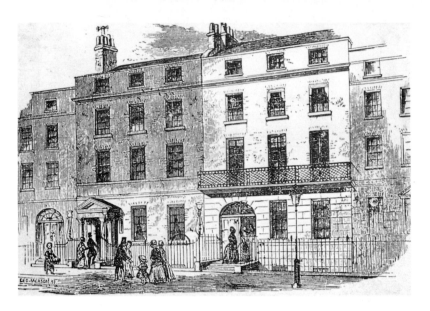

The original home of the GBI in Harley
Street, opened in 1845.

The daily governess.

The Asylum for Aged Governesses in Kentish Town,
opened in 1849. 'This home is intended simply as a
Home – for the disengaged and unprotected. It has
been placed under the care of a separate Committee
of Ladies, including two of rank, not better known for
their position in Society, than for their clearness of
intellect, their ready comprehension of business
details, and their active and enlightened
benevolence.'

High spirits were generally frowned upon in the schoolroom.

Students at Charlotte Mason's 'House of Education', 1893–4.

The GBI was one of the first charities to use illustrations to soften the hearts of potential donors.

Miss Elkins with her pupils, c. 1933.

How may the remaining counties be grouped? Into a centre triangle enclosed in a square.
What three counties form the centre triangle? Stafford, Worcester and Warwick.
What three counties form the north side of the square? . . .

And so on. The struggling pupil might find encouragement in the answer to 'What is the character of the English people?' Which was 'Brave, intelligent and very persevering.' [13]

Some writers showed more ingenuity than Dr Brewer in providing aids to learning. John Box, around 1860, produced *Metrical England* which helped the pupil to learn a series of historical milestones and at the same time master the metres of classic poetry, a level of erudition far above the average governess. Each line of the book gives one historical event, and the metre in which it is written gives the century in which it occurred. The key gives examples: Iambic – thirteenth century, anapaest – fifteenth century. The figures for the tens and units of the date are indicated by the first letters of the first two words of each line, by the following code: $a=1, b=2, c=3, d=4, f=5, s=6, v=7, l=8, n=9$ $o=0$.

'Swiftly sweeping o'er the sea the Norman brings his chivalry.' (1066)
(Trochaic)
'Vile outrage stretched Becket in blood at the altar.' (1170)
(Amphibrachic)
'All freemen joined the tyrant to defeat' (1215) (Iambic)
'A day of glory Scotland won at Bannockburn' (1314) (Choliambic)
'Agincourt's famous fight is the pride of his reign' (1415) (Anapaestic)
'Sailed over the sea to the throne of Charles the Second.' (1660)
(Dactylo-epitrite)
'Feared naught brave Wolfe who fell in victory's hour.' (1759)
(Spondaic) [14]

Mrs Markham's *History of England*, first published in 1823, was another textbook in common use in the private schoolroom. It is a full and interestingly told history, and the book is dotted with engravings and diagrams, with conversations at the end of each chapter on what has gone before:

Mrs M. Shall I tell you something of the domestic habits of the English in the fifteenth century?
Mary. Oh! do, Mamma; I shall like that very much.
Mrs M. . . . Some houses had chimneys, but in many the fireplace was in

[55]

the middle of the floor and . . . the smoke found its way out through the rafters.

Mary. A fire in the middle of the floor! How very dangerous that must have been!

Mrs M. There is in the great hall at Penshurst, in Kent, a fire-place of this kind . . . In these halls, while the nobles and their guests sat at table, they were entertained by singers, minstrels and dancers. Over their heads were the perches for their hawks, and at their feet . . . dogs gnawing the bones that were thrown to them; and besides all this, there was all the bustle and confusion of the numerous and noisy attendants, who, it should appear, were allowed to bawl and shout and talk to each other.

Richard. Well, I am sure I had rather dine in our neat little dining-room, with only our quiet Thomas to wait upon us, than in one those great halls with all that noise and dirt. [15]

Mrs Markham was the pseudonym of Elizabeth Penrose (1780– 1837), the wife of a Lincolnshire clergyman. She had been educated at a school in York where, according to a fellow pupil, 'nothing useful could be learnt'; but her love of reading led to a love of history. When she was sixteen, an uncle wrote of her,

Eliza, though a merry girl, devours folios of history with much more appetite than her meals, except when we have bantam eggs; then, indeed, she is like a conjuror devouring his balls.

Mrs Penrose published companion volumes on the histories of France, Germany, Greece and Rome, all carefully designed to make them suitable for children. In her 'advertisement' or preface to the first edition of her *History of England*, she says that she has 'dwelt little on cruelty and fraud, as being hurtful to a young mind to contemplate'. She may have underestimated the resilience and curiosity of the average young mind; but she produced a vivid and imaginative book for its time, from which it must have been quite pleasant to learn. It was so popular that 98,000 copes had been printed by 1857, and it was still in use by governesses in schoolrooms up until at least 1911.

Science, when it was taught in the schoolroom, was dealt with as an 'accomplishment' and consisted of the learning by rote of facts that should be of interest to any educated person and could be used in conversation. Only toward the end of the century did the heuristic method of teaching science become popular, whereby children were encouraged to find things out for themselves, and then only among the most enlightened teachers.

As it became recognised that arithmetic, in moderation, could be as useful to girls as it was to boys, special textbooks were designed for their use. *The Young Ladies' New Guide to Arithmetic* was published by John Greig in 1798, and was introduced by him as being better calculated than other works on the subject 'for the attainment of this useful accomplishment among the Female Sex'. It was a laborious attainment: in the section entitled 'Notation or Numeration', the pupil is instructed on how to express any number in figures up to septillions, and given exercises in writing nine figure numbers 'in words at length'.[16]

Despite these helpful books, the teaching of mathematics by governesses continued to be very poor, because it was taught by women who had little understanding of the subject themselves. A Miss Grant, arriving in 1870 as one of the first pupils at St Andrews School in Fife (later St Leonard's) wrote that 'hitherto I had been taught by a beloved but entirely unmathematical governess, who decreed that certain sums must be worked by certain rules, but was quite unable to explain why, and if my answer did not correspond with the answer in the key, it was simply marked "Wrong" and we went on to another'.

· 6 ·

The market place

What kind of woman became a governess in the nineteenth century?

The practice of giving dowries was dying out by mid-century, and the competition for eligible husbands was as hot as ever. Unless she was an heiress, a girl had to rely on beauty, charm and accomplishments to release her from a state of dependence on her father into a state of dependence on a husband. A rising imbalance in the population –five per cent more women than men, which was in part due to an increase in male emigration – made the goal of marriage increasingly hard to attain. For those who missed the mark, the alternative was spinsterhood in the parental home. For a girl of the upper or middle classes, in a reasonably well-off family, this might not be a dreadful prospect; to be the unmarried daughter left on the parental shelf was humiliating but at least it offered security. But for the daughter of a middle class family whose parents could not afford to keep her or, indeed, became dependent upon her, the only option was to teach, and for those with least educational attainment and who could not afford further training, teaching meant becoming a private governess. For orphaned girls and widows, with insufficient income to maintain themselves, becoming a governess was an obvious resort, since it provided a home of a kind as well as a small income; but above all it was a respectable existence. Though some girls no doubt found pleasure and satisfaction in the work, many adopted the profession unwillingly, and entirely for reasons of financial pressure.

In one of a series of essays about women, Anna Jameson (1794–1860) wrote in 1846 that in the case of

> the woman who has no home, or is exiled from that which she has, the occupation of governess is sought merely through necessity, as the *only* means by which a woman not born in the servile classes *can* earn the means of subsistence;

but 'a woman who knows anything of the world would, if the choice be left to her, be anything in the world rather than be a governess'. It led, she said,

> to nothing that I know of but a broken consitution, and a lonely, unblessed old age. It is at the most an occupation affording the means of a present subsistence and that a very poor one, with the prospect, at best, of half starving on a charitable pension of £15 a year from some benevolent institution or perhaps a little annuity of £30 or £40, scraped together by the toil of some twenty years – the best years of existence.[1]

While she urged governesses to do their utmost to put aside each year a proportion, however small, of their salary in anticipation of their old age, she admitted that most would find this impossible.

> The very circumstances which throw a young woman on her own exertions for support, generally throw upon her the care or maintenance of one or more members of her own family; there is some home whereto a few pounds bring needful help, – a sister to put to school, – a mother to support, – a father's or a brother's debts to pay.

She found ample evidence of this in the first annual report of the newly established Governesses Benevolent Institution. Out of thirty-three cases of indigence recorded, thirty of the governesses had been supporting one or more relatives out of their meagre earnings, often contriving to pay for the education of younger siblings. One had devoted all her earnings to the education of her five nieces, who all became governesses in their turn.[2]

There was very little alternative to teaching for a woman from a 'respectable' background who wished to retain her social position. As a governess in a private home she could hope to do this, but putting aside her pride and determining on this course of action was only the first step on her difficult path. It was not easy to obtain a situation.

As Mrs Jameson remarked,

> It used to be only the titled and the rich who required governesses for their daughters. There were few women either inclined to the task or by

education qualified for it, and it was generally fulfilled by the poorer relatives of the family. It is within the last fifty years, since marriage has become more and more difficult, – forced celibacy with all its melancholy and demoralising consequences, more and more general, – that we find that governesses have become a class, and a class so numerous, that the supply has, in numbers at least, exceeded the demand.[3]

This was despite the steady increase in families looking for people to educate their daughters in the home. The growing and increasingly affluent middle class regarded the keeping of a governess as not just a convenience but a status symbol.

Until the beginning of the nineteenth century there had been no particular way for a governess to find work except by word of mouth and the personal recommendation of a helpful friend or previous employer. Mrs Sarah Trimmer (1741–1810), a woman of exceptional piety, was a pioneer in the founding of Sunday Schools, which in the 1790s were the only schooling many children of poor families would receive since they worked on farms or in factories during the week. She wrote on education and religion, produced textbooks for charity schools, and was widely known for her philanthropic works. 'Morning visits to this exemplary family were not permitted,' wrote Mrs Papandiek in her journal,

> for Mrs Trimmer was employed in writing her excellent works on education, while the eldest daughter, acting as book-keeper, was in the accounting room, and the second daughter Sarah, was instructing her younger brothers and sisters in the schoolroom. [4]

Such was Mrs Trimmer's reputation that many people wrote to her for help and guidance, but it seems a little surprising that a woman in search of a good governess to take charge of the motherless children of a gentleman friend should, in 1707, write to Mrs Trimmer and ask if she herself would undertake the task. Mrs Trimmer responded with great courtesy and not a trace of sarcasm that she was most regretfully unable to oblige as she was fully occupied in caring for her own husband and ten surviving children.[5]*

But she undertook to find a suitable young woman for the position that had been offered to herself and, in so doing, she saw another outlet for

---

*She was in fact a woman of positively tedious sanctity, though she was clearly much loved by her close family (who admired her 'faculty of reading aloud for a greater length of time than most people are capable of'), and respected by all who knew her. But she had a knack of making almost any happy situation less happy by seeing and pointing out its moral dangers, and she was sadly lacking in sense of humour: 'Cinderella' she judged to be a tale fraught with danger for the young reader, in that it encouraged vanity, love of dress, and a dislike of step-mothers and half sisters.

her charitable energies. She became known as an unofficial employment exchange for young governesses. She found her hard-working daughter Sarah a situation looking after the daughters of the Duchess of Devonshire, though she had some doubts about allowing her to go into such a notorious Whig household. [6] Sarah had rather grandly rejected an offer from the Royal family, since she and her mother judged that a governess there would be too much 'restricted in the mode of communicating instructions'. (Another governess had indeed resigned from the post for this reason.) A male relation of Mrs Trimmer's, a Mr Roberts, however, seems to have gained her approval to teach writing in the royal schoolroom. She was a strong character; when we hear that Charlotte, her eldest girl who was so useful with the accounts, had been sought in marriage by Mr Ernst, one of the King's pages, 'but it was not consented to, much to the annoyance of the young people',[7] we can reasonably wonder if it was the Palace that blocked it or the firm hand of Charlotte's mother again.

In time Mrs Trimmer settled a large number of deserving young women in suitable governess posts, finding for anxious mothers the kind of reliable females whom they sought but did not know how to go about finding. This kind of help was much needed, particularly by the would-be governesses, the great mass of whom always had to fend for themselves.

The advertising columns of *The Times* of 1815 are not lengthy, but in every issue, among the advertisements for housemaids, dairy maids, surgeons' apprentices, lady's maids and barmaids, there are always two or three of governesses offering themselves for employment in daily or resident positions. Some are phrased with touching dignity:

> A young lady, well educated in English, French, writing, geography, (with use of globes), arithmetic and the fashionable works, having but a small income wishes to add to it by devoting a few hours each day for the instruction of one or two young ladies in the above branches of education, offering most respectable references.

Some dare to ask for 'a gentleman or nobleman's family', others are happy to offer themselves to 'any respectable family' and are prepared to do plain and ornamental needlework as an inducement. Many, by the wording of their entry, betray a palpable desperation: ladies of 'the most respectable connections', of 'genteel address', 'of the first respectability' are willing to do almost anything that will put a roof over their heads. One offers herself as 'a preparatory governess, a companion to a lady or superintendent of domestic concerns'. Another would be 'a governess to young children, a lady's maid or companion'. All can produce 'most respectable', 'unexceptionable', 'undeniable' references. None refers to the salary she might hope for.

There are very few employers advertising for governesses, perhaps two or three each week.

By 1835, there is a change in *The Times'* columns. Three times the number of governesses are advertising, but they are selling themselves more effectively. Most offer more than one language, drawing, music – guitar, piano, harp – arithmetic, geography 'with the use of globes', dancing, and 'the usual branches of female education'. Many qualify this list a little with the words 'the rudiments of . . .' Some seek to protect themselves by stressing that the children must not be of more than a certain age, usually rather young. The sheer numbers of advertisers mean that each must try to make her entry in some way outstanding – there is no place for modesty.

> First rate daily governess: A lady, whose tuition has met with extraordinary success wishes to attend a few young ladies. Her instructions comprise German, Italian and French, all three of which she speaks like the best informed natives, music, with unusual delicacy and finish, having learned in Germany, and every essential thoroughly, except globes and drawing. Can be highly recommended by families in the best circles.

Mr Falkener, of 3 Old Bond Street, was a man who knew a commercial opportunity when he saw one: the demand for trained governesses was growing and this need could be matched to the concerns of parents about the future of their plainer daughters. In January 1835, he was offering 'references of the highest character to parents or guardians wishing to place a young lady for three or four years' in his care. Having taught her, with the help of 'emminent masters and a resident Parisian governess' all the necessary subjects, he then undertook to provide her with 'an eligible engagement as governess'. By 1850 several others had followed his example and were advertising for 'governess pupils'.

A number of small governess employment agencies were now operating. They appealed to 'the nobility and gentry' to scan their lists of English and Foreign governesses – 'letters the only expense to principals'; it was the governesses who had to pay the fees. Few of these agencies were well or honestly run and the fact that none of them seems to have survived for very long is a reflection not only on their efficiency but also on the fact that many of the women trying to get jobs as governesses were less than honest about their abilities. The agencies could not live up to their promises of providing 'highly qualified ladies', for very few such ladies existed.

In 1858 Dinah Maria Craik (the popular novelist and author of *John Halifax, Gentleman*) published anonymously *A Woman's Thoughts about Women*, a book in which she urges, with cloying expressions of respect, that men give women their right of 'something to do' and the education to do whatever it is efficiently. With its author's repeated professions of pleasure in the role of 'the weaker vessel' and in a position of subservience to a loving man, this book would be found more than provocative by feminists of today, and it cannot have been entirely to the taste of those pioneering women of the nineteenth century, even those who were educationalists rather than suffragettes.

Mrs Craik describes as 'harmful and blasphemous' the

outcry about 'the equality of the sexes'; the frantic attempt to force women, many of whom are either ignorant of or unequal for their own duties – into the position and duties of men. A pretty state of affairs would then ensue! Who that ever listened for two hours to the verbose confused inanities of a ladies' committee, would immediately go and give his vote for a female House of Commons? or who, on the receipt of a lady's letter of business – I speak of the average – would henceforth desire to have our courts of justice stocked with matronly lawyers and our colleges thronged by 'sweet girl graduates with their golden hair?' As for finance, in its various branches – if you pause to consider the extreme difficulty there always is in balancing Mrs Smith's housekeeping-book, or Miss Smith's quarterly allowance, I think, my dear Paternal Smith, you need not be much afraid lest this loud acclaim for 'women's rights' should ever end in pushing you from your stools, in counting house, college or elsewhere.

No; equality of the sexes is not in the nature of things. Man and woman are made 'for' and not 'like' one another . . . That both sexes were meant to labour, one 'by the sweat of his brow', the other 'in sorrow to bring forth' – and bring up – 'children', cannot, I fancy, be questioned.

Of the natural vocations of men and women Mrs Craik says that 'one is abroad, the other at home: one external, the other internal: one active, the other passive.'*

*In the copy of her book which I read, this passage is sidelined in pencil, with the note, apparently by a contemporary hand, 'Give them equal education, and then see!' This is an idea that apparently did not occur to Mrs Craik.

She is pleading that girls should have enough education to give them 'something to do' in their spare time after marriage, and something to fall back on in the event of their not finding a husband, and it is these single women with whom she is most concerned. In her chapter on female professions she is eloquent on the lack of alternatives offered to the spinster who has to support herself. Apart from compulsory wifehood in Australia, or voluntary watch-making in the home, single women have but four choices of career, she says: teaching, literature, art and the stage, and of these only teaching is an available option for the widow, the reduced gentlewoman and the girl-orphan. This literature would be unsuitable, only geniuses will make a living or a name out of it; painting is a subject in which women could excel, but since their delicacy would preclude them from attending 'life' classes or anatomical dissections, they have no possibility of ever getting to the top; the life of an actress 'poses great danger to temperament, character and mode of thought', and so any woman of respectable background must reject it.

Thus, in effect, says Mrs Craik, there is only one avenue open to the average single woman of refinement, with the result that the great mass of half-educated women thrown on their own resources become governesses, and it is lack of foresight in the education of these people that has created the low standard of governessing of the day.

> Just as 'young men enter the church, young women of all classes and all degrees of capability rush into governessing, because they think it is a 'respectable' profession to get on in, and are fit for nothing else. Thus the most important of ours, and the highest of all men's vocations, are both degraded ... by the unworthiness and incompetence of their professors.

Mrs Craik maintains that parents are looking for education on the cheap and, while lavishing expense on house, dress and entertainments, they pay their daughter's governess only 6d. an hour for daily tuition, or £20 a year if she lives in.

> Moreover the market, is so overcrowded, that the result is 'thousands of incapable girls and ill-formed, unscrupulous women professing to teach everything under the sun, adding lie upon lie ... often through no voluntary wickedness, but sheer helplessness, because they must either do that or starve!

Having exposed all this iniquity, Mrs Craik sets about putting it right. Governesses must reform themselves. Every one who has not a true vocation,

a pleasure and facility in teaching, an honest knowledge of everything
she professes to impart, a liking for children and a strong moral sense of
her responsibility towards them,

had 'better turn shopwoman, needlewoman or lady's-maid – even
become a decent housemaid, and learn how to sweep a floor' rather
than continue in her dishonesty. Few of them would starve for want of
work, and the result would be that the remainder would be more sought
after, the value of their labour would rise, and their employers would be
much better served.[8]

Accurate though this conclusion might be, it was as well for
governesses that others were proposing less draconian but far more
sensitive and realistic solutions to the problem. Already in 1836 in
Brighton a boarding school had been founded by the Revd. Henry
Venn Elliott which was described in its prospectus as 'a nursery for
governesses for the higher and middle classes'. This was one of the first
serious attempts, as opposed to the opportunistic ones, to make
governessing a profession to be trained for positively, rather than a last
resort for the impoverished semi-educated female. St Mary's Hall (as it
is still called today, as a girls' public school) took its pupils from the
usual source for governesses, the daughters of clergymen of limited
means. They were charged £20 per year, not enough to cover the costs
but this was a charitable enterprise. Seven years later there was a long
waiting list for its one hundred places. The regime was strictly
disciplinarian and the punishments administered for quite minor
misdemeanours were the kind that are heard of in the schoolrooms of
private houses later in the century; lying flat on the floor, eating meals
alone at a table, sitting stitching in enforced silence, or being sent to bed
by daylight.[9] The potential young governesses were learning the ropes
of the profession by their own dreary experience.

· 7 ·

'The dullest life ever dragged on by mortal . . .'

All things considered, in the nineteenth century an expensive education for a daughter was not a sound investment for a middle-class father. Even in statistical terms it was a risky one. Supposing he had five girls out of, say ten children: it was quite possible that during their childhood or adolescence he would lose one or two from measles, whooping cough, dyptheria, smallpox, scarlet fever, consumption or one of the other hazards that they might encounter before they reached adulthood. Even if they survived all these, the conditions of childbirth were such that it was likely that at least one of them would die while giving birth, a risk each young woman would be expected to run for as long as her strength would bear it, and often longer, even in the most affectionate families. Supposing, once educated, she lived to a good age; after marriage there was nothing she could do to capitalise on it, so there was little gain for either the family that gave the daughter or the family that received her in marriage. Thus there was no point in spending more money than was absolutely necessary to improve a girl's mind when what guaranteed her chances of a good marriage were primarily her personal fortune and, less importantly, her outward appearance and genteel behaviour.

What she actually knew was of no moment, and excess intelligence could even be detrimental. All a girl needed to learn could be easily taught by decent spinster women with a little learning and a knowledge of genteel behaviour who were grateful for employment and a roof over their heads, and who, above all, came cheap. This left funds available for the much more essential education of the boys, who must in time provide for families of their own.

What cost little was, as so often, little valued, and a governess was treated as a superior servant, with some variation according to the family who employed her. There was nothing new in this. For a long time disrespect for governesses had been the norm, whether they were scholars or ignorant.

Mary Wollstonecraft, in her *Thoughts on the Education of Daughters* which was published in 1787, was one of the first to point out how shameful it was that governesses should be shabbily treated by their employers. She devoted a chapter to their problems, entitling it 'Unfortunate Situation of Females, Fashionably educated, and left without a Fortune'. Such women, she said,

> if not entirely devoid of delicacy, must frequently remain single. Few are the modes of earning a substance, and those are very humiliating. Perhaps to be a humble companion to some rich old cousin, or what is still worse, to live with strangers, who are so intolerably tyranical, that none of their own relatives can bear to live with them . . . it is impossible, the many hours of anguish such a person must spend. Above the servants, yet considered by them as a spy, and ever reminded of her inferiority when in conversation with the superiors . . . should any of the visitors take notice of her, and she for a moment forget her subordinate state, she is sure to be reminded of it . . . the concealed anxiety impairs her constitution; for she must wear a cheerful face or be dismissed. A teacher in a school is only a kind of upper servant, who has more work than the menial ones.
>
> A governess to young ladies is equal disagreeable. It is ten to one if they meet with a reasonable mother, and if she is not so, she will be continually finding fault to prove she is not ignorant, and be displeased if her pupils do not improve, but angry if the proper methods are taken to make them do so. The children treat them with disrespect and often with insolence. In the meantime, life glides away, and the spirits with it, 'and when youth and genial years are flown' they have nothing to subsist on, or perhaps, on some extraordinary occasion, some small allowance may be made for them, which is thought a great charity.[1]

Mary Wollstonecraft knew well that she was talking about. She had done her time both as a governess and as companion to a Mrs Dawson in Bath, a woman of unreliable temper who had used and discarded many other women in the post before Mary.

An excellent example of the type of woman who had to suffer the indignities of working as a governess is Ellen Weeton, letter writer and keeper of a remarkable journal. She wrote for posterity and so that her daughter should know the details of her life, keeping a copy of virtually every letter she wrote. Her correspondence was immense. Her journal, in which she chronicles a life of hardship and sorrow, served as a safety valve for the emotions of a frustrated woman of some intellect; it is written in an unrepetitive and readable style. Put with her letters, we have a vivid account of provincial life in the early 1800s with all the petty spites and jealousies of the striving and rising lower middle class.*

Ellen Weeton was born in 1776, the daughter of a ship's captain, a slave trader who died in 1782 while harrying an American man o' war. His widow failed to establish her right to the prize money due to him and, with two young children to keep, found herself facing penury. So, as women suddenly thrust on their own resources had done for two hundred years, she turned to teaching. She opened a small village school in Upholland, in Lancashire. She had enough education to have taught her own children to read and write, but the school was not a great success, her income from it never exceeding ten or twelve shillings a week.

From the age of twelve her daughter Ellen, always known as Nellie, taught in this dame school and did the family housework as well, a life of drudgery which in time made her ill. On her mother's death, Nellie, then twenty one, took over the school; she also took in lodgers, to supplement her income which had fallen to seven shillings weekly, barely enough to feed her. By digging into her own small inheritance she managed to provide for herself and for her younger brother until he had completed his education and clerkship and had become an attorney.

From then on, Nellie's life became typical of an impecunious spinster of that date. She was alternately neglected and spurned by her relations, including her ungrateful brother and his vindictive wife, and wooed by them when they thought her small savings might become available. Her life became a sad struggle for survival and maintenance of her self-respect, during which she held two positions as a governess. The first she found in 1809, having answered an advertisement in *Gore's General Advertiser*:

---

*Both the journal and the letters were written in a firm and always legible hand with a quill pen, though steel pens had been introduced in 1803. Prepared quills were bought by the score, and her friends appreciated her skill at mending them. She wrote to one in 1825, 'Why did you not remind me, when I was at Wigan at Christmas, to mend or make you some pens? I am sure I am as willing, as able; don't forget the next feathery opportunity. Bring some quills with you, or old pens to 'renovate.'

WANTED: in the neighbourhood of Kendal, a GOVERNESS to superintend the education of a Young Lady. None need apply but such as can give good references as to ability and character.

She was engaged at 30 guineas a year, a rather generous salary for that time, but it was not easily earned. She was employed by the wealthy son of a Preston banker. She travelled by mail-coach and post-chaise to take up her position in his very attractive house three hundred yards from the wooded shore of Lake Windermere. Alas, Mr Pedder was a man of exceptional meanness whose preferred occupations were drinking, wife-beating and being offensive to the governess. He had married his seventeen-year-old dairymaid after an elopement to Gretna Green, and Nellie's job was to teach the daughter of an earlier marriage. After her epileptic pupil died accidently in a fire, Nellie stayed on for some time as companion to the young wife rather than face the hostile world again.

In 1812 she took a situation as governess to the four elder children of Joseph Armitage, a wool trader who had retreated to a country house four miles from Huddersfield because of a Luddite attack on his previous, more accessible home where he and his wife had been fired upon and had stones thrown through their bedroom window. Nellie's experiences at High Royd present a detailed picture of a governess's life with a middle class family at that period.

Again she found herself in a fine house, where there were four indoor servants. It was set in 'pretty and romantic country', but she seldom had a moment to explore it, though she loved walking. She was intensely lonely. Her mistress was pleasant and communicative to her only when not pregnant, and as she ultimately had fifteen children this was seldom. Nellie was a chatty and gregarious person, and letter writing was the only outlet for her volubility as she sat alone in her room. But her duties were so many that she had little time even for this.

My time is totally taken up with the children; from 7 o'clock in the morning, till half past 7 or 8 at night. I cannot lie any longer than 6 o'clock in a morning; and if I have anything to do for myself, in sewing, writing &c., I must rise sooner.

The children, when Nellie took her position,

seemed to have been allowed full liberty to a riotous degree; yet Mrs A. seems to expect that I shall now, speedily, bring them to the exactest order, the task is a most arduous one!

They were, she said, 'well ordered' in front of their parents, but out of their sight are as unruly, noisy, insolent, quarrelsome and illtempered a set, as I ever met with . . . The eldest girl for some weeks would not study a single lesson. She sat with book or slate before her, doing nothing . . . I requested, persuaded, insisted; but she would only smile carelessly in my face, and toss her head.

Mr and Mrs Armitage had given her full authority to discipline the children, in which Nellie was unusually lucky. She had on occasion to 'resort to the rod', but clearly hated doing it. In time they became more tractable and she even became quite fond of them. Much later, when she told them how difficult she had found them all at the start, they told her that they had used to call her 'Uglyface' behind her back.

Nellie was not averse to telling such stories or being funny at her own expense. Once, when returning from a walk, she met a fortune-telling pedlar woman, but refused to sample her wares, 'for she could only tell me that I must die a miserable old maid'. Regretting this later, and knowing her gaunt and angular figure not to be particularly attractive, she wrote,

> Alas, I cast the *silver* opportunity away and . . . may live in sorrow that I did so all my days. Foolish creature that I was! when the *hope* of a husband, and a fine coach, might have cheered me even to my last moments, thus ridiculously to have lost all chances of the wretch's last resource! Goosecap! noodle! ninny hammer! no name is too bad for me!

She records, also, that during one of the happier moments between herself and Mrs Armitage, when the latter 'being freed of her burden' was for a short period in good humour,

> I wrote a message on a slate and sent it by one of my youngest pupils. She wrote underneath it, that she would comply with my request as soon as she returned from my Lady Kitty's (the necessary) [the lavatory] but having received a very pressing invitation, she was under immediate engagement, and could not then stay a moment!

But such moments of levity were few; far more often Nellie was sadly lamenting her lot, the long hours, the lack of time to keep her clothes in repair or to read a newspaper (which she had to order and pay for herself),

> as I am never for a moment free of the children . . . I don't complain of this; it is no more than my duty; but certainly a governess is more a prisoner than any servant in the house.

She was obliged to supervise the children's play even when they were safely in a enclosed yard when, as she observed, the nursery maid could have done her turn.

Nellie would not have resented the exorbitant demands made on her time and energy if only her employers had been more appreciative of what she did for their offspring. Three months after taking up her post she wrote,

> The children 'have really made great progress, since my arrival, in their books; but as Mr A leaves all domestic management to his wife, and she never examines the children, I sometimes feel myself suspected of neglect . . . of which I never can, or will be guilty.

And, three months later,

> I have never, since I came her, received the slightest acknowledgement of the improvement of my pupils. It appears like a tacit degree of dissatisfaction with me; and when I do labour hard indeed till my spirits sink with the daily anxiety and exertion of mind, and the excessive confinement I am kept in injures my health, it is really mortifying to be left to suppose that my services are considered as inadequate to the situation I hold.

Her weekly account of the children's education was listened to with indifference, and her request for particular books with which to teach them was turned down.

> The expense seems to be an object, and I am surprised at it; for those who choose to keep a governess should not be afraid of a few shillings in books, and I did not exceed in my proposal ten or twelve shillings.

She had determined to buy some on her own account and lend them to her pupils, when Mr Armitage partially relented, to the extent of ordering some books himself, but of his own choice.

For the governess's own use, the only book offered by her employers was 'an Encylopaedia, which is not an everyday kind of reading,' she said sadly. 'There are some people,' she concluded

> with whom we cannot soon become acquainted . . . and others who are like old friends at the first interview. The former seems to be the case with Mrs Armitage and me. The idea of receiving wages and being, in truth, a servant, keeps my spirits down, and throws a degree of reserve over me, which I sometimes think has a correspondent effect on Mrs A . . .

Nellie suffered sadly in her longing for congenial company in her isolated life. Too 'jaded' often at night, when the children were gone to bed, even to take up her pen, she sat alone in the schoolroom, stitching and mending by the light of a single candle. 'I really think my neck is grown longer with trying to get near enough to the light to see to thread my needles.' She longed 'for some society'; but she felt that among family and servants there was nobody in the house with whom she could be on equal terms and she knew nobody in the surrounding neighbourhood, so had to put up with it. She wrote to a friend,

> I can give you nothing entertaining here in regard to myself; were I to tell you how I live, it would be a dullest account of the dullest life ever dragged on by mortal. I want for nothing, in the common acceptance of the word, but I go on in that monstrous tenor, in which there is no enjoyment; happily, however, for me, I can derive amusement from the oddity of my own thoughts, and have many a hearty solo laugh . . . as to plain every-day chit-chat, I was never in the way of it, and am unacquainted even with the theory. I know nothing of my neighbours, good or bad – as to fashion, I might as well be blind or deaf for what I can either see or hear. Visits, balls, plays, concerts, card-parties, equipages, scandal, tempest, war, trade, and all the other epithets of busy, bustling life, are to me words without meaning; my own ideas must either entertain my correspondents or not.

Luckily they did. Her letters were so full of humour and charm that they must have given great pleasure. But she often reminded her friends that she had long awaited a reply.

> I am writing to you upon paper which I bought in London at 5d a Quire, so don't be saucy and call it shabby. I shall inclose yours in one to Miss Braithwaite on a sister sheet; and sure it was bought in Lunnon too, for did I not buy it there my own sel; and if I could have known how long I should live, I would have bought as much as would have lasted my life; and, alack a day, I did but buy one Quire, and sorrow to me, I may happen to outlive it, and then what will I do? . . .
>
> Have the literati of Wigan commenced a Newspaper yet? I apprehend they have not, as I have seen no announcement. Perhaps if they knew – the learned ones of Wigan – that so able a pen as mine might be engaged in their service, they would proceed; tell 'em, will you?

When, after two years, Nellie left High Royd of her own accord, and with no apparent rancour on the Armitages' side, there was still little evidence of any recognition of what she had done for their family. The parents do not come well out of the story of her departure. Only the children cared.

I could weep when I think of our parting the night before I left. I had seen them all put to bed, when, hearing some noise, I thought they were quarreling, and went to see. I found them all weeping at the idea that that was the last night I should be with them; the next morning they rose at five, and walked me part of the way (I had to walk four miles to the coach) and when they left me went weeping home; the servants were very angry that I was not sent in the car.

Always generous with her time in writing letters, Nellie was careful in her use of paper. The recipient of a letter had to pay the postage at that time, and two sheets cost more than one. She would 'cross' her pages, writing diagonally over the original lines – 'I can seldom find it in my heart to leave a shred of unscrawled paper' – and resented having to leave the necessary space to address the sheet after folding it. (Envelopes were not introduced until 1840.)

She received many letters in reply to hers, which must have been some consolation in her dreary life. But if an intelligent and literate woman of thirty seven found the loneliness of being a governess almost intolerable, how much more agonising it must have been for a young girl. It was not unusual for governesses as young as sixteen or seventeen to be engaged. Although Nellie Weeton, at a particularly low moment, felt that she was 'a tenfold closer prisoner than any other governess in this neighbourhood', she was probably only giving vent to her frustration, for her situation was typical rather than unusual.[2]*

Even where governesses were treated with respect, simple disregard for their emotional needs was widespread. Mrs Jamieson appealed in 1846 to women's better nature, pointing out that it was

> a great mistake to regard the human being who dwells beneath your roof, and in the shadow of your protection, merely as an instrument to be used for your own purposes. She also has a life to be worked out . . . You may help the working out of this life, or you may put an extinguisher on it.

Few regarded her words. 'You should cultivate cheerfulness,' said one lady to her pale governess, irritated by her appearance.[3]

*Nellie Weeton was never again employed as a governess, for she was shortly afterwards encouraged by her odious brother Tom, whose iniquities she always forgave, into a disastrous marriage. By the terms of their mother's will, Tom could claim £100 of his sister's tiny fortune when she either married or died, and this seems to have been his callous motive. After seven years of misery, Nellie left her brutal husband and spent the next few years desperately trying to obtain access to their only child, a daughter. He had dictated the terms of their Deed of Separation, to which in physical fear and under duress she had agreed. It was not until 1839 that the Custody of Infants Act was passed, whereby a mother might gain access to her infant children, and even the right to care for them, if they were under seven years of age. There is evidence in church records that Nellie Weeton ultimately succeeded, but no letters are available after 1825.

Anne Brontë was nineteen when she took her first governess position. In her novel *Agnes Grey* her picture of the life of a young governess in two families, is based largely on her own unpleasant experiences. The Bloomfield family, with its odious and ungovernable children, whose parents refuse to allow the governess to discipline them while blaming her for their excesses, is said to be based on the Ingham family of Blake Hall, near Mirfield in Yorkshire. Anne's first post as governess was with the two elder children of their large family for two rather unhappy terms in 1839, and she found her charges, as her sister Charlotte noted in a letter, 'unruly and violent'. Direct descendants of Mr and Mrs Joshua Ingham claim that, though some incidents in the fictional story may have been exaggerated, the reality of Anne's life was not dissimilar to Agnes Grey's experiences. A younger sister of Anne's pupils told her granddaughter that she remembered all the children on one occasion running screaming round the garden and refusing to obey their governess's calls to come to their lessons, a scene that has a close parallel in an incident in the book, when the father's wrath falls upon the governess. More than once the Ingham children are said to have reduced Anne to tears, but family tradition suggests another side to these stories: Mrs Ingham, who died in 1899, told one of her grandchildren that she had once 'employed a very unsuitable governess called Miss Brontë, who had actually tied the two children to a table leg in order to keep them quiet while she got on with her writing'.[4] Anne herself in a letter said that though she was not empowered to inflict any punishment on her 'excessively indulged' pupils, their mother was extremely kind, and Charlotte described Mrs Ingham as 'a placid, mild woman'. So the reality at Blake Hall may not have been as horrific as the fictional account. But it would be a mistake to suppose Anne's desciption of the life of a governess in this or in her next position to have been based on anything but truth. Within her own family she had ample experience to draw upon of how governesses were treated. Charlotte Brontë worked as a private governess and resented it even more than her sister. She complained in a letter to a friend in 1839 of her then employer's callous treatment:

> I said in my last letter that Mrs Sidgewick did not know me. I now begin
> to find that she does not intend to know me; that she cares nothing in the
> world about me, except to contrive how the greatest possible quantity of
> labour may be squeezed out of me, and to that end she overwhelms me
> with oceans of needlework, yards of cambric to hem, muslim nightcaps
> to make, and, above all things, dolls to dress. I do not think she likes me
> at all . . . I can see now more clearly than I have ever done before that a

private governess has no existence, is not considered as a living and rational being, except as connected with the wearisome duties she has to fulfil . . . One of the pleasantest afternoons I have spent here – indeed, the only one at all pleasant – was when Mr Sidgewick walked out with his children, and I had orders to follow a little behind . . .

When Charlotte came 'to the lowest state of exhaustion' and showed her depression, she was taken to task 'with a stress of manner and a harshness of language scarcely credible'.

On the other hand, a cousin of the Sidgewicks considered Charlotte to be far too touchy. Urged to hurry up when the party was waiting for her to accompany them to church, she took offence; and on not being invited to go with them on another Sunday, she became deeply depressed at being unwanted. She may have been over-sensitive, but there is no doubt that her sense of natural justice rebelled at the distance that convention put between her and her employers.

In her biography of Charlotte Brontë, Mrs Gaskell relates an incident in which one of her small charges 'said, putting his hand in hers, "I love 'ou, Miss Brontë," whereupon the mother exclaimed, before all the children. "Love the *governess*, my dear!" '[5]

Children emulated their elders in looking down on the women who taught them. Many people deplored the disrespect which they showed to their governesses and attached the blame firmly to the parents who were setting them a bad example. In 'The Young Lady's Friend' a writer drew attention to 'the instinctive homage' that should be due to 'mental culture and refined manners', and conjured up a picture of a governess humiliated by the young:

Can there be any sense in the half-educated daughter of a lawyer or merchant treating her more mature and more accomplished teacher as an inferior? . . . Nothing can be meaner than the false pride exhibited by some girls towards the ladies who give them lessons in music, drawing or languages: some have even been known to pass their instructress in the street without acknowledging the acquaintance.

One can almost feel the heat of of the affront burning in the cheeks of the snubbed governess as she turns aside to hide her humiliation, gazing blindly into a shop window. The writer had perhaps some personal experience of being cut dead in such circumstances.

Charlotte M. Yonge, in *Womankind*, says 'Insolence to a governess is a stock complaint', and she does not mean insolence from children in this case, for she goes on, 'In real life I never heard it from anyone by birth and breeding a lady.'

·8·

'The despotism of fashion'

It is not surprising that when, in the middle of the nineteenth century, it slowly began to be accepted that to educate girls might actually be desirable, there were few women capable of the task of instructing them. It was necessary to make use of male teachers, but that meant precautions had to be taken: when Queen's College first opened as a day school for girls in London in 1848 the lecturers were all men, so the classes had to be attended by a rota of voluntary 'Lady Visitors'. They were chaperones, whose job was to make sure the students were not lured into the corridors and assaulted.

Many of those women teachers and educationalists of real determination, who refused to accept the status of women's education as it was, founded or allied themselves to one of the progressive girls' schools or colleges that started to come into being in the second half of the century. They were then able to carry on the struggle from positions of some authority. The speed with which they brought about change was quite remarkable: during the first half of the nineteenth century there was hardly anything recognisable as secondary education for girls, and yet by its close many schools had women teachers who had been educated at university. The twenty women teachers employed by the redoubtable Lawrence sisters at Roedean in 1900 were all graduates, or held equivalent qualifications.

The perseverance and ultimate success of those nineteenth century female educationalists in bringing women's education into line with men's has been very amply chronicled and will not be pursued further here. Though full educational parity was still far from being achieved, by the end of the century the main bastions had fallen and the benefits ultimately filtered through even to the governesses.

In the mid 1800s the history of the governess begins to diverge from that of the school teacher. Collectively, and through sheer numbers, she was a power in the land, but a negative one, since the girls who came under her exclusive care stood little chance of achieving more than the most basic knowledge.

By contrast, some girls' private schools in the second half of the century were offering a wide and balanced range of subjects, properly taught by experienced teachers. The prospectus for Wimbledon House School in Kemptown, Brighton, opened by the Lawrence sisters in 1885 (the forerunner of Roedean), listed an impressed number of classes: physical training was mentioned first, and included outdoor games, swimming, riding, dancing and gymnastics. Domestic economy and needlework were not forgotten, neither were the 'accomplishments' of drawing, writing, painting and music. The bulk of the curriculum was, however, solid learning: in this order were listed Bible history, English language and literature, languages ancient and modern, history, geography, natural science, mathematics and religious instruction – the latter in accordance with the views of parents. These subjects were what female educationalists considered to be necessary to produce the physically and mentally developed woman. Older pupils could be prepared for Girton and Newnham, the Cambridge colleges which had been established in 1873 and 1880. Learning was to be for learning's sake, ultimately with a view to competing in a male-dominated world, and not simply to add attraction to young girls coming on to the marriage market.

Parents of the professional classes, who intended their daughters to be able to earn their own living and who liked the ideas on offer, sent their daughters to the schools run on these lines. But these few progressive schools were out of the reach of most middle class parents, if not financially then socially. When Cheltenham Ladies College was established in 1858, with Miss Dorothea Beale as headmistress, there was strict vetting not only of the means of the parents of potential pupils but of their position in society as well. There were many parents, in any case, who mistrusted the principles of the progressive schools, as being too much like boys' schooling, and as being dangerously avant garde.

Many parents still looked to the traditional schools, with their emphasis on elegant accomplishments, that had been appearing all over the country since early in the century. The most fashionable were to be found in Brighton, where in 1836 there were said to be at least a hundred small boarding schools for girls.[1] By the end of the century Southport was described as 'the Brighton of Lancashire; one part of it,' said a school inspector, 'seems made of nothing but schools, judging by the brass plates.'[2] There was good reason, however, for caring parents to be uneasy about the standards in these traditional schools, for there were many examples of horrific conditions to alarm them during the first sixty years of the century. Tales of overcrowding, ill health, poor food and bitter cold were abundant. The register of Cowan Bridge School, which the four elder Brontë girls attended, shows that in the first two years after it opened seventy two girls were entered; within two years twenty eight of them had been removed of whom at least six soon died as a result of conditions and treatment in the school.

So middle class families usually fell back on the solution for their daughters that their parents had used: for reasons of fashion, finance, family custom or fear of the unknown, vast numbers of parents continued to engage private governesses, so that they remained at least ostensibly in charge of their daughters' well-being and curriculum.

The nominal fees in a typical fashionable boarding school were between £120 and £150 a year per girl, and this sum could be quadrupled by the cost of 'extras'. A governess at the same date, on the other hand, would be paid £20 to £40 a year plus board, and if she taught two or three daughters, or girls from more than one family, there was no comparison in terms of value for money. It was a positive economy, with very similar educational results. In the middle of the century, any father could reasonably argue that a governess could teach his daughters just as well as a school, for the standard of teaching in the average girls' school was abysmally low.

In her autobiography, Frances Power Cobbe, (1822–1908), champion of women's rights, describes female schooling in the 1830s as 'at that moment more pretentious than it had ever been before, and infinitely more costly than it is now; and it was likewise more shallow and senseless than can easily be believed.'[3] From 1836, she spent two years as a pupil at a Brighton boarding school where 'extras' brought the cost for her parents to £500 a year, and where the emphasis was, as usual, on the 'accomplishments'.

> Not that which was good in itself, but that which would make us admired in society was the *raison d'être* of each requirement. Everything was taught in the inverse ratio of its true importance. At the bottom of the scale were Morals and Religion, and at the top were Music and Dancing: miserably poor music, too.

They learnt the fashionable modern languages:

Such French, such Italian and such German as we spoke may be more easily imagined than described ... Naturally after (a very long way after) foreign languages came the study of English ... our English studies embraced one long, awful lesson each week to be repeated to the schoolmistress herself by a class, in history one week, in geography the week following. Our first class, I remember, had once to commit to memory – heaven alone knows how – no less than thirteen pages of Woodhouselee's *Universal History*!

She tells of dismal daily walks and pointless punishment:

I have seen ... no less than nine young ladies obliged to sit for hours in the angles of the three rooms, like naughty babies, with their faces to the wall; half of them being quite of marriageable age, and all dressed, as was *de rigeur* with us every day, in full evening attire of silk or muslin, with gloves and kid slippers.

Music at this school, as at other schools and in the homes where girls were educated by governesses, was taught to all, and even those with no ear or aptitude were obliged to spend long and agonising hours trying to learn to sing or to play harp and piano, some learning the new instruments, the accordion and the concertina.

Frances Cobbe said one day to her German music teacher, 'My dear Fräulein, I mean to practise this piece of Beethoven's till I conquer it.'

'My dear,' responded the honest Fräulein, 'you do practise that piece for seex hours a day, and you do live till you are seexty, at the end you will *not* play it!' 'And yet,' said Frances, 'so hopeless a pupil was compelled to learn for years, not only the piano, but the harp and singing!'[1]

Hannah More, who was given at times to entertaining flights of fancy, may nevertheless have been quoting from life when she told of a girl who started music aged six, and having practised four hours a day till she was eighteen (leaving out Saturdays and thirteen days when she was travelling,) clocked up 14,400 hours of playing scales. The point of the story was that at the end of it all she married a man who couldn't stand music.

This tale is given credence by a school inspector's estimate that the average, upper middle-class girl would have 'sat before her piano during 5,520 hours at a cost to her parents of at least £100 by the time she left school at eighteen'. A Royal Commission report in 1895 claimed that in the middle of the nineteenth century music had held a 'perniciously important position' in the average girl's educational curriculum; the main objection was that music was taught indiscriminately to all as an essential accomplishment, 'regardless of whether they had sufficient musical ability to give themselves or their friends the faintest pleasure as the result'.[5]

A veneer of education was nevertheless what parents found adequate for their daughters and the proliferation of small schools run on these lines would not have taken place had there been no demand for them. The object of it all was still marriagability, and the girls themselves were apparently unaware that for them schooling could have any other end in view. At Frances Cobbe's Brighton school,

> All the pupils were daughters of men of some standing, mostly country gentlemen, members of Parliament, and offshoots of the peerage . . . It seems to me the young creatures there assembled were full of capabilities for widely extended usefulness and influence . . . But all this fine human material was deplorably wasted.

'Nobody dreamed,' said Frances, 'that any one of us could in later life be more or less than an "Ornament of Society".'[6]

It was against the vacuity of home education, however, that the novelist Catherine Sinclair (1800–64) took up the cudgels. Writing in 1836, she launched an attack, not without wit, in *Modern Accomplishments*:

> Lady Howard's utmost ingenuity was exercised in devising plans of study for her daughter, each of which required to be tried under the dynasty of a different goveness, so that, by the time Matilda Howard attained the age of sixteen, she had been successively taught by eight, all of whom were instructed in the last '*method*' that had been invented for making young ladies accomplished on the newest pattern.

Though slightly less attention was paid now to deportment and manners than had been the case in the previous century, the concentration on 'the accomplishments' was even more intense.

The question is whether by opting for a governess education parents got in any way a better education for their daughters than if they had sent them to a fashionable school. The answer is, very rarely; the type of education which young women brought with them into the homes where they became governesses is suggested by the critical Taunton report of the Schools Enquiry commission published in 1868. Some of the schools inspected were for the 'daughters of persons whose income range from £150 to £600 per annum', which meant small professional men, whose daughters would find few jobs other than governessing to suit their social standing. A girl would come from home at about ten years old, able to do a little reading and sewing, and would stay till the age of fourteen or fifteen. At school

> she is perfected at reading, learns spelling from a book, from which she repeats half a column daily; learns geography and English grammar – both by rote; does sums out of an arithmetical textbook twice or thrice a week, and reads Goldsmith's History of England. After two or three years this course is extended to include chronology, geology and mythology, with other branches of science and general information . . .

This sounds rather good until we find that these subjects are all learnt by committing to memory Miss Richmal Mangnall's *Historical and Miscellaneous Questions*. The report goes on:

> How little a girl can manage to learn during five years spent in such a school will hardly be believed by those who have not had ocular proof of it. So far as I could discover most girls in private school carry nothing away but reading (which is generally good), an angular and scratchy handwriting, and a very indifferent skill with the needle . . . I remember having gone to a ladies' (day) school . . . where there were some 25 girls paying £6 or £8 per annum. The list of the school-books which they used, including Greek and Roman history and geography and nearly every branch of science – would fill a page, yet not one could do the simplest sum in the addition of money, or answer any question in English grammar except in the words of the book which she had got by rote. Further examination of the pupils would no doubt have disclosed equal ignorance in other subjects, but the mistress seemed so much distressed by the children's performances that I gave over questioning them. She was a well meaning and may have been painstaking woman, a widow who had started a school to support herself, engaged a master for music and dancing, and then gone on teaching the other subjects, without the least notion of her own incapacity.

In a girls' school in another large town the inspector 'found a lesson in geography going on.

> The chief mistress, an elderly person and rather deaf, was sitting knitting with a geography book open on her knee, the children stood round, and she questioned them from it thus:
> 'What is separated from Scandinavia by a narrow sea called The Sound?'
> 'What island in the South of England is remarkable for its beauty?'
> When I asked her whether grammar was taught, she answered, 'Yes, they learn a verb every day.'

The inspector concluded that 'they might as well have said their lessons to the armchair as to her,' and it is obvious from the rest of his report that this school was not an exception but rather was typical of the schools in the area. He considered that the boarding schools catering for girls from similar backgrounds as the day schools were not much better; the only difference was that when a girl went home at the age of sixteen she took with her in addition to what she had, or had not learnt, 'an air of affectation and constraint' and 'two or three pieces of ornamental needlework, each of which has occupied her three months . . .' These were lovingly framed by the proud and 'usually satisfied' parents, and of course can still be found in antique shops today, at prices which would stagger their creators.

The summary of the Commission's report makes no bones about who is to blame. 'The present inferiority for girls' training is due to the despotism of fashion or, in other words, the despotism of parents or guardians.' [7]

In the chapter of the Report devoted to girls' education one of the Commissioners, Lord Lyttelton, wrote:

> There is a long established and inveterate prejudice that girls are less capable of mental cultivation, and less in need of it than boys, that accomplishments, and what is showy and superficially attractive, are what is really essential for them . . .

If girls were found to be inferior to boys in learning mathematics, grammar and science, he said, it was because they had no teachers capable of instructing them in these subjects. His conclusion was an attack on the attitude of middle class families who ought to have demanded decent secondary education for their daughters as well as their sons. He condemned their

> apathy and want of co-operation, often their active opposition . . . They will not pay for good teaching when they might have it, they are themselves the cause of deterioration in competent teachers . . . and their own want of cultivation hinders it in their children.[8]

The Taunton report caused anger and made many enemies among the establishment, but it was immensely helpful to the pioneers of female education.

Thus the schools that trained potential governesses and the schools that were chosen by parents as an alternative to governess education stood equally condemned. It is hard to argue with the conclusion of the Report that the poor quality of the middle class girl's education at this time should be laid firmly at the feet of parents; and it follows that those parents who eschewed the better schools that began to appear in the second half of the 1800s and stuck to governesses, by continuing to under-pay them and to require so little of them, were responsible for the teaching ability of the average governess remaining abysmally low. They were also responsible for the fact that the gradual improvement in the pay and position of schoolteachers was not reflected in that of governesses. By the 1870s the annual pay of an elementary school-teacher was approaching £100, while that of a governess remained much lower. Parents advertising usually offered from £50 to £70, and though governesses occasionally asked for more, they were still in no position to demand it.

Maria Shirreff, born in 1816 and one of the Founders in 1872 of the Girls' Public Day School Trust, wrote of her mother that she considerd learning in women 'not only unnecessary, but undesirable', and of the governess she employed to care for her daughters, that 'she probably could not have formulated a single rule of education and would undoubtedly have failed in any examination'.

'The recommendation of an English governess must rest more upon her moral than her intellectual qualifications', said another writer, and not in any tone of disapproval.

In Ireland the situation was little different. Responsibility for the early education of George Bernard Shaw, who was born in Dublin in 1856, was divided between his uncle, Rector of St Bride's Church, and Miss Hill, a governess who tried to give him a taste for poetry by reciting such lines as,

Stop, for thy tread is on an Empire's dust . . .

an attempt which, Shaw said, only moved him and his sisters to derisive laughter. She also taught him to add, subtract, and multiply, but failed to teach him division,

because she kept saying 'two into four, three into six' and so forth, without ever explaining what the word 'into' meant in this connection. This was explained to me on my first day at school, and I solemnly declare that it was the only thing I ever learnt at school.[9]

In the 1870s Beatrix Potter, a lonely and intelligent child who learnt to read from Scott's Waverley Novels, was abandoned in her early teens by her devoted governess, Miss Hammond. The woman had found herself outstripped by her pupil who had come to know more than she did, and so she was unable to teach her anything further. Later Beatrix expressed gratitude that her education had been neglected, since school might have 'rubbed off' some of her originality.

I fancy that I could have been taught anything if I had been caught young; but it was in the days when parents kept governesses, and only boys went to school in most families.[10]

The remark implies a general acceptance that governess education meant hardly any education at all.

The 'governess nursery' of St Mary's Hall in Brighton, which I described earlier, had been started in 1836 for philanthropic reasons and was well run by the standards of the day. Some of the less well known schools, however, having exploited the need of impecunious parents to make their girls self-supporting to sell places at their establishments, then grossly abused their trust. The conditions under which many girls lived and worked were sometimes so appalling that learning was well nigh impossible in the battle simply to survive malnutrition, typhus and tuberculosis and cruel treatment. It was not unusual for girls to sleep several in a bed, and hygiene was an unknown concept.

Lowood, the dreadful orphanage in *Jane Eyre* is modelled by Charlotte Brontë on the Clergy Daughters' School at Cowan Bridge, where she and three of her sisters spent less than a year from 1824 to 1825; conditions there led to the deaths within months of Maria and Elizabeth, the two elder girls. The reality of Cowan Bridge was probably no less horrifying than that of the fictional school; according to her husband, 'to the day of her death [Charlotte] maintained that the picture drawn in *Jane Eyre* was on the whole a true picture of the Cowan Bridge school as she knew it by experience'. And yet this was a school that had been established entirely to do good, to train at a low cost young girls from families of straightened means and to equip them with the education that would enable them to earn their living as governesses; the subscribers were the most upright and reputable of philanthropists, and included Hannah More and William Wilberforce. One of the trustees, The Revd. William Carus Wilson, who lived in nearby Casterton Hall, was in control of the domestic and scholastic arrangements. He was a well-meaning man, reputed to love children, but with no knowledge of management, hygiene, or anything relating either to children or to the running of a school. Most of the staff were his relations, and there is no reason to suppose that they were not as distressed as he was when the children sickened and died. This sad school was run not with evil intent, as seemed to be the case with its fictional counterpart, but with the ignorance and incompetence typical of the day. Nine years after its founding it moved to the healthier surroundings of Casterton. Charlotte wrote later, 'the accommodation, the diet, the discipline, the system of tuition, all are, I believe, greatly improved'. Despite her exposure of him in *Jane Eyre*, which caused a great deal of anger and controversy, Carus Wilson survived with his reputation relatively intact.*

After leaving Cowan Bridge, Charlotte was for a time patchily educated at home by her aunt, before spending a further eighteen months at a better, happier school, run by a Miss Wooller, where she later returned in 1835 as a teacher. Depression and overwork eventually brought this to an end, and she wrote later to the headmistress that she remembered 'my incapacity to impart pleasure fully as much as my powerlessness to receive it'. Intelligent minds such as hers must have suffered great frustration at having to teach from Miss Mangnall's *Questions*, still used thirty five years after its publication, as one of the text books at Miss Wooller's. It was to be the mainstay of countless ill-trained teachers and governesses for many years to come.

It may be that the Brontë sisters, when they worked later as governesses in private families, may have used their own intelligence and ingenuity to try to enthuse their charges, though their accounts suggest that the insubordination of the children and the lack of parental support for their governesses' disciplinary effort made this impossible. But Elizabeth Sewell, writing in *Principles of Education* thirty years after Charlotte and Emily worked at Miss Wooller's, bemoaned the low standards of the teachers who had got their education in such schools:

> Of governesses in general, 'What do they know?' They themselves will answer – in all humility and truthfulness – 'Nothing'. [11]

---

*In 1844, the Revd. W. Carus Wilson, was described as being 'so well known as the kind and active superintendent of an institution for the Education of future Governesses', and is recorded as offering places in Old Casterton Hall, in his parish, which had been adapted as a temporary or permanent refuge for six to twelve old and poor governesses. It is to be hoped that these ladies found there a happier way of life than did his pupils at the Cowan Bridge school.

· 9 ·

Charity begins in hostels

B y the middle of the nineteenth century training for schoolteachers
had begun to improve. It was being suggested by some enlightened
people that qualifying examinations and certificates of proficiency
should be introduced for governesses also, but not particularly with the
interests of their pupils in mind. The intention was more philanthropic,
that the status of governesses themselves should be thus improved, so
that they should gain more respect and higher salaries. Unsuccessful
efforts were made by the pioneering Governesses Benevolent
Institution to hold exams for teaching diplomas, but they attracted
candidates of such low quality that the scheme never got off the
ground.[1]

By 1850 there were approximately 500 certificated women teachers
in England. (This figure compares interestingly with the figure of
twenty one schoolmistresses licensed to teach in Paris in the year 1380
by the cantor of Notre Dame alone.[2]) Several colleges had been
founded where women could train to be elementary teachers, but the
low numbers of qualified women they turned out made little impact for
some years on the dearth of female teachers for girls' schools.

In the census taken in 1851 there were 21,373 women who gave
their employment as governess. That they were in the main poorly
equipped in knowledge and teaching skills still appeared to be of little
concern to most of the parents who employed them. Well after the
accession of Queen Victoria to the throne in 1837 the common belief

persisted in Britain that women had neither the mental capacity nor the need for serious education.

The education of the Queen's children was for a long period in the care of Lady Lyttelton (mother of the Schools Enquiry Commissioner), who became royal governess in 1842. She said once, 'I know very well I was born to be a schoolmistress', and she took pleasure in giving their first simple lessons to the Prince of Wales and the Princess Royal, whom she addressed affectionately as Princey and Princessy. She had three sub-governesses, nurses, nursery maids and nursery staff under her control, so her job was mainly administrative. Having had five children of her own, she had experience to back her judgement, and she had sensible theories on the management of children. Her royal charges were reasonably naughty, but Sarah Lyttelton had unusually advanced ideas on how to discipline them. She wrote to a daughter-in-law on the subject of a granddaughter's crying fits,

> I can't wonder you are uneasy about them – *j'ai passé par là!* But there is no occasion, believe me, to suppose they mean *bad temper* at her age. As to checking them, I fancy taking very little notice is not a bad thing. I own I am against punishments; they wear out so soon, and one is never sure they are fully understood by the child as belonging to naughtiness. It is odd that the Princess has exactly the same cry of 'Wipe my eyes!' all the time she is roaring.

She took sensible decisions for the royal children's well-being. When she first arrived in their nursery she found the eldest child, the Princess of Wales, dressed in Garter Blue velvet, Brussels lace, white shoes, pearls and diamonds and looking 'too comical'. Some time later she speaks of the princesses as being 'dressed in coarse straw hats, and brown holland frocks and blouses'. She had few brushes with the Queen, who referred to her as 'so agreeable and so sensible,' and when she finally left the royal service the Queen recorded that all the nurses and maids were in tears, 'she was so beloved'.[3]

The Queen's children were all well taught, but many of her aristocratic subjects were as educationally deprived as their middle class counterparts. Above the Norman gateway of Windsor Castle was a room with deeply embrasured, low, stone-mullioned windows. At one time it had been used as a state prison, but in the 1860s it was schoolroom to Victoria, Louisa and Mary Grey, the three daughters of General The Hon. Charles Grey, equerry and private secretary to the Queen. Their studies were directed by a harsh German *Fräulein* who made them learn daily verses from the scriptures by heart like parrots. They also memorised strings of dates starting with Nimrod, the Babylonian captivity and Alexander the Great.

'Alaric, King of the Goths, and Attila, King of the Huns,' Louisa remembered,

> seemed to me a mysterious pair of twins on a par with Romulus and Remus . . . We plodded daily through three new dates, steeple-chasing over centuries until we finally reached the accession of Queen Victoria.

This useless and unhappy period, for the governess was also physically unkind to the children, eventually came to an end, and Fraülein Rebentisch was said later to have gone mad as a result of contemplating Prussia's annexation of Hanover. She was replaced by an English governess who was chosen, as governesses were at that time, according to Louisa, for her refinement and high principles, rather them for any ability to teach. She could not even keep order, and was mercilessly teased by the children who placed biscuit crumbs in her bed to prevent the poor woman from sleeping. For the girls, at least, Windsor Castle became a happier place.[4]

Among the inadequate governesses there were some who were reasonably well educated and whose teaching ability was sadly wasted in households where the atmosphere was in no way conducive to learning. This could be because the parents only required the usual 'accomplishments' or, as often, because they did not give the governess the necessary support for the discipline she must impose on her pupils. Charlotte Brontë, during one of her periods as governess, complained in a letter about the children in her care,

> . . . more riotous, perverse, unmanageable cubs never grew. As for correcting them, I quickly found that this was out of the question; they are to do as they like. A complaint to [the mother] only brings black looks on myself.[5]

Other parents were too kindly or indulgent with their children for an intelligent governess to practise her craft. In 1827, in *A word in favour of Female Schools,* Mrs Broadbent tells of

> an amiable girl who lived as governess in an excellent family . . . who wrote a letter to her mother . . . which said 'I know that I ought to be satisfied, as their parents are so, but, indeed the little I can do with these children, in the way of improvement, is quite mortifying. We are so constantly in the carriage, going to this place or the other, that we have not time for anything.'

The same writer tells a story of a mother who, in despair of finding a first class governess for her daughters, enlisted the help of her brother, describing to him all the abilities and attributes she required to be embodied in a young woman of twenty-five. The brother replied that if he should come upon such a paragon he would instantly marry her.[6]

It could happen that a governess finding herself transferred into a huge ancestral home would avail herself of the heaven-sent opportunity to acquire the education she had hitherto been unable to obtain. One such was Miss Georgina Johnstone, one of five sisters, two of whom became governesses in order to help finance the education of some nephews. Through a friend, she was found a place instructing the daughters of the Duke of Argyll and, for fourteen years, moved with them between Argyll Lodge near Holland Park and Inveraray Castle on the shores of Loch Fyne. The youngest girl, Lady Victoria Campbell, was ten when Miss Johnstone first laid eyes on the family in 1864. At the time, they were staying in Brighton, having swimming lessons and enjoying donkey rides on the downs. On entering the sitting room of their lodging house she was disconcerted 'to find a number of girls with a bewilderingly close personal resemblance and a rapidity of speech and action that rather daunted the staid, deliberate little lady, who found herself looking rather timidly at those who were to come under her not very dominant personality'.

She might well be daunted for though her pupils were to prove intelligent and well-behaved, they had little desire to work and she had absolutely no idea of how to teach. As daughters of an officer in the army of William IV, she and her sisters had been brought up in the country and had had no schooling of any kind. However, under the Argyll roofs she set about acquiring the knowledge her remarkable brain hankered for with 'an insatiable craving'. With two well furnished libraries at her disposal she taught herself all the languages of Europe, and at the end of her time with the family was studying Sanskrit and Gaelic. She used to work at night, kneeling upright at the schoolroom table in order not to fall asleep. She persuaded the minister of the tiny loch-side town of Inveraray to teach her astonomy, and a developing passion for botany made her ardent in the pursuit and indentification of fungi. The girls soon found that being late for lessons brought no recrimination if they brought with them to the schoolroom a new or interesting toadstool.

One of her pupils wrote later that 'with this gift of instucting herself there came no aptitude at imparting knowledge'. This unperceptive remark reflects the fact that the lessons Miss Johnstone set were rarely learnt, and during readings from Macaulay's *History of England* or a session with Colenso's *Arithmetic* she could easily be diverted with discussions on a recent debate in the House of Lords or the oncoming Franco-German war.

'My dears', she would say at the end of the morning, 'our lesson has been sadly neglected; we must hope, though, that our conversation has not been altogether unprofitable.'

The family as a whole was aware that they all 'owed much to the rare intelligence and interest which she brought to bear on all passing events, and to the cultured atmosphere that hung around this learned lady'.

It is clear that Miss Georgina Johnstone, or 'Pock Pudding' as she was called by her charges because of her 'intense Englishness', was a natural and gifted teacher, of a type almost unknown in the governesses of the day. That she had had no education but was entirely self taught explains why she did not use the teaching methods that the family would have been used to in previous governesses. There were no lists of figures to be learnt, no studying page by page of Miss Mangnall's turgid questions. To learn history from the works of Lord Macaulay, whose books were in the library and whom they knew as a visitor to Argyll Lodge, was certainly more likely to stimulate the interest and imagination of teenage girls than to pore over the pages of 'instant' historical knowledge compiled by Dr Brewer.

Whether or not the Duke and Duchess regarded Miss Johnstone as 'a puzzle', as her pupils did, they undoubtedly appreciated what they had in her. The Duke asked for her assistance in correcting proofs of his book, *The Reign of Law*, and amused his publisher by regularly arguing at length with her at the luncheon table over details of punctuation and literary style.[7]

Such a governess and such a position were both unusual; the continued undervaluing of the governess class led to sad tales of neglect and tragedy. Concern expressed by many people over the unfortunate position of elderly, ailing or unemployed governesses had led to the formation, in 1843, of the Governesses' Benevolent Institution, 'with a view of remedying the existing evils in Female Education, and of removing them in future, and of benefiting Governesses in general'. These aims were ambitious but, after 150 years of existence, the founders of the GBI would be gratified to know how significantly the Institution contributed to achieving the first two, and that in 1991 it was still 'benefiting governesses in general'.

Queen Adelaide donated money and headed a long list of royal and noble patrons of the Institution, which was launched by the Duke of Cambridge. In an inaugural speech he 'strongly advocated the claims of governesses to the charitable consideration of the public when no longer able to fulfil the duties of their profession'. *The Times* noted in its report of the occasion that the Duke looked in excellent health and that the meeting was 'excedingly numerous, but that at least three fourths of the audience consisted of the softer sex'. The 'but' is significant in demonstrating the writer's belief that such a preponderance of women meant that it was a mere fashionable gathering and that the subject was not being taken very seriously.

Indeed, at the start, it seems to have been hard to find enough money to achieve any of the founders' aims. In the first year the Ladies' Committee, which was formed to decide on elegibility of governesses for temporary financial help, received 102 applications. They were able to respond to fifty six of the worst cases; for the remainder, apart from a few whose references were not satisfactory or who wanted loans which were not available, they could do nothing, simply for lack of funds. 'The assistance afforded being necessarily very limited, as compared with the wants of the assisted,' the members of the Institute responded with increased effort, and as year by year the number of governesses applying for assistance rose, so did the sum of money available to distribute among them. At the Annual General Meeting of 1847 the GBI was able to report that during the preceding year applications had been received from 422 penniless governesses for financial help, and that £559 had been divided between 207 of them. This amounted to just under £3 per governess, and cannot have relieved very much hardship, but annuities had also been awarded to sixteen other indigent governesses of advanced years. After this meeting dinner was enjoyed by the company, with toasts and votes of thanks, and *The Times* correspondent commented, 'We must not forget to mention that the presence of ladies gave animation to the festivities of the evening'.

In the first year, a free annuity of £15 per annum was awarded to a governess whose application had been successful in a ballot of subscribing members. She was chosen from among thirty seven other worthy applicants, all either ill, old, destitute or all three. Miss Anne T. drew extra sympathy and votes by virtue of the fact that she had regularly given away all her salary to charity; this Christian lack of care for the morrow received its due reward.

Soon a Provident Fund was set up and governesses were encouraged to subscribe towards the purchase of annuities for themselves. Seventeen years later, at the time of the death of the devoted and tireless first Secretary of the Institution, the Revd. David Laing, the GBI was providing free annuities for ninety nine aged governesses, all securely funded from invested income. Another 427 were receiving annuities from their own earnings.

A handsome house, 66 Harley Street, had been acquired by the Institution in 1845. This was adapted as a hostel in which governesses, who were temporarily unemployed, might find refuge and a breathing space while looking for their next post. They had, of course, first to provide suitable references, and it was preferred if one letter came from a subscriber to the Institution.

The house did not look like a hostel. It had not so much as a brass plate on the door, and there was an air of dignified refinement about it. There was a fine drawing room, in which the governesses could read, talk or do their needlework, a handsome dining room, and a smaller room where the residents could meet friends privately. The bedrooms were of a good size, and as it was necessary for them to be shared by up to four women, they were curtained off in sections to give them each some privacy.

For 15s. a week governesses could have board and lodging; laundry and wine had to be paid for separately. They could stay up to one month, which could in certain circumstances be extended to three months by agreement with the Ladies' Committee. During that time assistance would be given in finding new situations. After one year 250 governesses had been helped into employment.

Another important step was taken in 1848. Recognising that the lack of educational qualifications was one of the main reasons for the low status of governesses, the Governesses' Benevolent Institution set up a college in No. 67 Harley Street, next door to the residential Home, with the help of money donated by the Hon. Amelia Murray, a Maid of Honour to Queen Victoria. This lady made the principal objects of her concerns the slaves of the Southern States of America and English governesses, a significant linking of causes. The newly formed Queen's College offered lectures, mostly by the staff of King's College, conducted tests and awarded certificates of proficiency. Though the college was set up 'for the education of young ladies generally – of governesses especially', the fees (£9 9s. per term or £26 per year, in 1851) were unfortunately not much less than most governesses might earn by a year's work, and excluded many who might have benefited; but it was another step in the right direction. It is a measure of the success of Queen's College that it gave their early training to three young women who became famous head-mistresses, Dorothea Beale of Cheltenham Ladies College, Elizabeth Day of Manchester High School, and Frances Mary Buss of the North London Collegiate School for Girls.

The patronage and active participation of the Duke of Cambridge and a long list of other members of the aristocracy made it possible to raise funds for the GBI by holding social events. In June 1848 a 'Grand Fancy Sale' was held in the grounds of the Royal Hospital in Chelsea, attended by a gathering of four thousand people, *The Times* estimated, including many people 'of rank and fashion'. They strolled among the stalls, which displayed many 'costly and fancy articles', buying bouquets of flowers and listening to the great Jenny Lind singing 'some of her favourite airs'. A total of £2000 was raised by the two-day event, and most of it was applied to another valuable long-term project, the Asylum for Aged Governesses which opened in 1849 in Kentish Town. Here the surroundings were more salubrious than the address now implies: at that time Kentish Town looked across open green fields to Highgate. Nineteen governesses were initially accommodated in this, the first of a series of permanent homes run, as now, for aged and retired governesses by the GBI.

Till the end of the century, the annual reports of the Institution are filled with tragic accounts of governesses who have sacrificed their own health and security to support aging parents and educate large families of siblings.

Emulating the GBI, a Governesses' Institution was formed in Liverpool; another GBI in Scotland, and in London another 'Temporary Residence for Governesses' was set up. At its 1857 AGM it reported proudly that its rooms were always full. In 1871 the 'National Union for the Improvement of the Education of Women of all Classes' was founded, specifically to press for the founding of day schools for girls, where good training could be given in the art of teaching in order to raise the status of all women teachers.[8] Awareness of the problems of the governess was spreading but there was still a long time to go before governesses ceased to be among the most neglected and misused members of the teaching profession.

To a woman forced to depend entirely on what she earned, the possibility of illness was a constant worry, and many governesses with failing health had to rely on charity. In 1853 the 'Institution for the care of Sick Gentlewomen in Distressed Circumstances' was in the process of moving from Chandos Street to 1 Harley Street and was badly in need of re-organisation. The not-yet-famous Florence Nightingale, then aged thirty-three, was engaged as Superintendent to pull it together. Interviewing her, Lady Canning, chairman of the Committee, was impressed by her 'quiet and sensible manner'. She might not, had she heard it, have appreciated Florence's scornful description of the Institution as 'a Sanatarium for sick governesses run by a Committee of Fine Ladies', nor her happy acceptance of a friend's advice to 'trample on the Committee and ride the Fashionable Asses rough-shod round Grosvenor Square'.

This, in effect, was what she did. She dazed the committee with her revolutionary ideas, antagonised many of them, replaced most of the staff and reorganised the finances. She halved the running costs and doubled the efficiency, perhaps the first time that such a thing had been attempted in relation to a health service.

The governesses, who formed the majority of the patients, must have felt the improvement, for many sent her adoring letters, referring to her as 'darling Miss Nightingale', 'our sunshine' and 'dearest, kind Miss Nightingale'. She felt deepest sympathy for the impoverished, struggling women, and frequently assisted them from her own pocket. She made it possible for one governess whose money had run out to have a convalescent period after her illness rather than at once re-enter employment. Another was sent to Eastbourne at Florence's expense for a holiday, with arrangements that she should be visited and taken for drives while there.

The most common illnesses among the governesses were mental breakdown and cancer. The most unpleasant task that Florence had to undertake, as she wrote to her father in 1854, and one in which the doctors and the committee refused to help, was that of personally discharging the patients. The governesses showed no wish to leave, since the Institution was 'the cheapest lodging they can find, with the added luxury of taking medicine and sympathy'. She had to make a rule that all, except the dying, had to leave after two months. 'Otherwise, there is no incentive to get well.'

She said of the Institution many years later.

> I think that the deep feeling I have of the miserable position of educated women in England was gained while there (or rather, of half educated women) . . .[9]

These same women were struggling, like fish in a near dry pond, to find any other pool in which they could make their living. Too genteel for manual labour, unqualified for any profession, determined at all costs to maintain 'respectability', they floundered in poverty and despair. The governess market was so overcrowded in Britain that for some hope lay in the chance of finding positions in the colonies. In the 1860s a scheme to help governesses to emigrate to Sidney, Australia, was started by a group of women led by Emily Streeter. Even she, on arrival, had great difficulty in getting a teaching position, and like many others found herself working as a needlewoman, a job she would have despised at home. There were some successes among the emigrants, but many disillusionments.

Those who remained in Britain fought frantically for work, answering advertisements and queuing despondently outside employment agencies. A menial clerical job, copying documents or addressing letters for an agency, would attract hundreds of applicants. One recorded 250 women applying for a job worth £12 a year, and another 810 applications for a clerical position at £15. Some 120 women applied to an agency that had not even advertised a vacancy, such was their desperation.[10]

The problem was as much one of prejudice against women office workers as of over-employment. In 1851 the national census recorded only nineteen female clerks and book-keepers. In 1881 the figure had risen but was still only 7000.[11] It is not surprising that those who managed to find work in private households were prepared to do almost anything to keep it, suffering on occasion indignity and abuse, and frequently neglect and thoughtless treatment. Anything was better than the streets.

· 10 ·

Fighting for respect

Whatever the circumstances, a governess had to maintain her appearance of gentility; one of her best selling points was the fact that she was, or appeared to be, a gentlewoman. She was described in one issue of the *Quarterly Review* as 'a being who is our equal in birth, manners, and education, but our inferior in worldly wealth'. This was a kindly way of depicting her, since the typical governess was the spinster daughter of a poor clergyman, of little education and of means so slender that she would work for a pittance. But it is an insight into the perception of the kind of family that increasingly came to provide her employment. As affluence spread downwards through the social classes, 'keeping a governess' became a status symbol in the household of the small professional man. Nellie Weeton recognised the reason for her employ with Mr Pedder: 'I am only kept here from ostentation, not out of real kindness to his wife.'

Adaptable as they ever had to be, governesses saw their advantage and learned to play the snob card, using their refined accents as a protective shield and their knowledge of the world gathered through various posts to safeguard their positions. If she could establish her own superiority over her employers in worldly experience and in social contacts, a governess could forestall the urge found in many families to emphasise their newly found social position by humiliating their employee.

In his *Book of Snobs*, published in 1846, Thackeray created the immortal Miss Wirt, governess to the Ponto family, who had brought this skill to a fine art. She is not only a social paragon but also a remarkable musician. After dinner on the first night of his stay at 'The Evergreens', Miss Wirt entertains the company with a performance on the piano of variations of 'Sich a gettin' upstairs'.

First Miss Wirt, with great deliberation, played the original and beautiful melody, cutting it, as it were, out of the instrument, and firing off each note so loud, clear and sharp that I am sure Stripes must have heard it in the stable.

'What a finger!' says Mrs Ponto; and indeed it *was* a finger, as knotted as a turkey's drumstick, and splaying all over the piano. When she had banged out the tune slowly, she began a different manner of 'Gettin' up Stairs', and did so with a fury and swiftness quite incredible. She spun upstairs; she whirled upstairs; she galloped upstairs; she rattled upstairs; and then having got the tune to the top landing, as it were, she hurled it down again shrieking to the bottom floor, where it sank in a crash as if exhausted by the breathless rapidity of the descent. Then Miss Wirt played the 'Gettin' up Stairs' with the most pathetic and ravishing solemnity: plaintive moans and sobs issued from the keys – you wept and trembled as you were gettin' up stairs. Miss Wirt's hands seemed to faint and wail and die in variations: again, and she went up with a savage clang and rush of trumpets, as if Miss Wirt was storming a breach; and although I knew nothing of music, as I sat and listened with my mouth open to this wonderful display, my *caffy* grew cold, and I wondered the windows did not crack and the chandelier start out of the beam at the sound of this earthquake of a piece of music.

'Glorious creature! Isn't she?' said Mrs Ponto. 'Squirtz's favourite pupil – inestimable to have such a creature. Lady Carabas would give her eyes for her! A prodigy of accomplishments! Thank you, Miss Wirt!' – and the young ladies gave a heave and a gasp of admiration – a deep breathing gushing sound, such as you hear at church when the sermon comes to a full stop.

Miss Wirt put her two great double-knuckled hands round a waist of her two pupils, and said, 'My dear children, I hope you will be able to play it soon as well as your poor little governess. When I lived with the Dunsinanes, it was the dear Duchess's favourite, and Lady Barbara and Lady Jane MacBeth learned it. It was while hearing Jane play that, I remember, that dear Lord Castletoddy first fell in love with her; and though he is but an Irish Peer, with not more than fifteen thousand a year, I persuaded Jane to have him. Do you know Castletoddy, Mr Snob? – round towers – sweet place – County Mayo. Old Lord

Castletoddy (the present Lord was then Inishowan) was a most eccentric old man – they say he was mad. I heard His Royal Highness the poor dear Duke of Sussex – (*such* a man, my dears, but alas! addicted to smoking!) – I heard His Royal Highness say to the Marquis of Anglesey, "I am sure Castletoddy is mad!" but Inishowan wasn't, in marrying my sweet Jane, though the dear child had but her ten thousand pounds *pour tout potage!*'

'Most invaluable person,' whispered Mrs Major Ponto to me. 'Has lived in the very highest society'; and I, who have been accustomed to see governesses bullied in the world, was delighted to find this one ruling the roast, and to think that even the majestic Mrs Ponto bent before her . . . I hadn't a word to say against a woman who was intimate with every Duchess in the Red Book.

Piano practice takes up a great deal of time in the Ponto household, as in its non-fictional counterparts.

In fact, the confounded instrument never stops; when the young ladies are at their lessons, Miss Wirt hammers away at those stunning variations and keeps her magnificent finger in exercise.

I asked this great creature in what other branches of education she instructed her pupils? 'The modern languages,' says she modestly; 'French, German, Spanish, and Italian, Latin and the rudiments of Greek if desired. English of course; the practice of Elocution, Geography, and Astronomy, and the Use of the Globes, Algebra (but only as far as quadratic equations); for a poor ignorant female, you know, Mr Snob, cannot be expected to know everything. Ancient and Modern History no young woman can be without; and of these I make my beloved pupils *perfect mistresses*. Botany, Geology, and Mineralogy, I consider as amusements. And with these I assure you we manage to pass the days at the Evergreens not unpleasantly,'

Only these, thought I – what an education! But I looked in one of Miss Ponto's manuscript song-books and found five faults of French in four words; and in a waggish mood asking Miss Wirt whether Dante Algiery was so called because he was born in Algiers, received a smiling answer in the affirmative, which made me rather doubt about the accuracy of Miss Wirt's knowledge.[1]

Miss Wirt, though the subject of a little pardonable enhancement, is probably nearer to the type of the well-placed mid-Victorian governess that the better known Thackeray creation, Becky Sharp.

'Looking ladylike' was no easy matter for a woman who had no money beyond what she earned, and there was never any kind of uniform for governesses, as for other staff, which an employer might have been expected to supply. The wages on which a nineteenth century governess had to keep up appearances varied not only according to the demand for her services but as to where she was employed. Miss Maddocks on the Isle of Man, where prices were admittedly lower than on the mainland, is recorded as having been paid only £12 a year in 1812; in London this would have been the level of salary paid to a 'daily' governess. (This was at a time when the average agricultural wage was over £30 a year.) As late as 1869 an advertisement in the *Daily Telegraph* offered only 7s. a week (£18 a year) for a governess to teach English, French, music, needlework and drawing to three children daily from 10am to 6pm.[2] The advertiser would have been flooded with applications, though the lucky woman chosen would not even get her keep, as she would if she had been living-in.

A resident governess, mid-century, could usually expect a salary in the range of £20 to £40, from which deductions were sometimes made for laundry costs.*

By the next century the governess might well be obliged to keep herself during the holidays, but at this time she had no such worry, for she seldom had a holiday, except what 'time off' she could afford to take between posts. On this meagre salary, from which she might be sending money home to a widowed mother, a governess had to buy or, more likely, make the clothes to maintain her ladylike appearance so that she could appear in the street or, on occasion, in the drawing room, without shaming her employer.

Nellie Weeton, on £30 a year, took pride in the neat, though much mended, appearance of her clothes.

> I have, for some years, entirely given up all kinds of needlework which has no real utility to recommend it. When I sew, it is to make necessary clothing and to keep it in repair . . . I consider it as so disgraceful to wear rags, or any part of my apparel with ever so small a hole in it, that I daily find at least a *little* employment for my needle; for I am too poor to buy new, frequently. My cloaths, if examined, would be found to have fewer holes and more patches and darnings, than those of almost any other person; yet I think I am respectably dressed, and as neat in my *every day apparel*, as any of my acquaintances.

*By way of comparison, a female domestic servant, living-in, at the same date, would be paid between £9 and £12 per annum, with keep and uniform provided. She would be allowed a half-day off on alternate Sundays, and some hours of freedom during the week to compensate for long working hours, from 5 or 6 in the morning until after the family went to bed at night. It was customary, also, for female servants in country areas to be allowed Mothering Sunday off, when they were expected to go home to their mother bearing the traditional simnel cake.

This pride was reflected in her attitude in relation to her employer's uncaring behaviour. She said in a letter:

> I am staying at home this afternoon (Sunday 17) for want of a decent bonnet to go to church in. Mrs A knows this, but neither offers me a holiday, nor a conveyance to Huddersfield, to buy one; and I'll stay at home these two months before I'll ask her.

Nevertheless, she accepted with pleasure a present from the Armitage grandmother, despite its being in a rather unlikely colour:

> Mrs Armitage senior had presented me with a new scarlet stuff gown, in which you may suppose I look very glowing. She is a very generous, charitable, hospitable woman.

Normally, her dress, like that of most governesses, was 'very plain, that I may pass unnoticed; a dark print, no way remarkable in the make of it, and a bonnet, likewise plain'. On holiday on the Isle of Man in 1812, when she did a great deal of walking, she wore 'a slouch straw hat, a grey stuff jacket, and petticoat; a white net bag in one hand, and a parasol in the other'.

If the financial strains were great, greater still was the strain of necessary economies on a governess's pride.

> The tragedy of these women was the disparity between the material and social expectations that they were encouraged to adopt by their upbringing and the manner in which they were treated by their employers. A governess was a servant; her worth was calculated according to her rating on the labour market, which put a higher premium on a good cook and only a slightly lower value on a competent housemaid.[3]

Picture a young woman, perhaps in her early twenties, closeted with the children all day, and only allowed into the drawing room occasionally as a kindness when there are no important visitors being entertained. By the nature of the position she has been put in, she has to consider herself too well bred to converse with the servants, and her loneliness during long evenings sitting in her room can be imagined. If on one of her incursions downstairs she catches the eye of one of the sons of the house, she is almost certain to be summarily dismissed – even the curate and the doctor she must avoid, since too long a conversation with either could arouse her employer's suspicions that she might be committing the unforgiveable sin of flirting. Nellie Weeton was in love only once in her life, and then with a clergyman, who visited her employers on several occasions. From the start of their acquaintance she was aware of the social difference between a governess and a clergyman. and she resolved to be 'cautious of being in his company more than I could help, lest my heart should involuntarly form an attachment that might cause me years of unhappiness'. But she lost her heart to him all the same.

'I cannot say I ever met with a man I thought so agreeable . . .' she wrote,

> I never did before feel such a sentiment, as I did whilst he was here; as I still yet do. I avoided him as much as I could without appearing singular, during his stay. I was as reserved as possible, lest he should perceive my sentiments.

Though she joked in a letter to a friend, which she implored her to burn, 'Such a man should not go loose – he should either marry, or be confined . . .' she suffered much, and longed for him to be gone from her life. Yet she felt the social gulf to be so great that she never considered attempting to find out whether her sentiments might be reciprocated.

Mrs Craik, in her *Thoughts on Women*, asked 'lady-mothers whether they would not rather take for a daughter-in-law the poorest governess . . . than a "person in business" – milliner, dressmaker, etcetera?' implying that a governess was a cut above the rest. But in reality none of these possibilities would be allowed to arise.

The governess must at all times 'keep her place', for if she did not she would lose her livelihood, and a good reference when she left was her only hope of keeping herself from the workhouse. There was little hope of her progressing in any way up the social scale.

This was the lot of the average governess, but there were obviously exceptions, in particular among governesses employed in above- average households. Anna Jameson was born Anna Murphy, the daughter of a painter of miniatures who had developed a wide circle of aristocratic patrons. This enabled Anna, at the age of sixteen, to become governess first to the daughter of the Marquess of Winchester, and later for four years in the family of a member of parliament, Mr Littleton, who later became Lord Hatherton. A warm and lasting friendship developed between the governess and the Littleton family, and thirty years later Anna wrote a letter to a friend, 'I am staying at present with Lord and Lady Hatherton. We have had a large aristocratic party . . . all very gay; but my chief delight has been the society and affection of my *ci-devant* pupil, Hyacinthe Littleton.' Anna had become known by then as a writer, and her governess past had done her no damage socially.[4]

Miss Georgina Johnstone, the Campbell family's beloved 'Pock', was another exception: unlike Miss Weeton, who said that her first employer only 'in the presence of guests treats me with respect and even humour', Miss Johnstone argued happily with the Duke of Argyll over the lunch table, and discussed literary and scientific matters on a level with him. She dined downstairs with the family, if not always, certainly frequently. Her pupil relates that

> Politically she abhorred Mr Gladstone and his works; but personally she was amusingly under the sway of his courteous manners and his gratitude when, as occasionally happened, he dined at Argyll Lodge, and she was ready with some needed bit of information in the after dinner discussions.

Schoolroom tea was a very lively party which brothers and guests would often join, attracted by the bursts of conversation and laughter around the scones and gooseberries, with the small, prim figure of Miss Johnstone presiding happily over it all.

The family kept in touch with 'Pock' long after the girls were married, exchanging letters and visits.[5] Fifty years later one of her pupils criticised her own grand-daughter in words that seem to reflect the tones of her remarkable governess:

> You do not appear to have the zest for life that I had at your age; but keep your elbows off the table, and read Sir Walter Scott, and the rest may come.[6]

Ruskin would have heartily approved of Miss Johnstone's treatment at the hands of her employers. In 1864, the same year that she took up her employment with the Campbell family, he appealed for more respect to be paid to governesses, if only to do honour to their pupils. In a speech in Manchester Town Hall, he said,

> And give your daughters not only noble teachings, but noble teachers. You consider somewhat, before you send your boy to school, what kind of a man the master is; whatsoever kind of man he is, you at least give him full authority over your son, and show some respect to him yourself; if he comes to dine with you, you do not put him at a side table; you know also that, at his college, your child's immediate tutor will be under the direction of some still higher tutor, for whom you have absolute reverence. You do not treat the Dean of Christchurch or the Master of Trinity as your inferiors.
>
> But what teachers do you give your girls, and what reverence do you show to the teachers you have chosen? Is a girl likely to think her own conduct, or her own intellect, of much importance when you trust the entire formation of her character, moral and intellectual, to a person

whom you let your servants treat with less respect then they do your housekeeper (as if the soul of your child were a less charge then jams and groceries), and whom you yourself think you confer an honour upon by letting her sometimes sit in the drawing room in the evening?[7]

Poor Nellie Weeton, in a letter, said of the position of governess,

It is rather an awkward one for a female of any reflection or feeling. A governess is almost shut out of society, not choosing to associate with servants, and not being treated as an equal by the head of the house or their visitors, she must possess some fortitude and strength of mind to render herself tranquil or happy; but indeed, the master or mistress of a house, if they have any goodness of heart, would take pains to prevent her feeling her inferiority. For my own part, I have no cause of just complaint; but I know of some that are treated in a most mortifying manner.

It was not only in regard to their personal dignity that governesses were thoughtlessly treated. Their comfort and working conditions were not considered of importance either. It was not an uncommon arrangement for the governess to share her bedroom with the pupils with whom she spent her days. This was, as Mrs Jameson said, 'a cruel invasion of her privacy in her only place of refuge'.

The schoolroom where she taught, and where she spent her lonely evenings, was often one of the most cheerless rooms in the house. Mrs Jameson told in parable-like style of the family of a nobleman of great wealth, whose apartments in one of the finest houses in London were extravagantly furnished. The governess's rooms were different –

You went up a back staircase to a small set of rooms, with a confined, gloomy aspect; – the study was barely furnished – a carpet faded and mended; – stiff backed chairs, as if invented for penance – a large table against the wall – the map of Europe, and the Stream of Time – a look of meanness, coldness, bareness, which would have chilled at once any woman accustomed to a *home* . . .[8]

Despite this story, Mrs Jameson advised governesses that in general the higher the rank of their employer, the greater the courtesy with which they would be treated, 'such courtesy being ever in proportion to the wideness and impassability of the distance which society has placed between you and your employer'. In a grand household they would have more solitude, but more independence than in a middle class household. In the latter, they could expect more companionship or sympathy but might suffer more 'petty affronts', in their ambiguous and difficult position. On the whole, she advised the younger governess 'who has yet to earn her experience', that she might have more chance of happiness by starting with a middle-class employer. But, she said ominously, 'to you it is not the beginning of your career that will be the hardest and saddest part of it'. She follows this with pages of gloomy advice on how to survive the depression and health hazards attendant on this 'monotonous and unnatural existence'. She advocates for the 'hours of solitary rest', that the young woman 'remember and apply one-half of Johnson's precept, "If you are solitary, be not idle," – (the other half you had best forget).' Needlework, she says, is good, but leaves the thoughts too much at liberty. When, after months of continuous exertion 'a listlessness or deadness of spirit' creeps over the young governess, she should ask for a short respite, a few days of change of scene and air, and hope it will be granted. 'If taken in time, it may prevent much and incurable mischief.'[9]

It is hard to imagine that anyone reading such well intentioned and practical advice should continue on a course of becoming a governess, but then as Mrs Jameson said herself, 'I never in my life heard of a governess who was such by choice'.

Nellie Weeton, with middle-class comployers, was not always treated kindly, and when contemplating leaving her second post she reflected that her employers would have to replace her with a young person, for they would not have a chance of finding another woman of Nellie's years (thirty seven), experience or attainments who would submit to the privations and humiliations that she had experienced.

She told how a relation of her master's who lived nearby had kindly invited her to dinner (the mid-day meal). 'Such is the liberality of *my mistress*, that I am to stay with the children until dinner is quite ready, and to return . . . as soon as I have eaten and then go again to tea . . . I objected, preferring to stay at home entirely to visiting in such a way . . . As long as a governess, or any other person, is admitted into the company of her superiors, she should be treated as an equal for the time, or else it is better not to invite her at all.'

Maria Edgeworth, a defender of governess, observed in 1822 that in well bred families the governess was no longer treated as an upper servant, but rather as a friend and companion of the family. However she disapproved of the household in which she was actually treated as an equal; that was going too far, and would encourage a governess to neglect her duty. She suggested that in less happy situations some blame might lie with the governesses themselves, for the way they were used.

A governess must either rule, or obey, decidedly. If she do not agree with the child's parents in opinion, she must either know how to convince them by argument, or she must with strict integrity conform her practice to their theories. There are few parents who will choose to give up the entire care of their children to any governess; therefore there will probably be some points in which a difference of opinion will arise. A sensible woman will never submit to be treated, as governesses are in some families, like a servant who was asked by his master what business he had to think; nor will a woman of sense or temper insist upon her opinions without producing her reasons. She will thus ensure the respect of enlightened parents.[10]

From her comfortable position as a successful author, Miss Edgeworth surely overestimated the capability of a governess, terrified of losing her job, to stand up to overbearing employers who were fully aware that education was a buyer's market.

7 JULY, 1887

THE LADY REGISTRY OF RECOM-MENDED SERVANTS.

For Rules, see No. 124.

——◆——

A LADY wishes to recommend a nice-looking girl of fifteen and a-half as SCHOOLROOM MAID, UNDER HOUSEMAID, or UNDER NURSE. She has been well brought up, and is a very good needlewoman and knitter.—Address Miss Gadesden, Ewell, Surrey.

A LADY wishes to recommend a very respectable, cleanly, active, elderly person to take charge of a house where one servant is left while family are away. Would help clean; highly recommended, having been in family as housemaid many years; moderate remune-ration.—Address Mrs. Wheeler, Whitehall Road, Woodford, Essex.

MRS. SCOTT wishes to recommend a lady as GOVERNESS to one or two children, or as COMPANION to a lady.—Address Miss Raven, 22, St. Ann's Road, Wandsworth.

MRS. TAYLEUR can highly recommend a LADY'S MAID to one lady. Age twenty-five; wages £20. A good plain sewer, milliner, and dressmaker.—Apply to Mrs. H. Tayleur, Brynyffynon, Ruthin.

A governess could not afford to quarrel with her employer for, to be able to advertise in *The Lady*, she needed her recommendation. This was in the Rules.

· 11 ·

The Lady joins the fray

In the latter part of the nineteenth century a governess might be treated more humanely by employers, but finding a job had become no easier, and there were still complaints by governesses who were employed to teach having to do menial household jobs like mending the family linen.

The Lady magazine was first published in February 1885, at £1.8s. per annum. It flourished from the start, responding sensitively to requests from its readers, and giving them what they wanted. Its attractions were regular and well illustrated articles on fashion and the activities of 'society', on household management and cooking, on music, on the theatre, and on gardening. There were features too on public affairs, on books, on running bazaars, on the management of servants; a political column, 'From the Ladies' Gallery', kept readers abreast of matters in Parliament. There were stories and competitions, and a very popular service in which the readers' handwriting was analysed and their characters explained. A weekly column entitled 'Law for Ladies' featured discussion on subjects relevant to women like 'Landlord and Tenant' and 'Mistress and Servant', with advice on legal problems such as Breach of Promise of marriage.

An 'Exchange and Sale' column was well subscribed, and in November 1885 an Employment column was added. This very rapidly became flooded with advertisements from women desperate to earn money in their own homes. Every possible form of handwork was offered by 'ladies in distressed circumstances' and of 'reduced means', and soon a few governesses began to advertise. The repetition of the same advertisements week after week, for there was no charge for those seeking work, shows that these governesses did not get many answers. It was deeply disheartening.

The popularity of *The Lady* meant a wide readership, and it became a useful forum for debate on matters beyond the immediate household. If the magazine could not provide many jobs for governesses, it did give a good airing to some of their problems.

In May 1885, a correspondence starting with a passing reference drew attention to their difficulties in finding employment and of their inadequate pay.

In these days, when the want of suitable employment for gentlewomen is attracting so much attention, and when for want of it so many ladies are driven to swelling the ranks of the much overstocked governess world (for which most of them are utterly unfitted) it is a matter of surprise that wood-engraving is not attracting more attention . . .'

This drew an attack on mistakes made by parents in 'the early training of girls':

Many an incapable and therefore ill-paid governess would have been happy and useful if her mother had allowed her to learn to work with her hands instead of voting it unladylike.

Another correspondent wrote,

I have found it is too often the idea that, if ladies can do nothing else, they can in some subject or other teach; but it is merely a delusion and a snare. In the present day, unless they have been trained to do it from the beginning, or at least are so proficient in the special subject they profess as to have passed some examination of a college, if not a university, they have no chance of success.

This was true. At last women were achieving a level of education through colleges and examination systems that meant that girls' schools could demand qualifications of their women teachers and could afford to reject those without any. Within a very few years only those parents educating their children privately would accept unqualified teachers, and only unqualified teachers would accept the £60 or £70 a year that these parents would offer. In a girls' private school they could earn up to 50 per cent more.

The next letter in *The Lady* correspondence denies the advantages of teacher training for girls and goes on in a strain that reflects attitudes of a hundred years earlier in respect of women's physical capabilities. The solution it advocates is reminiscent of medieval society. It comes as a shock to find that it is signed by a woman:

> It is not true that if a girl is qualified either to teach one special branch of study or to undertake private pupils that she can be sure of earning her living. There are many young ladies who have studied at conservatoires and are thorough musicians and who are excellent linguists, but they are not able to find occupation. Besides, if they find it, after perhaps waiting a long time, teaching at two shillings a lesson is not an enviable lot, and no adequate compensation for the years of training and labour they have gone through. The examinations governesses and female teachers have to pass at present require so much labour that the strain upon the nervous system of the candidates often injures their constitutions for life. The first care of the parents should be to provide for the future of their daughters as it is always a sad case if a girl has to face the world, however she may be prepared for it. Physiological and statistical facts prove that woman was never born to take up the struggle for existence. Nature has intended her for quite another sphere, and if she leaves that sphere, willingly or unwillingly, nature will be against her. The root of the evil lies at the abnormal social conditions of the present century. In catholic countries many girls go into a convent, and are thus saved from endless humiliations and sufferings. Well educated women who are energetic and able to work would do best to emigrate to America or Australia and societies should be formed to assist them to that purpose.

Another letter writer complained that there were far too many governesses in Britain, and that more and more women were being educated to join the profession, only to find that it was appallingly badly paid. This writer, too, suggested that they should emigrate, this time to New Zealand and the West Indies, where, she said, there was a great shortage of educated English speakers, and where they would find themselves not very well paid but at least they would be shown respect and treated like ladies.

Governesses wrote to complain of the duties they were expected to perform – in addition to teaching they had to take total charge of the children from dawn to dusk, to make their clothes, to do any housework required of them and to act as companions to the mothers. The point was made that they would earn more by calling themselves 'cook', 'housemaid', or 'nurse' rather then 'governess' or 'lady help', and yet would be doing much the same work. The governess, moreover, unlike a servant, was expected to pay for her own laundry, and was not allowed a regular 'day off'.

One governess wrote suggesting that they all get together and form a union – 'Unity Is Strength'! Another inveighed against governesses who, 'because they have a small income of their own', or 'don't want to curb their tempers and live at home, elect to go out as governesses for their board alone, asking for no money.

> Do they ever think that by doing so they make it more difficult for the girl who is obliged to earn her living and must obtain an engagement with a fair salary? I have often heard it said that ladies who are willing to pay their cooks thirty or forty pounds then say 'Why should I pay Miss X fifty pounds when I can have a governess for nothing?'

A male correspondent wrote saying that people should not be hard on 'the ignorant governess'. Few of them would take the job willingly if they could find any other available to them.

The Lady governess correspondence now swung in another direction, following an article on the abuses governesses suffered at the hands of the agencies that they applied to in their desperation to find jobs. These agencies, specialising in supplying governesses 'to the nobility and gentry', had been proliferating throughout the country since mid-century. In every issue of *The Times* in the 1880s there were advertisements inserted by seven to ten employment agencies for governesses in London alone. Their names varied, but the use of the words 'institute' or 'institution' gave them an air of solidity. Others relied on the personal, cosy sound of names like 'Mrs Faithfull', 'Madame Aubert', or 'The Ladies' Agent' to give their clients confidence. Claims to provide the most qualified teachers and the most highly remunerated posts and the boasts of the most genteel clientele were universal.

The Lady article pointed out that, though applying to specialist agencies ought be the wisest course for this huge class of unskilled labour, this was not the case:

> Girls and women, maids and widows, learned and ignorant, they flock to the educational agencies who are ever tempting them with their advertisements of work for them to do. And now they find to their bitter cost that of a dozen agents to whom they apply ten at least are harpies, eager to prey upon their helplessness and inexperience, pocketing their hardly earned fees, encouraging them in their vain hope and never putting an hour's work in their way. It is not only the ill-qualified, either in aquirements or in past experience, who are thus treated.

Letters from governesses who had been duped in this way then flowed freely. The practices of these agencies were simple and cruel. They advertised tempting vacancies which by chance had just gone when the applicant, having often walked for miles, appeared on the agent's doorstep. However, the agent would assure the disappointed governess there were many others in the offing, and the payment of a fee, usually five shillings, would ensure that the governess was informed immediately when a suitable situation appeared. She would also be asked a sign a form agreeing to pay to the agency a percentage of the salary she received during her first year's engagement. As one governess put it, if the employers were also asked to forfeit an equivalent sum on engaging a governess they might be less inclined to give her notice on the slightest pretext.

Sometimes, after weeks of waiting, and a few unanswered letters, the governess would call again at the agency, and be received with cool disdain and the assurance that 'her name would be brought forward in the books'. Or else she would spot another advertisement in the name of the same agency, offering a situation with identical details to those she had requested, even down to the locality she preferred. She would rush to the agency, to be asked, 'Ah, but do you teach the violin?' When she answered that she did not, she would be told that in that case it was not worth her while applying. In vain did she protest that this requirement had not been mentioned in the advertisement. Once again money, time and effort had been spent on a fruitless journey.

Sometimes a brave governess would argue her rights with an agency, and would then receive by post details of situations entirely unsuited to her needs or abilities, though sometimes she would not discover this until she arrived at the prospective employer's house for interview. It was also, of course, not unusual for a governess to travel many miles for an interview to find that the employer was already suited, sometimes because the agency had seen the employer's own advertisement in a journal, and had simply passed it on to the governess. On other occasions, the same employer's address would be given to far too many applicants, who would be turned from the door, with aching feet and hearts and bruised, resentful spirits. In this manner, the dwindling funds, the physical energies and the mental endurance of these unfortunate women were dissipated.

There was, inevitably, some response in *The Lady* columns to this correspondence from those agencies who felt they were neither 'harpies', 'traps for the unwary', 'unethical', 'collectors of windfalls' or 'bloodsucking', as they were variously described. They wrote to the magazine defending themselves and denying the accusations, protesting that their own particular businesses were reputable and that fees were never charged without positions being secured for clients. A letter writer, signing himself 'A Man of Business', claimed that his four daughters were all governesses and had all held excellent positions gained through the services of agencies. One agent claimed to charge the employers more than she did the governesses, another that it was hard for her to make any profit because of the cost of postage and telegrams. One agent switched the attack on to the governesses themselves, resenting the sweeping generalisation that all agencies were unscrupulous and immoral. She claimed that 'in our daily work we meet with those governesses who are neither educationally, socially nor morally what they represent themselves to be, but we do not brand the whole of the profession as uneducated, dishonest and untruthful'.

Certainly honest agents existed, particularly outside London. A powerfully phrased letter winging in from a outraged lady operating in Bristol left no doubt in this reader's mind about her probity.

Agencies were as easy and cheap to set up as small schools had been 200 years earlier and, as then, it was a simple way for a widow or spinster to make a living. Certainly some failed governesses must have turned their hand to the agency business, knowing its workings as they did. An advertisement which appeared in a weekly religious paper in 1898 is informative: 'Agency to be disposed of. Easily worked. Handsome profits. Best Principles.'

Though some agencies performed a service that was valued by the governesses who used them, there were undoubtedly a great many rogues who thoroughly deserved to be castigated for their callous and unethical behaviour. It was pointed out ironically that a very high proportion of those agencies which made their living out of the fees from poor governesses, and profited from their lack of experience, were in fact run by other women, taking advantage of the misfortunes of their own sex. Dog was finally eating dog.

It might be thought that by 1885, when these letters and articles in *The Lady* were published, there were other occupations open to the kind of women who had hitherto felt obliged to become governesses. Campaigns had indeed been organised to persuade more businesses and professions to train and employ women. Emily Davies (1830–1921) was a largely self-educated clergyman's daughter and a leading light in the promotion of the cause of women in education, becoming in 1874, for a short period, Principal of Girton College. She had since 1860 been writing and lecturing on the subject of widening the scope of female employment. Regretting the traditional attitudes that forced women who had no vocation for teaching into becoming governesses, she had pointed out then how many wives and daughters had shown an aptitude for business, working in and sometimes managing family firms without injuring their 'distinctive womanhood'. She showed how many jobs that appeared eminently suitable for women were debarred to them simply by tradition: for example, managing shops, such as drapers and hosiers, or assisting chemists and druggists in their work which was, after all, 'a sort of scientific cookery'.

'It is scarcely credible, though I am afraid true,' she wrote in the 1860s, 'that at this moment it would be useless to ask a respectable hairdresser to take a female apprentice.'

She urged that the current economic, social and moral objections to employing women were based on custom only, and were confused and mutually contradictory. It was maintained that in a well supplied labour market, the introduction of female employees would lessen each person's share of the available wealth. But surely, she said, unproductive women were more of a burden on society than productive ones? 'No man in his senses would keep two or three of his sons doing nothing, in order to give the rest a better chance of getting on.'

Another fallacy was that to train women in a profession or to run a business was money wasted, since they would throw up their business on entering marriage. No so, said Emily Davies; the business could pass on to others, and the professional training in a wife could only be of value. She quoted the Revd. Charles Simeon: 'If you have a thousand pounds to give your son, put it in his head rather than in his pocket.' The advice was equally applicable in the case of daughters.

She dealt easily with the moral argument, as she called it, that helplessness in women was not only becoming but was useful, as a stimulus to exertion in men. Single men, she said, do not feel stimulated by the vague knowledge that there are a good many women in the world requiring to be supported, and married men would in any case have their families to provide for.

The social reasons for keeping women idle she found the most foolish, and she dealt with them at their own level. Women, it was said, were meant for the domestic circle, and 'public life' was injurious to them. Was there any woman, Emily Davies asked, who led a more public life than the Queen, and yet was there any more admirable wife and mother to be found among her subjects? Fathers, who would shake their heads at the idea of taking their daughters into their own counting houses, allowed them to stand behind a stall at a bazaar, or to lead off at a charity ball – far more public scenes, and where, indeed, publicity was essential to success.

She stirred the consciences of liberal minded people, pleading with them as employers to take a lead in opening up the fields of medicine, trade, banking, and prison work to women.[1] Her arguments and those of other like-minded men and women eventually had effect, and by the end of the century there were many more avenues of employment open to women in general. But an analysis of what they were reveals a great dearth of the kind of opportunity that a woman of governess class would be inclined to take.

It must be remembered that the potential governess is the daughter of a small tradesman, poor clergyman, army officer or the like. She is short of money, so no capital is available, and she has no training. Her education is usually fairly limited and her experience of the world non-existent. She has been brought up as 'a lady'.

In 1898, in enterprising mood, she buys a copy of the *Dictionary of Employments open to Women*, newly published by the Women's Insitute, in hardback, and priced at one shilling and sixpence. The aim of this slim volume is 'to indicate every means of honourable livelihood at present open [to women], and to give a bare outline of the qualifications required, and of the remuneration that may be expected'. The intention is to help relieve the 'painful overcrowding in some of the better known occupations for women', as well as to increase awareness of concerned people of the harsh working conditions of millions of females.

Of some 302 occupations listed in alphabetical order in the directory, she finds that 189 are manual labour, ranging from agricultural work (paying up to 15s. a week) to working at home stuffing dolls for a doll-maker, which means working from ten to nineteen hours a day, average weekly earning seven shillings. Also in this category are:

Bacon-curer: Hours: These are short. Wages: 6s. to 12s. a week.
Bargewoman: General information: The life is not suitable for inexperienced women who have no friends on the boats.
Barmaid: Hours: Up to 100 a week in licensed houses. Wages: 10s. to 15s. a week. [There were 80,000 or more women employed as barmaids in 1898]
Boiling water seller: Women in the poorer districts boil water for their neighbours at the rate of ¼d. per kettle or pot.
Leather Cigar-Case closer: Hours: 50 a week. Wages, average: 7s. to 9s. a week.

None of these will be considered by our middle class job-seeker. She will also have difficulty finding somthing suitable in the next category; there are some sixty two occupations which are neither heavy nor menial work, and where the pay might be enough to live on, but which she would find socially too demeaning:

Artificial teeth maker: (earning up to £5 per week, in a dentist's
  workroom.)
Post Office Clerk:
Laundry inspectress:
Registrar: (paid according to the number of births and deaths
  registered)
Hairdresser:

In the end, there are fifty one occupations that she could confess to
with confidence to her father, the rector.

Of these, eighteen, which include accountancy, medicine, draughts-
manship, hotel management, fashion design and phrenology, require
skills or qualifications she does not have, or else require a long training
or apprenticeship, usually scantily paid, if at all. Five are too risky; life
as an author or as a table decorator depends on popularity or on
certainty of regular work. Four require capital, which she does not
have; there is no hope, without it, of becoming a farmer, an art dealer, a
house agent or the proprietor of a 'cyclists' rest'.

Only three women have yet become bankers, the *Dictionary* says;
some have done well as magazine editors, and one or two as dealers in
exotic birds, but the openings are few: another five of this type to cross
off.

She has not the expertise in any particular subject to become a
travelling lecturer, and dog and cat breeding require special knowledge, so two more gone.

Of the remaining seventeen, most would pay her much less than the
£100 a year she has reasonably set as her target. She could manage
artificial flower-making or working as a professional 'reader aloud', but
would get only about £50 for either. As a Deaconess, her pay would be
only £75, as a Bible Woman, £25, and as a District Visitor, for which
being a 'lady by birth' is a requirement, £60.

The only possibilities remaining to her from her list of respectable
jobs are to be a Book-keeper (£150), a Chaperon (£100 +), a General
Clerk (£80–£100), a Travelling Companion (£100−), an Indexer for a
publisher or newspaper (£125 +), a Baby-Farm Inspector (£150), an
Inspector of Schools (£300), or a writer of verses for cards (£200, for a
good one). Or a Teacher.

She looks up Teacher, in all the different categories of school. In
every category training or expertise is now required. Where an
applicant has none, the salaries are very low during a long pro-
bationary period. Of course increasing numbers of women are now
opting for training and further education; but there were many like our

job-seeker who do not have so much courage or determination, or indeed enough money.

So she turns to Teacher, private. The book says the position of a governess has changed greatly for the better in the last fifty years. It says salaries can be expected of £100 or more, resident. (And there would be no need to pay for lodgings. And she would have a respectable address. And some security.) It also says that higher education has increased the number of trained women seeking posts as private governesses and that this, with the general impetus given to learning, has caused parents to expect greater efficiency in those who teach their children. There is still a large demand for governesses, it says, and that while there is an improvement in the status and salary of highly certificated teachers, those who are not specially qualified are worse off than ever, owing to the limited number of persons ready to offer them employment.

But she knows better: so many of her relations are governesses. And so she sets out for the agency and the job she always knew she would have to take in the end.

By 1890 the Governesses' Benevolent Institution had been in existence for forty seven years. The members of the original committee had all died, leaving behind them a soundly based organisation which was funding 288 free annuities to aged governesses and had so far responded to over 33,000 applications from others in temporary difficulty, with grants and help with travel and medical expenses. It was still at 66 Harley Street, an oasis at which the unemployed governesses could find temporary respite. The hostel was always full. At Chislehurst, in Kent, the Institution owned twelve 'pretty cottages' for retired governesses, the successor home to the 'Asylum' in Kentish Town, where the residents were given an annual income of £43 a year and medical attendance. There were two bedrooms in each cottage, as the inmates were all required to have a relative or companion to live with them.

One of the most useful functions of the Institution, however, was still to act as a free governess employment exchange, with no charge being made either to employer or to employee. It took the simple form of two registers. In one the governesses, after supplying references to the registrar from two respectable parties who knew them well, and on obtaining the approval of the Board, could enter their own particulars. In the other the ladies who wanted governesses could enter the details of the situations, the number of pupils, the subjects to be taught and the salaries they offered. Either side could examine these books and write directly to those whose particulars appealed to them. Business was thus conducted entirely between the principals themselves, and all they had to do was inform the superintendent at once when they were suited. Surprisingly this service was sadly under-used by employers, despite advertisements inserted by the Institution in the Personal columns of *The Times*.

What was needed was a really well run agency, properly founded and financed, with an impeccable reputation. Help was at hand, and came from the office of Messrs Gabbitas and Thring, that pillar of respectability and eventually international repute that had been established in Sackville Street, Mayfair, in 1873. The founder, Mr Askin of Askin and Gabbitas, barely survived taking on the dynamic Mr John Gabbitas as partner in the firm's first year, and soon his death necessitated the seeking of another partner, though the name was not changed until 1895. Mr Thring was a nephew of Edward Thring, the famous headmaster of Uppingham from 1853 till 1887 and founder of the Headmasters' Conference. As Gabbitas and Thring the business did a flourishing trade, leading their competitors in the efficient supply of qualified teachers to all the leading boys' public and preparatory schools. Mr Gabbitas was the dominant partner. He had an imposing presence, a compelling personality, and was said to be a tireless and energetic worker. He terrorised his employees by his insistence on efficiency and perfection, and was reputed to enjoy striding into the office in the morning and picking a quarrel with the first person he laid eyes upon. He had a remarkable memory not only for the names of his clients but for their qualifications and past engagements.

Mr Gabbitas had two peculiarities. The first was that he would make no concession to modernism. Until he died, in 1904, the offices in the handsome house in Sackville street were very Dickensian. Communication between floors was by speaking tube, the caller attracting attention by blowing down the tube into the whistle that plugged the other end. This means of internal communication was common in tall London houses well into the twentieth century. But Mr Gabbitas' long refusal to invest in a telephone, which would have been an invaluable asset to his business, caused surprise and irritation. It was not until after he retired, and after the headmaster of St Paul's School had stormed round to complain of this inconvenience, that a telephone was finally installed. In deference, presumably, to the late senior partner's feelings, it was located on an upper landing, so that every time it rang a clerk had to run up the stairs to answer it.

The second significant trait in Mr Gabbitas' character was that he could not stand women. He would not employ them and he would not accept them as clients. It was this that gave Sydney Truman, a young employee in his office, the idea of breaking away and forming a separate agency, run on similar lines to Gabbitas and Thring. It would cater, however, for the vast and inadequately served market for governesses and women teachers, for whom there was till then no national agency. In 1901 he set up in Holles Street, Mayfair, as 'Mr Truman's Agency for Governesses'. In 1905 Mr F. E. Knightley, also from Gabbitas and Thring, joined him, and they signed articles of partnership to become Truman and Knightley. Sydney Truman held the chairmanship until he retired in 1958.

A typical entry in the long lists of available governesses published weekly by Mr Truman in 1904 read,

> Gentleman farmer's daughter, aged 19. Churchwoman, HIGH SCHOOL EDUCATION. English subjects, French, German, Latin, Elem. Maths, Music (Cert.) Dancing, Elem. Science. Fond of country life, good walker, cycles and plays games. Resident, £25.

Another, a trained teacher of twenty eight who could teach much the same subjects plus chip-carving, drilling and *repoussée* work, asked for £40 a year with (in bold type) Senior Oxford Local Certificate.

Despite the wording of the first, these two were probably advertising for daily posts, as the asking salaries would have been very low for resident governesses at that time; the average annual wage of an agricultural labourer in England was £48, and it was known for governesses to earn as much as £100. The would-be governesses applying to Mr Truman were not obliged to pay any fee on registration, and would only pay them thereafter if they obtained appointments.

At last governesses had a reliable agency working for them and with them, and in 1913 they had another. Gabbitas and Thring, not to be outdone, shook off the shade of Mr Gabbitas and took women on to their books. Yet even up to the Second World War the typists were all male, and there were very few women on the staff.

· 12 ·

'I'll deal with you later . . .'

Many governesses suffered much abuse and misuse, but the suffering was not all on one side. During the latter half of the nineteenth century and, indeed, at the beginning of the next, children in the schoolroom suffered much at the hands of their governesses. This harsh treatment was a reflection of the changing standards in the ordinary household during the first part of the century; these solidified into a new morality during the early years of Queen Victoria's reign.

The *mores* of the Regency period were a hangover from the eighteenth century: an earthy sense of humour and a fairly casual attitude to sexual morality and even to religion were usual in the upper classes. The use of euphemism was not thought necessary when referring to intimate matters. Lady Lyttelton, born in 1787, used far more explicit language when discussing pregnancy and childbirth than did her daughters-in-law. In 1815 a wet-nurse advertising her services in *The Times* candidly offers 'a good breast full of milk'; another, offering the same in 1850, calls it 'a good medical recommendation'.

These easy attitudes took a sharp knock when the young Queen came to the throne, but the history of the previous fifty years made this inevitable. The new generation, not unnaturally, blamed its predecessor for the social wrongs it observed as it grew up, and the young instinctively rebelled against the practices of their parents. Throughout the century writers exposed the iniquities rife in British society, the use of child labour in mines and factories, lack of education for the working classes, the poverty and slum housing conditions in both urban and rural communities, the injustices in the agricultural industry. Those who did not actually see these horrors could read about them. From the early 1800s a sense of unease grew among the nobility and the established moneyed classes, and particularly among the younger generation who were gradually replacing those who had been a part of the free-thinking, free-loving life of the previous century.

The Evangelical movement that was active among the middle and working classes is considered to be in part responsible for preventing revolution in England in the nineteenth century. Preachers encouraged their flocks to accept their God-given lot. They must find solace for the pain and distress of this world in the promise of comfort in the next. Another factor prevented the rumblings of discontent in the industrial areas getting out of hand: this was the instinct for self-preservation of an aristocracy that had so recently seen its counterpart cruelly massacred a short way across the Channel by a population crushed and brutalised into reaction against its oppressors. The subsequent Terror caused alarm in Britain, and not only in the aristocracy. A gap in living standards as great as existed between the upper classes and the lower in Britain could only ultimately lead to trouble.

Thus a combination of guilty conscience and of instinct for survival helped to cause a shift in attitudes that, as time went on, produced a swelling tide of good and charitable works and the implementation of political reform of an inequitable legal system. With it came a reassessment of religious attitudes, and a new appreciation of the values of hard work and plain living, both of which were considered to be good for the soul. Upright behaviour and a crushing code of morality became the ostensible standards of the Victorian family, led in exemplary fashion by the purity and the God-fearing life of the young Queen and her impeccable consort.

The adult Victorian male of reasonable means was in a position, if he wished, to preach upright living and, privately, to practise otherwise. His wife was not, but her chance to kick over the traces would come in the Edwardian era; his servants had more than ever to watch their step, and were expected to do without drink and, in the case of female servants, without friends of the opposite sex, on pain of instant dismissal without a 'character'. This would mean a return to the rural poverty from which they usually came, or else a job in a factory. But it was his children above all who became the innocent brunt of the new thinking. They must be raised to accept discipline and learn not to complain. Noisy behaviour was thought to be unacceptable: a child should be seen, neatly arrayed in clothes that could not comfortably be played in, while not being heard. Larking and romping were discouraged, and other displays of childish high spirits were generally frowned upon. The perfect child behaved like a miniature adult, and even in the most indulgent homes the reading in the evening round the family fireside was of tales of a moral and uplifting nature, often of mild misdemeanor followed by horrific retribution. The stories of Maria Edgeworth and of Mrs Sewell, which were hugely popular with the middle class Victorian parent for reading aloud, seem to the modern day reader not only priggish in the extreme but in some cases certain to be psychologically damaging. The Calvinist Revd. W. Carus Wilson, Charlotte Brontë's headmaster, published a book of improving stories, *The Child's First Tales*, in 1836, illustrated by the crudest wood-cuts, showing criminals being hanged, men in chains, and children in their coffins. Mr Wilson wrote in words of one syllable, for the child who had just learnt to read, tales of death and torture intended to console and elevate the infant mind. To the little child grieving by its mother's death-bed he argued: 'Well, if you love her, you would wish her to have what will do her most good.' 'Yes,' eagerly replies the grieving child, 'that I would.' 'Well, to die will do her the most good.'[1]

Boys newly out of the nursery escaped the severity of their home life by being sent to boarding school, which might or might not be an improvement. As their sisters grew to adulthood they were treated with more humanity; but for the younger children in the schoolroom, daily life could be very hard. It became quite normal for a governess to be given complete control not only over the lessons but over the general well-being of the children once they had left the nursery, and many women seem to have used this position as an outlet for the frustration in their own lives. The more important strict adherence to the teachings of the established church became, the more harsh became any correction administered for deviations from the rules. A lie, the theft of a sweetmeat, a refusal to admit guilt, unpunctuality, a suggestion of insolence, disobedience, inability to understand a lesson – any of these minor misdemeanours could incur punishments far in excess of what they deserved. The words of Hannah More, regarded as harsh when she wrote them in 1799, were now an acceptable part of schoolroom thinking. Children, she said, were 'beings who bring into the world a corrupt nature and evil dispositions'. Original sin was not just a concept – it was manifest in children's behaviour and must be thwarted. If this thinking was too strong for some people, justification for strict discipline could also be found in the writings of Rousseau, still a strong influence on educational thought. He claimed that children came pure into this life, but they had to be adapted to the world they must live in – they must be hardened and prepared for 'the yoke of necessity'.

Children were beaten, starved and mentally battered into submission. With the increased power given to governesses by parents, many of whom were sure that discipline was, in a Christian sense, the most loving regime that they could impose on their young, there was also a withdrawal of communication between parent and child. The governess ordered everything in their daily lives, and many children educated at home became as remote from their parents as if they had been at boarding school. Thus the abused, the despised, neglected and unloved were put in charge of the totally defenceless.

During the 1870s in the strictly Presbyterian family of the Fergussons of Kilkerran, in Ayrshire, a governess was left to look after several children while their father, Sir James, performed his duties as a Member of Parliament and of the government in London, and then as Governor in various of Her Majesty's colonies. The first Lady Fergusson had died in 1871, and the children had not been raised to expect much gentleness in their motherless life. One of the books in their nursery was entitled *Mother's Last Words*, and was given, presumably, for their solace in their bereavement. This is an edifying tale by Mrs Sewell of two orphan boys who, beset by poverty after the death of their mother, 'a worn out woman, ghastly pale', attempt to earn their living as crossing sweepers.

> Oh, yes, we'll work like honest boys,
> And if our mother should look down,
> She'd like to see us with a broom,
> And a crossing of our own.

They narrowly avoid the snares of dishonesty into which their cold and hunger nearly lead them, and when the younger boy falls ill 'his happy soul escapes to its home on high'. The elder brother is not so lucky (probably because he once very nearly stole a pair of shoes) but he grows up an honest, if lonely, apprentice, and eventually is allowed to join his mother and brother in eternal summer.*

The Fergusson governess was strict to the point of cruelty, and believed that pain was a good persuader. The elder son, Charles, on one occasion watched his sister Susan Georgina having her piano lesson. The governess stood beside her, brushing her pupil's long hair as she

*The illustrated ballad *Mother's Last words*, first published in 1860, was so popular that 1,088,000 copies were printed.

played. Whenever she heard a wrong note she brought the bristles of the hairbrush down hard on the back of the girl's hands until finally they were bleeding. At last, unable to bear the sight of his sister's pain and tears any longer, young Charles rushed to her side, crying out 'For shame!'

For this outburst, he was confined to his room without supper, and his name was added once more to the list of beatings to be administered when next his father returned from abroad. The children, not surprisingly, came to dread their parents' brief periods at home. Their young stepmother was either too frightened or too uninterested to interfere.

The extraordinary licence that governesses enjoyed for the physical abuse of their pupils was quite common. Sometimes it extended to nurses, though few used it. Clementine Churchill recalled being 'beaten unmercifully' by her nurse at the age of four in 1889. It was not a habit peculiar to the British: the power of the governess to call down punishment from the parents was known in Europe too. Princess Stephanie of Belgium, later wife of Rudolph of Austria who died at Mayerling, had a hideous childhood.

She was born in 1864, and at the age of six was taken from the care of her loving nurse and put with her elder sister Louise in the charge of a French governess, Mademoiselle Legrand. The family lived in the royal palace of Laeken, just north of Brussels. The governess obliged the children to rise at 5am in summer, 6am in winter, and to dress in total silence before windows that were never closed all the year round. They were helped by a maid, who might not address them, and Mlle Legrand would make surprise visits to their bedroom to make sure her rules were not being broken.

After visiting their mother in her room, they started lessons at 8.30 in a study which was 'like an icehouse' in winter, when their teeth would be 'chattering with cold'. Their fingers were so stiff with chilblains that they could barely hold their pens, but the governess seemed not to notice the cold, from which they deduced that her clothes were lined with fur. An 'all round' education was what was required and they studied all day except for three hours spent at games, walking and, rather surprisingly, gardening, all under the supervision of the governess.

The girls usually had lunch and dinner with their parents and ten minutes before each meal Mlle Legrand would conduct them to their mother's boudoir where the Queen was generally expecting them. In Stephanie's words,

She came forward to meet us, and asked how we had behaved. I always trembled at the prospect of this assize, but neither my entreaties before we entered the *boudoir*, nor my anxious glances after we had gone in, would withhold the governess from telling the Queen about the most trifling incidents of the day. Outbursts of temper, disobedience, lessons badly learned, rudeness, curt answers (I was always very plain spoken), undue liveliness – everything was reported by the censor, blamed and punished. This painfully exact record of our sins of omission and commission was a continual torment to us.

The punishments administered by the governess were very un-pleasant. Often I had to kneel on parched peas; but the punishment I dreaded most of all was confinement between double doors. There I would be kept locked up for hours, or even for entire days.

It is hard to believe that the parents authorised such cruelties, which were often the result of 'injustice and calumny' on Mlle Legrand's part, whose word was trusted more than that of the children. In fact it is questionable how much the Queen actually knew of what the odious governess was getting up to, for when the girls eventually persuaded their mother to watch them 'covertly' at their lessons and she saw her strike Louise, she instantly dismissed her.[2]

It is hard for us now to understand why these abused children did not manage to complain more effectively to their parents about blatant injustice and ill-treatment on the part of their governesses, but the immediate problem of communication must be remembered. The degree to which members of the aristocracy were engaged in politics and in London society meant that they were frequently absent from the family home where the children were left in governess care, so that intercourse between the two generations would be very infrequent. The complexity of life and sheer size of large country houses often made it difficult for children to get to their parents and, even if they did, to speak to them alone. In many families the barrier that existed between the schoolroom and the drawingroom was breached only at specified hours, usually for a period between afternoon tea and dinner, when there would usually be visitors or other relations present before whom exchange of confidences was difficult. Whispering was rude, and how could a frightened child know whether the governess might not be standing at the door listening with her sharp ears? House-parties at weekends would mean that the mother was busy and preoccupied, with little time to listen to childish complaints. It was simpler for the parents to believe the governess when she said the children were naughty, than to believe the children when they said the governess was cruel. The visible effects of blows or deprivation would impress a mother, but these would rarely be evident. While there is no reason to suppose that there was less love between parents and children in aristocratic families than in middle class ones, there was usually a greater degree of blindness in the former about what was going on behind the parental back.

Another thing the children had to contend with was that inherent feeling in parents that what they suffered in their own youth did them no lasting harm and, therefore, was probably right, with perhaps some modification, for their children. Parents in the 1950s and 60s were still accepting that little boys were likely to be unhappy at their preparatory schools; it had always been so, and it was probably a necessary preparation for life. It only dawned on parents in the 1970s and thereafter that boarding schools not only could but should be humane and pleasant places, and that after selecting one they should constantly check to ensure that their child was indeed happy.

The predominant reason, however, for the inability of children to protect themselves by telling tales about their governess was the same that prevents children reporting physical or sexual abuse today: fear of retribution from the perpetrator. Parents, if they believed the tales, might well only warn rather than dismiss the tyrant, and what fearful revenge could a child then imagine her taking when next the father and mother were away? The risks incurred by complaining were unquantifiable and the reaction of parents uncertain.

Victoria, Louisa and Mary Grey, in their schoolroom in Windsor Castle, were children of loving parents, but they were in no doubt that Fräulein Rebentisch would vent her rage upon them if they dared to complain of her unkindness to their parents. And so Victoria dared say nothing when she was made to walk for miles suffering the pain of a broken chilblain on her heel. Little Mary, learning to read, 'was often battered and pinched till her poor little arms were pulp'. It was the casual question of an uncle as to how they liked their governess that finally brought about their deliverance. 'Startled by the answer he received, he went straight to our mother about it, and she, horrified at his disclosure,' sacked Fräulein Rebentisch.[3]

Lord Curzon wrote that his sadistic governess, Miss Paraman, 'represented a class of governess and a method of tuition (in entire independence of the parents) which have both disappeared. With children who are constantly with their parents such a system would be incapable of concealment.'

His description of her is a series of memories of pain and humiliation:

In her savage moments she was a brutal and vindictive tyrant; I have often thought since that she must have been insane. She persecuted and beat us in the most cruel way and established over us a system of terrorism so complete that not one of us ever mustered up the courage to walk upstairs and tell our father or mother. She spanked us with the sole of her slipper on the bare back, beat us with her brushes, tied us for long hours to chairs in uncomfortable positions with our hands holding a pole or blackboard behind our backs, shut us up in darkness, practised on us every kind of petty persecution, wounded our pride by dressing us (me in particular) in red shining calico petticoats (I was obliged to make my own) with an immense conical cap on our heads round which, as well as on our breasts and backs, were sewn strips of paper bearing in enormous characters the words Liar, Sneak, Coward, Lubber and the like. In this guise she compelled us to go out in the pleasure ground and show ourselves to the gardeners. She forced us to walk through the park at even distances, never communicating with each other, to the village and to show ourselves to the villagers. It never occurred to us that these good folk sympathised intensely with us and regarded her as a fiend. Our pride was much too deeply hurt.

She made me write a letter to the butler asking him to make a birch for me with which I was to be punished for lying and requesting him to read it out in the Servants' Hall. When he came round one day with a letter and saw me standing in my red petticoat with my face to the wall on a chair outside the schoolroom and said 'Why, you look like a Cardinal!' I could have died of shame.

She made us trundle our hoops as young children, all alone, up and down a place in the grounds near the hermitage where were tall black fir trees and a general air of gloom and of which we were intensely afraid. She forced us to confess to lies which we had never told, to sins which we had never committed, and then punished us savagely, as being self-condemned. For weeks we were not allowed to speak to each other or to a human soul.[4]

Much of George Curzon's childhood in the 1860s, by his own account, was spent in tears, so it is surprising to discover that he apparently bore Miss Paraman no great ill-will in later life, saying that 'she taught us good habits – economy, neatness, method and a dislike of anything vulgar or fast.' His parents had such a high opinion of her that, after Lady Scarsdale's death, Lord Scarsdale gave the governess a gold necklace that his wife had wanted her to have.

Reading a letter written by Miss Paraman to Lord Scarsdale two years after George had gone to Eton, one begins to doubt whether his subsequent account of memories of her cruelty were not exaggerated.

Many thanks for your kind and good wishes, and the cheque you kindly enclosed. I am very glad to hear all are well.

I fear Mrs Senhouse is in a very bad state, dear George has written me nice kind letters and seemed much concerned to find his grandmama so worn and looking so thin and ill. I suppose the dear boys will soon be home again. My kindest love to all the dear children and good wishes,

Yours ever most truly, E. M. Paraman[5]

A brilliant dissimulator or a maligned disciplinarian? Probably the truth about Miss Paraman lies somewhere between the two.

A more surprising example of parental ignorance of schoolroom matters was in the household of George and Mary Lyttelton, whose children were the grandchildren of Sarah, the sensible royal governess. They were loving and conscientious parents, close to their children, and the schoolroom was not at the end of a far-away wing, as in some houses. It was actually between Mary's boudoir and George's study, and they often passed through it while the children were working at their lessons. Mary would smile at them, and George would murmur 'Absurd monkeys' as he went by. Despite this, they were incapable of choosing the right kind of women to look after their offspring.

The Lyttletons had a succession of indifferent governesses, among whom a Miss Nicholson stands out as being particularly unpleasant. Lucy, the eldest daughter, wrote in later life that her usual punishment was being put in a large, deep old-fashioned bath which stood in the dark behind heavy curtains in a corner of the schoolroom. Perhaps even more frightening, she was sometimes imprisoned between the double doors that are often positioned, about a yard apart, in the width of a wall separating rooms in eighteenth-century houses. She was 'often whipped', and she remembered being made by Miss Nicholson to walk on the Parade at Brighton with her hands tied behind her and being frightened by the possibility of meeting a policeman in this state, which was hardly a cheerful holiday memory for a child. Later this unhappy girl was cared for by an expert in psychological oppression called Miss Pearson, whose 'stern and upright mind and high and stern sense of duty' seem to have afflicted Lucy with a morbid sense of her own sinfulness. She wrote later '. . . it was well for me to have my faults exposed to me with an unsparing hand, though it cost me many times of almost despairing tears, and a good deal of bitter repentance'.

Despite miserable memories of this kind, the Lyttelton children all seem to have considered themselves to be members of a particularly happy and close family, and the governesses' punishments have to be considered in the light of the fact that even the children's adoring mother, Mary Lyttelton, used a rod on her two-and-a-half year old daughter's hand when she had been naughty. Children at that time accepted the physical pain regularly inflicted upon them by their elders as a normal part of life.[6]

· 13 ·

The governess in war
and peace

Generally speaking, domination by the governess of schoolroom life continued up to the First World War. It was by no means always as brutal as the examples given, but in principle parents thought it right not to interfere. Under a benign rule the schoolroom could be a happy and productive place, but an insensitive or vindictive woman had a power that could make childhood a time of fear and subterfuge. This was a fact of life that many children had to accept and live with.

The three Tennant daughters, Peggy, Katherine ('K') and Nancy, came at the end of a hugely extended family. Sir Charles Tennant, who had seventeen children in all, was eighty-one when his last child was born, two years before his death. The three girls were not untypical in their acceptance of the gloomy regime imposed by their governess 'Cauy' (pronounced Coy). She was about thirty-five years old and poorly educated and, like others who felt inadequate in their jobs, became a bully. In later years, when one might suppose that time might have mellowed the memory, 'K' still remembered her as 'horrible'.

Between 1910 and 1913 Cauy taught the girls to read and write from *Reading without Tears*, a book relied upon by many governesses. Her demands for perfection amounted almost to mania. If one letter were written incorrectly on a page she would insist on the whole page being re-written. Nothing she taught was made in any way interesting, which didn't appear to matter very much to their mother and stepfather since the girls were educated 'really only with marriage in mind'. Though 'K' remembered little that she learnt from her governess, she had vivid recollections in later life of her piano lessons: Cauy's method was to hit the girls' fingers hard with pencils when they made mistakes. In the afternoons she would take them for 'long, dreadful walks' when she would move at such speed over the ground that the children had to run to keep up with her.

In this family, too, the parents were frequently away from home, Broadoaks, in Byfleet, and never visited the schoolroom when they were there. Though girls and governess always joined the dining room party for lunch, it was at a separate table, so their poor relationship with her would not have been easily apparent. In any case, for a long time all the girls were 'far too frightened' of Cauy to dare tell their father and mother how much they disliked her or how unhappy she made them.

When the parents were not there, the schoolroom maid would bring lunch up to the schoolroom. Peggy remembers that:

> It would be something simple, like chops or chicken and lots of rice puddings, but excellent because Mother loved good food and always had very good cooks. Cauy would make meals a misery. She was tremendously greedy, and she would eat up everything, all the extras and some of mine as well, and leave me one little bit, especially when there were sausages. If I got one sausage I was very, very lucky.

One of Cauy's more subtle cruelties was to forbid visits to the nursery where their adored Nanny, daughter of a Scots miner, still ran a loving regime, caring for two younger stepbrothers. The governess and the nanny loathed each other, and perhaps Cauy feared that the nanny, if she were to be told of the children's sorrows, might pass the tale on to the parents. Or perhaps, as is equally likely, she was simply jealous of someone who commanded the love she could not herself gain from the children.[1]

It is entirely to Lord Curzon's credit that he reacted to his own childhood unhappiness in a positive way. In 1906, when the family were newly returned from India on the completion of his Vice-Royalty, his first wife died. His two elder daughters, Irene and Cynthia, were old enough to need formal education, and he determined to select their governesses himself. It was not that he took their education very seriously – they were aware later in life that they had only been educated with marriage in view – but he wanted to ensure that they did not have a woman like Miss Paraman inflicted upon them. The applicants who came before him must have found it an alarming experience, for he was not only very famous but also imposing and critical. One, on arriving in his library at Carlton House Terrace, was so nervous that he would reject her for 'her extreme chinlessness' that she kept her feather boa closely round her face throughout the interview, and only when she took up the appointment in the family home of Hackwood, near Basingstoke, was her deformity revealed.

Curzon could reasonably have asked one of his female friends or relations to help him in the task of interviewing the women, which might have made the sessions less harrowing for them and more successful for himself, but he did not. In his very full life he had acquired no knowledge of children and their peculiarities, or any sense of what children needed. As long as a governess looked respectable and could show adequate references which said that she was neither cruel nor dishonest he would engage her.

The result of Curzon's method of selection was an endless stream of incompetent governesses passing through Hackwood – few of them stayed for more than a year – and a complete lack of any systematic education for his three daughters. Of them all, only one endeared herself to her charges, as a person of no great intelligence or education, but kind and gentle. She left them after a short while to get married.

Each new arrival would start their history lessons at the Druids and had usually left the household by the time Julius Caesar was conquering Britain. 'Once we crept up as far as the Plantaganets,' Alexandra, the youngest daughter, remembered, 'but by that time we were on the rocks and the governess went.'

'Handwork' was a subject they all taught in some form to the three girls. They learned to paint Beatrix Potter characters on silk, to press flowers, to make pen-wipers and cut 'terrible little paper doileys' which they pressed on their reluctant relations as presents. They were taught arithmetic too, but never got beyond learning tables by heart, simple addition and subtraction, with short and long division. Learning by heart was a prominent feature of their lessons: one governess made them memorise all the famous speeches from Shakespeare plays, but also a selection of pieces of miscellaneous information 'with no surround to them'. The shade of Miss Mangnall and her *Questions* was still haunting the schoolrooms of Britain.

As a member of the government in Asquith's wartime coalition, Curzon spent a great deal of time in London, but he always came down to Hackwood at weekends, which was when the inadequacies of the governesses were uncovered that led to the dismissal of each in turn. Governess and girls would have luncheon in the dining room with him, and he would entertain them by relating unnamed historical events, eloquently describing the characters and the situations and evoking vivid images. This would have given nothing but pleasure, had not the prospect of the inquisition that always followed hung over the listeners like a lowering cloud; for these expositions were followed by questions about the scenes he had portrayed: Who were the characters? What incident in history was it that he had described? The date? The place?

If the ordeal was fairly uncomfortable for the girls, who stood in considerable awe of their father, they could at least protect themselves by saying 'But we haven't got as far as that . . .'. But for the governess it was torture. The questions were then thrown at her, and inevitably her ignorance was exposed in front of her pupils, as she murmured miserably, 'I – er – I am so sorry, Lord Curzon, I didn't quite catch what you asked me'.

One woman was dismissed in more dramatic circumstances: a Miss Phillips, whom Alexandra remembered as 'pretty nasty', came to them during the latter stages of the 1914–18 war, and when she was found late one night by one of the servants in Lord Curzon's Hackwood library, suspicions were aroused as to her motives. Was she a spy? Could she have been looking for secret government papers? On Armistice Day, 1918, young Alexandra was 'having a frolic round the schoolroom table' in celebration of the victory. Either her exuberance or the reason for it inflamed the governess, who threw a heavy inkwell at her. Suspicions of German sympathies thus confirmed, Miss Phillips was sacked.[2]

Other girls remembered their schoolroom days less with distress than with recollection of tedium. Agatha Christie in the 1890s knew a family whose governess

> instructed her pupils in natural history, little else. A great deal of picking of leaves and berries went on – and a suitable dissection of the same. It was incredibly boring. 'I do hate all this pulling things to pieces,' confided my small friend to me. I entirely agreed, and indeed the word Botany all through my life has made me shy like a nervous horse.[3]

The Baird sisters, some of whom went on to found St James' School, West Malvern, remembered their time in the schoolroom as happy and irresponsible. It was clearly extremely productive as well. Six of the seven Baird girls had 'a clever Scotch governess', Miss Alexandra Somerville, who engaged their interest in their work, teaching them languages, arithmetic, geography and other subjects. She took them right up to the level of the Cambridge University entrance examination, no mean feat for a single teacher, and for a governess at any time highly unusual. Miss Somerville was paid probably not more than £100 a year.[4]

At the start of the First World War, as a small girl, Daphne Price walked daily across Belgrave Square, through the gardens, in tightly laced black boots, holding her nanny's hand. She had lessons with the daughter of Sir Otto Beit, who lived at No. 49, the tall house on the corner of Grosvenor Crescent. Running fast through the hall, all but knocking over the footman who opened the door, she would rush upstairs at great speed, not so much in eagerness for her lessons as for fear of meeting Sir Otto, who she remembers as 'rather fierce'. Safely arrived in the schoolroom on the third floor, she and Muriel Beit were taught by an English governess who rejoiced in the spendid name of Miss Thrasher, but who in no way lived up to it. She was a demure and proper person. Her pupil, years later, 'could not imagine her ever to have been young and skittish', but she was kindly and well educated, from a simple rectory background. She sat at one end of a long table covered with a green baize cloth bordered with heavy fawn coloured braid, her two pupils sitting to her left and right, twisting their pencils in and out of the holes in the braid when lessons became boring. The girls sat well forward on their plain wooden chairs, and very upright, with their backs perfectly straight. They could not do otherwise, for vertical boards had been made by a carpenter and were attached by brackets to their chair backs in order to ensure their good posture.

Miss Thrasher had the usual supply of textbooks that many governesses preferred – aids to teaching as much as aids to learning – including Mrs Markham's *History of England*. This book was first published in 1823, long before Miss Thrasher was born, yet Daphne remembered it with pleasure many years later, with its numerous engravings of fortified castles and recumbent kings on tombs and with each chapter followed by a questionnaire in the form of conversation between a mother and two children. 'Tell me, Mamma, did not the Vikings. . . ?'

The books from which Miss Thrasher taught were her own property, carried from family to family, and growing slowly more out of date. Some of them were the very same copies she learned from herself as a girl. Books were expensive things for governesses to buy, and as a parent said who employed a governess between the two World Wars, 'One didn't think of paying for their books . . .'

There was a 'break' at eleven o'clock, when a footman brought a tray of milk and biscuits up to the schoolroom. The children would carry them to the big bow window that looked out into Grosvenor Cresent to watch the event that occurred every morning on the dot of eleven o'clock. A beautifully equipped open carriage stood in the street, with smartly dressed grooms holding the heads of the two horses. From the front door of 1 Belgrave Square, Baron Koch de Gooreynd emerged, attired for the park. He climbed into the driver's seat; the grooms, in their frock-coats, fawn trousers and top hats, mounted to stand behind him with folded arms, and off they would clatter for a rapid circuit of Belgrave Square before passing again on the way up to Hyde Park for the Baron's morning drive. The spectacle over, Miss Thrasher would call the little girls back to the schoolroom table.

Though she taught well, Miss Thrasher taught in English only and, as it was still widely held that for a girl to be well educated she should know two foreign languages, the afternoons were spent learning French and Italian with other teachers, a regime that went on until Daphne was seventeen, and 'came out'.

Sir Otto Beit took a particular interest in what went on in his daughter's schoolroom; very unusually for a parent of the day, he would draft a programme of work that Miss Thrasher had to follow, and he would make sure that it was adhered to. A the end of each term he would come to the schoolroom and conduct an inquiry into what they had learnt of geography, history, arithmetic and English literature. This was a harrowing experience for the girls and still worse for Miss Thrasher, who was even more frightened than Daphne was of her employer.[5]

Meanwhile, the young Pakenhams were being raised in Oxfordshire in the care of a series of governesses. Mary Pakenham recorded in her memoirs that, like many country-house bred children,

> . . .the only people that Pansy and I knew were our governesses, and willy-nilly we knew them very well indeed.
>
> Most of them were unhappy women who did not like children. At any rate they did not like us. We were more than revenged, however, for anything we suffered at their hands, by the dullness and ignominy of the life they led under our roof, and by the fact that they were put in a horrible little bedroom facing north in a quarter otherwise devoted entirely to bathrooms, sinks and housemaids' cupboards. There was linoleum in the passage, and the noise in the early morning of the housemaids clumping down two steps and getting brooms and pails soured their tempers for the day.

The reader's sympathy goes entirely to the governess. The customary dislike that indoor servants showed for governesses could be enjoyably expressed in early morning clatter outside her bedroom, and it is easy to imagine her lying in her sleepless bed, gazing at the shabby ceiling with tears of anger and frustration in her eyes.

With her nerves already well frayed, she joined in the schoolroom each day after breakfast a bunch of intelligent and rebellious children, who, like many others, were predisposed to dislike any outsider put in charge of them, and not unhappy to be disliked in return. The fact that the governess was empowered by their parents to make momentous decisions in their daily lives did not endear her to her charges.

Mary Pakenham relates one tale of governess foolishness and insensitivity. Her younger sister Pansy and her brother Frank had a favourite toy – a wooden knight mounted on a horse on wheels – which they had named, with a precocious and mystifying felicity, Falsextus. The governess had decided that the Pakenham children had more toys than were good for them, and so she took a selection of these to give to 'poor Mrs Quartermaine in the village who had fourteen children'. The children believed that the inclusion of Falsextus, despite their protests, was done deliberately in order to distress them.

> Our only consolation was that she left her parcel not with Mrs Quartermaine, but at the cottage of an unknown man, a bachelor. Seeing one's governess make such a fool of herself was almost worth the loss of Falsextus.

Since this is the worst incident of governess cruelty that Mary Pakenham seems to have remembered, the question arises as to why the Pakenham children were so automatically opposed to the women who came in turn to teach them. They had nine governesses in all, and few of them stayed very long. The children's attitude must at times have caused much suffering among these unfortunate women

> I shall never forget our feelings of incredulous triumph when we realised that we had (unintentionally) given one a nervous breakdown before her second term was over. Later I realised that one could be more than a passive agent, and I was deliberately instrumental in the exit of one after only three months.

How this was achieved is not related; perhaps the memory was not entirely relished, for children can be both devious and cruel.

Only the first and the last of the Pakenham governesses were remembered with any pleasure. The first was Scottish, old fashioned and very strict. She laid down for her pupils a good foundation of reading and spelling, with elementary history and geography. Her geography book was elderly and was named *Aids to Accuracy*. It started with rhymed descriptions of journeys on various English railways.

'The Great Western Railway' began,

> From Paddington we take our start,
> Next, Hanwell meets the eye
> (Safe home for lunatics), then Slough;
> Change here for Windsor. Look out now,
> The Castle you'll espy.

More usefully, she taught them the names of the principal towns, rivers and capes of the countries of the world.

The last governess to teach the youngest children found favour with them, and she 'stuck us for five years. She often used to wonder why the dullness didn't drive her to drink.'[6]

Because of the way governesses were passed on from one family to another, it is occasionally possible to follow one and to see how differently she was viewed by successive employers. Miss King spent a part of her career in the beautiful Wilton House, near Salisbury, where she was governess to the Earl of Pembroke's only daughter, Patricia.

Patricia had previously had one unpleasant French governess (who threw to the ground and stamped on a bunch of flowers she had been given when she discovered that the nanny, whom she loathed, had been given some flowers too), and an English one (who had suffered from cyclical bouts of madness, according to the phases of the moon). However, Miss King, who arrived in 1915, was a great success in her post. She is remembered as 'a splendid person' and 'an excellent teacher', though not much good at maths. That did not matter; governesses were hardly expected to be good at maths, and the schoolmaster from Wilton village came in to give coaching. What the parents had wanted for their daughter was a pleasant person to teach her in most subjects, and in Miss King they got exactly what they were looking for. She taught Patricia to love reading – by the time she left her pupil had read all Dickens, Scott, Thackeray, Whyte Melville and more – and Miss King had inspired everyone's affection.

Eventually Miss King had schooled Patricia to the level of the Oxford and Cambridge Junior Certificate; then she accompanied her pupil and another young girl to Brittany, where they spent a period in La Baule, with the purpose of perfecting the young ladies' French. Miss King's own inadequacy in this language was demonstrated at the reception desk of their hotel. There had been some muddle over the reservation, and the girls were reduced to helpless giggles as their governess tried to deal with the situation, repeating loudly and desperately, in an atrocious accent, '*Mais je suis* Miss King, *vous savez? Je suis* Miss King!'

'We could speak French much better than she could,' says her ex-pupil, 'But she was such a remarkable woman. She was perfectly sweet, and we loved her.'

Miss King stayed until her pupil was launched into her first London 'season' and the family kept in touch with her in later life.[7]

Miss King's next engagement, from about 1923, was with relations of the Pembroke family, also in Wiltshire, teaching a thirteen-year-old girl. Despite the family recommendation, it was distinctly not a success. Her pupil remembers her now as 'not at all an attractive personality, and we simply didn't "click". She only stayed for a year or so.' They found that Miss King behaved rather grandly, and she seemed very upset when the family discovered that a nearby farming family was related to their governess: this fact, which to her employers was simply a matter of passing interest, was apparently to the governess a source of embarrassment. She had after all told her pupil that the sign on the King's Arms public house in the nearby village of Fonthill Bishop represented the arms of her family, implying, perhaps, rather grander connections than mere farmers. Perhaps it was true; it so happens that in the late 1920s the pub was run by a family called King; in 1990, however, the coat of arms on the sign outside the King's Arms pub in Fonthill Bishop is definitely that of the monarch.

It is hard to reconcile the 'beloved Miss King' of Wilton House with the snobbish and 'tiresome' woman who left little impression on the memory of her next pupil save that of being small, with iron grey hair and usually wearing dark clothing.[8] This shows how dependent a governess's success in a post depended on the predelictions and the whims of the family who employed her. A long retired governess recently considered the suggestion that there was one obvious way of finding out more about a family offering a employment:

'Oh, no,' she replied, almost in alarm,

> That wouldn't have done at all; you couldn't have asked to speak to the previous governess – you were in a very subservient position! I *never* thought of asking that.

When Miss Hilda Payne decided to become a governess in 1923, she made sure she always knew as much as possible about a post before she took it. She was, she claims a timid person.

> When I went to be interviewed, I was very shy, and full of butterflies. But when they interviewed me, I would ask them a lot of questions about their life, because it was going to be *my life* with them, you see.

She was sensible in her approach, for she knew that that life would not be an easy one. But she had her own good reasons for undertaking it.

> When I was in my early twenties, it wouldn't have been considered respectable for a young woman to travel alone, and I longed to travel. And then I decided. I went to see the rector, and I told him I was taking on a post as a governess. He said, 'Well, you are choosing a very unhappy life for yourself. It is a very awkward position in a family. You will be neither fish, nor fowl nor good red herring.' He wanted me to go to a missionary school, where I could travel and be looked after. But I decided no, I couldn't, because I wanted to be able to choose for myself.

And so she did, selecting her posts carefully, sometimes relying much on her instinct, and usually successfully. She was always, after the initial visit to the 'Universal Aunts' Agency, recommended by each family to others. Sometimes she had several families to choose from, who all wanted her. She achieved her aim of travelling, with people who travelled or lived abroad, but held posts in England too.

Miss Payne is refreshingly critical of those who employ governesses. Of one in 'an uncomfortable place' in Scotland, where she felt that her employer took pleasure in saying things embarrassing to the governess at mealtimes, she remarks dismissively, 'She was rather an uncouth sort of woman.'

Miss Payne has a strong personality and sharp sense of humour. It is hard to imagine anyone being less than polite to her. Only one family gave her a nickname. It comes as no surprise to find that throughout her working days she was called 'Miss Payne', but through no lack of affection. One mother said to her, 'You have been in the family so long; please call me by my Christian name. But I will continue to call you Miss Payne, out of respect.'

She now lives in retirement in a pretty farm cottage on the family estate of one of her employers, doing occasional coaching, visited and appreciated by those whose life she shared. She remembers the rector's words, but says, 'He said it would be an unhappy life. It was not an unhappy life, but it had its difficulties.'[9]

The sweetbread eaters

ADVICE TO GIRL GRADUATES

(After Charles Kingsley – at a respectful distance)

Dress well, sweet Maid, and let who will be *clever*.
Dance, flirt and sing!
Don't study all day long.
Or else you'll find,
When other girls get married,
You'll sing a different song!

Punch, July 5, 1890

Mrs Alfred Sidgewick's novel *The Grasshoppers*, published in 1913, begins:

> When Hilary Frere first expressed a wish to go to College her mother wept. Mrs Frere had not trained up her daughter in such a path as this. She had never seen any of the Women's Colleges. Nevertheless, like many others of the generation, she cherished a lively dislike of these institutions. The very name of one still sends an unpleasant thrill through the frames of many respectable and otherwise intelligent persons. It conjures up a vision of womanhood with the graces left out. It suggests an aggressive creature, brimful of knowledge to be gathered from textbooks, and lacking the modesty that recognises yet wilder,

deeper knowledge in other people . . . [she feared] a collegiate life would have the same effect on a girl as a vow of celibacy. It would lead her to dress in a disagreeably conspicuous fashion. She would cut her hair short, take to spectacles and burn her modish gowns, and it would fill her with the distrust of men and marriage that is fashionable amongst the glorified spinsters of today.

Needless to say Hilary goes to college, enjoys adventures there that are entirely to her liking, and most of her mother's fears are not realised. But the apprehension of this fictional mother was shared by many real-life parents, and was rooted in nineteenth century prejudice. One of the first girl undergraduates at Cambridge related that when her intention of going to college became known in the country district where she lived, her acquaintance 'could not have spoken worse of her if she had committed a forgery'. Another girl, having gained a scholarship, was told, 'You are surely satisfied now. You cannot want to *make use of it*.'[1]

This attitude persisted well into the new century, and it was the life blood of the governess class. There was a genuine dread among many otherwise intelligent people of what would happen to their daughters if they sent them not just to 'college' but to schools like Roedean, Cheltenham Ladies' College, and St James', West Malvern. A girl who played hockey seriously, who studied scientific subjects in laboratories, who dressed in a 'djibbah' and read the *Aeneid* in the original Latin might become, of all horrific concepts, a 'Bluestocking' who would then reject everything her parents had planned for her: the débutante season, the houseparties where she would meet 'the sons of people one knows' and the eventual 'suitable' marriage. If the landed gentry saw the dangers of public school education for their girls, so too did many others whose counterparts forty, fifty, and sixty years later would be scraping family money barrels and straining their resources in every way to get their daughters into the same schools.

The liberalisation of attitudes towards women's occupations brought about by the 1914–18 war made the reactionary element more wary still. The discovery that, while their menfolk were fighting, women could drive ambulances, work in factories and on the land, run businesses, do all manner of physical things hitherto supposed to be the preserve of males, and do them well, was a revelation to men and women alike, and not always a welcome one. A stopper had been removed from the bottle that could never be put back in; but there were many who would go on trying for a long time yet to stop the bubbles escaping.

Meanwhile, for many reasonably affluent parents, keeping a

daughter at home, safe within their loving control, was a way of keeping these alarming changes out of the family, and of perpetuating a system that felt safe.

The governess continued to be the answer to the education of girls in such families, but the war brought a subtle change in her position. The horrors that had been vicariously or actually experienced, the loss of husbands, brothers and sons and the decimation of households, brought a consciousness of the fragility of family ties into homes. Thus the war did as much for children as for women in changing the attitude of those who controlled their lives. Whereas in Victorian days children's faults and weaknesses had been sternly schooled out of them to make them behave like adults as soon as possible, now they became treasured and enjoyed because they *were* children, and allowances were made for the fact that they were young. Their innocence came to be cherished, and their vulnerability recognised; it was as if the loss of the greater part of one generation had made people aware of the value of the succeeding one. Books were written for small children to enjoy having read to them, rather than to frighten them into obedience. The practice grew of writing in the language of children, rather than of telling children's stories in adult words.

Parents started to take far more interest in what was going on in the nursery and schoolroom, and the traditional barriers that had separated children from their parents were disappearing. 'The inviolable rules that had governed our infancy had slipped. Our parents were no longer inaccessible – our governess no longer reigned supreme.' The girl who made this remark eventually persuaded her parents to send her to boarding school.

The changes did not happen overnight, nor were they universal. But from the end of the war in 1918 and as the nineteen-twenties wore on, the regime in the schoolroom underwent a fundamental reshaping. The governess, who had once ordered every minute of schoolroom life and who had educated entirely according to her own ideas, found herself consulting, discussing and sharing the problems with parents who apparently cared about what their daughters learnt. These parents were becoming aware of new standards in what the girls might achieve; the message coming from the women's colleges was not going unheeded and, reluctant though the universities had been to give educational parity, the world was coming to realise that women, with suitable secondary education, could compete successfully with men in all subjects at university level.

The governess who failed to educate or who had managed to conceal her own lack of education became far more liable to exposure, and she who bullied or punished too severely was no longer protected by the children's fear of her or their lack of communication with mother and father.

In many households another kind of restructuring also took place. After the war, with the male workforce substantially reduced, the reluctance to employ women in jobs traditionally held by men was fast disappearing. The country girl who had had domestic service as virtually her only opening if she wanted to leave home could now earn her living in a variety of other ways. In 1911 a female typist, for example, had been a novelty; after the war she was everywhere, and earning a decent salary. The cost of living, which had risen steeply during the war years, was going down again, but wages were rising. A shop assistant, who in 1906 had earned on average £83 a year, had seen that rise by 1924 to £120, and after the mid-1930s the figures would rise much more dramatically.[2] Housemaids, as a result, could no longer be hired in droves, and though the larger country and town houses still kept huge numbers of staff, wages improved and living conditions became more humane. Above all domestic staff were treated with greater respect, and the crippling hierarchy headed by butler, house-keeper and cook was gradually growing more benign as lines of demarcation became blurred.

At a higher social and educational level, more clerical and managerial jobs became available as prejudice toward female employees waned. It was a necessary development, again because of the post-war shortage of young men. Many young women of the middle classes, who might have hesitated before, now took these opportunities as the social stigma attached to such work started to disappear. Whereas before 'being a governess' had seemed almost the only option, now there was choice.

Fewer governesses were therefore available, but fewer were needed, as more parents were sending their daughters to boarding schools. It was no longer an *outré* thing to do. Thus employment of governesses became once again concentrated in the aristocracy and affluent members of the middle class: for, generally speaking, the larger and grander the household, the slower came the change.

Governesses had come out of the nineteenth century with a long tradition of inferiority behind them. It was to take more than a world war materially to change their status. Most of them were still spinsters or widows, so their social position was not strong: though some employers might go so far as to be kind, it tended to be the kindness of patronisation rather than of genuine good-heartedness.

The tone of the relationship that would exist between governess and employer would be set at the very first interview. This could take place in the home of the prospective employer, if in London, but it would be in the library, or in the dining room, rather than in the drawing room. The venue would be an indication that, if employed, the governess should not expect herself to be allowed into the heart of the family; her position was functional, and in the functional rooms she had her place, but not in the rooms where the family relaxed or entertained visitors.

The employer would usually refund to the governess the expenses she had incurred in travelling for interview, this having been agreed in advance with the agency who had put them in touch with each other, but was liable to jib at the cost of a cab if one had been used. Cabs were not for governesses, unless they were accompanying the employers' children.

Country employers often chose the neutral ground of the local railway station for interviews, rather than go to the trouble of bringing the applicants to their homes. Juliette Huxley, as a nineteen-year-old in 1916, sought a position as a governess through a London agency and was asked to meet Lady Ottoline Morrell in the first class waiting room of Oxford station.

> I duly arrived and waited some time in a musty solitude. It then struck
> me that there was another waiting room on the down-side of the station.
> I made my way to it, and there found two imposing and distinguished
> persons, obviously expecting someone.

Juliette had done 'just well enough' in her exams at her school in her native Switzerland – her highest mark was for 'composition'. She had no experience of teaching, but this did not deter the Morrells, although she would be expected to instruct their nine-year-old daughter Julian in French and general subjects. Lady Ottoline's own description of their first meeting in Oxford station 'where we sat together on a bench' suggests that they were more interested in the fact that Juliette was young, cheerful and active.[3]

Other women living in the country, when looking for governesses for their daughters, might stay overnight at a London hotel for the purpose of conducting interviews. They would spend a morning sitting in a quiet corner of the foyer, while the governesses arrived at fifteen-minute intervals, sometimes passing their rivals leaving as they came through the swing door. An hotel employee would have been engaged to bring each in turn to the table in the corner.

Late arrival would count as a bad mark, as would unsuitable or brightly coloured clothing or too 'perky' a hat. Too breezy or familiar a manner on first meeting was frowned upon, and sitting down or removing coat and gloves without waiting to be invited to do so did not go down well. It implied too much ease.

Sometimes the governess had to watch and wait while the prospective employer scanned again the written references that had been sent previously by the applicant. Occasionally she would recognise the hand-writing of a former employer on letters that the interviewer had obtained for herself. She would then be closely questioned on the detail of the references. She would know that a judgement was being made on her morals, her appearance, her accent and her manners. Her ability to teach would be taken for granted. It was the only attribute that she would not be required to demonstrate, although, if employed, teaching would take up the largest part of the time in her working day.

Many a governess thus had no opportunity of seeing in advance the home in which she might be destined to spend several years of her life until she arrived apprehensively with her luggage from the local railway station.

From that moment on, her position in the household was awkward and ambiguous. The parents would treat her with politeness and apparent respect, either out of sheer good manners or in order that the children might submit to being in her charge. But there came a point where the privacy of the family and its guests must not be invaded; the boundaries tended to be set at meal times.

In the morning the governess would accompany the children to family prayers, which still took place in many households, especially in Scotland. She would take her place on one of the line of chairs on the 'family side' of the diningroom. The nanny, on the other hand, would usually be seated on the 'servant side', next to the senior members of the staff, housekeeper, cook and butler. It was not unknown for a nanny to refuse to attend prayers because of this division between herself and the governess.

After prayers, the governess would take the children back to the schoolroom for breakfast, and keep them there during the morning lessons. For luncheon, assuming the children were of an age to join the family, the governess would also join the party in the dining room. Very often, she would be obliged to sit at a side table with the children, being given food by the servants after the main table had been served. If the schoolroom party was permitted to sit at the main table, the governess would sit in such a position as to be able to monitor their behaviour. She would not normally be expected to join in the general conversation unless specifically addressed, and then she had to take care not to express her views forcefully.

In the afternoon the governess would superintend the 'rest' period, the younger children lying on their beds for up to an hour, the elder girls reading improving books, perhaps lying on the schoolroom sofa. A brisk walk would come next, whatever the weather, unless some expedition had been planned. The adults of the family would have tea in the drawing room or hall at the end of the afternoon and, as it came to an end, the governess would bring the children down, changed into tidy clothes, to join their parents. She would bring them only as far as the door, ushering them through, and closing it quietly behind them, as their Nanny had done when they were younger. She would collect them again later, summoning them quietly from the door at the designated hour for bed.

The children in some households would dine in the dining room from the age of twelve or thirteen, the point at which boys went on to public school. The girls often had to wait until they were sixteen or seventeen. But it was very rare indeed for a governess to have dinner with the family. Even before the 1914–18 war, however, she might on occasion, and all else failing, be summoned to dine downstairs to make up the numbers of an unbalanced party or to satisfy superstition and raise them from thirteen to fourteen. Normally, though, she would spend the evening alone in the schoolroom, where her supper would be brought to her on a tray by a footman or the schoolroom maid. She would not be served the same fare as was appearing in the dining room – more likely something left over from the day before, or whatever else the cook deemed to be suitable. Harold Macmillan, towards the end of his life, was observed at a luncheon party peering at a dish he was being offered.

'And what is this?' he asked.

On being told, 'Sweetbreads', he replied, 'Ah yes, what we used to give the governess.'[4]

After supper, letter-writing or preparation of lessons for the next day would occupy the hours until bedtime. After the 1920s the practice of requiring the governess to help with the household mending had died out, but she might be expected during her leisure time to repair some of the children's clothes. In a generous household, from the 1930s on, there might be a schoolroom wireless to listen to.

There was no question of her leaving the house of an evening, as her pupils were in her charge by night as well as by day. In this her situation was very similar to that of the nanny who, also in a position of supreme responsibility for the younger children, was never off duty. But there the similarity between the two women ended. The 'teaching' remit that the governess enjoyed put her in a higher social category in the household. Only if there was a secretary employed and living in the house would she find an exact social counterpart who might join her at suppertime or for an evening's conversation.

There were some nice differences in the ways the governess and the nanny were treated which demonstrated their relative positions. For instance, the governess was paid by the term, and this was called salary, whereas the nanny was paid by the month, and it was called wages. A governess's earnings would normally be double that of a nanny. Though in the previous century they were often paid quarterly, by now the cook, the butler and the housekeeper were also paid by the month, and the other servants by the week, the payment period in each case representing the length of notice that each would expect to give or be given on termination of service.

The governess and the nanny dressed differently, and the difference went further than the nanny's nursery apron or white, starched overall. This was clear to see in the Royal Botanical Gardens in Regent's Park in London, a favourite venue for governesses and nannies in the afternoons. These were private gardens, but open to the families of members of the Royal Botanical Society, and their nannies and governesses held keys to the gates. There they would walk and sit, chatting to their friends while their charges played hoop-la or skipped along the gravel paths. Evelyn Northcroft, daughter of a Harley Street specialist, was taken daily to the park by her nanny in the early 1920s, and remembered being easily able to tell which were which as they sat on the benches: the nannies all wore pale grey dresses in the summer and, from October onwards, dressed in navy blue with matching felt hats. The governesses wore two-piece tweed suits and jerseys, of varying weight, all the year round. In effect, the nannies wore uniform and the governesses emulated the dress of their employers.

Another sign of the difference that placed the governess above the nanny was the mode of address. The nanny would be addressed by the family by her surname alone – for example, Jones – and by the children and the staff as Nanny or Nanny Jones. The governess would be addressed by all with the prefix Miss – Miss Smith or Miss Brown —though the children, and in some families even the parents, might use an affectionate abbreviation. This alone, however customary, could be an irritation to the nanny. It was compounded by the unacceptable fact that the governess would normally address the lady of the house as Mrs Perkins or Lady Perkins, whereas the nanny would call her Madam or My lady as did the rest of the staff. A governess wishing to stress her superiority when talking to a nanny or one of the servants would refer to their mutual titled employer as Her Ladyship, thus subtly putting herself onto the side of the family, who would normally use this expression when talking to inferiors.

As well as all this, in the nanny's eyes the governess was a usurper. She took away the attention and perhaps even some of the love of the children whom the nanny had nurtured since infancy, and this could not be easily forgiven. Yet it was very often to the nanny that the children would tell tales about the governess, knowing that their complaints would be faithfully relayed to their parents whom they might be shy of approaching themselves. Thus relations between schoolroom and nursery were more often than not strained to the point of open hostility.

In his book *The Rise and Fall of the British Nanny*, Jonathan Gathorne-Hardy tells of an epic battle between a nanny and a governess in the Weymouth family in the nineteen-thirties. The new governess, Miss Vigers, arriving to take charge of Caroline Thynne, assessed Nanny Marks as being particularly powerful, despite her diminutive size, and therefore a potential danger to herself.

From the start, Miss Vigers seems to have decided that there would be conflict and laid her plans accordingly. The very day she arrived she began to tell stories of how in her previous post at Lady Somerlyton's the nanny had tried to interfere with the education of the children. 'But,' said Miss Vigers, 'Lady Somerlyton kept the nanny firmly in her place.' Aware herself of the enormous social gulf which did and should separate a nanny from a governess, she tried to impress it both upon the children and on Nanny Marks. She openly abused her with being a 'mere servant' and of 'trying to put on airs'. Nanny Marks began to loathe Miss Vigers . . . she became slightly incoherent when Miss Vigers was mentioned.

Matters developed swiftly. Thinking, with a knowledge of the realities of power no doubt gained from her study of history, that she would greatly strengthen her position if she could get her hands on the Exchequer, Miss Vigers offered to organise the paying of the other servants in order to lighten the load on her mistress. Nanny Marks was furious. She stormed down and refused point blank to be paid by anyone else than Lady Weymouth – a concession immediately granted her.

There followed the battle of the knickers. Miss Vigers, consolidating her hold on Caroline, had all Caroline's clothes transferred from the nursery to the schoolroom. She found that a pair of pink knickers was missing and assumed at once that Nanny Marks had concealed them out of obstinacy. Returning, apparently calm but no doubt inwardly seething, to the nursery she demanded the knickers. Alexander

Weymouth, from Nanny's subsequent accounts, reconstructed the following conversation.

Nanny:	I haven't got Caroline's pink knickers.
Miss Vigers:	You must have got them: they're down on her clothes list, but they're not amongst the clothes you handed over to me.
Nanny:	I tell you, I simply haven't got them, Miss Vigers. They're not here, and what could I possibly have done with them?
Miss Vigers:	It's no good asking me what you have done with them. You've eaten them, I expect.
Nanny:	I've done no such thing. Come in and look for yourself.

Nanny now shut herself in the night nursery, leaving Miss Vigers to rout fruitlessly through the toy cupboards, under cushions, behind rocking horses. Finding nothing, she tried to get into the night nursery only to discover the door was being held fast. A tug-of-war developed, Miss Vigers shouting, 'Open the door! Open the door!' She was stronger than Nanny, so the door began to open; but now Nanny suddenly let go, the door flew open, and Miss Vigers overbalanced backwards. Before her enemy could recover her dignity, Nanny left the field having won, she always claimed in after years, not just a moral victory but a physical one, as Miss Vigers was still lying flat on her back. She also said it was proof of Miss Vigers' madness that she should accuse anyone of eating pink knickers.

Quarrels and arguments of this sort were continual. As month followed month, they began to wear Nanny out. She became obsessed with the idea, quite justifiably, that Miss Vigers was trying to drive her from Sturford. Miss Vigers once said to her, 'Yes, so far I've only got Caroline. But Alexander will be starting lessons with me soon. Even that little baby [Valentine] will belong to me one day.' Time is on the side of the governess. Nanny Marks fretted and brooded and eventually had some form of nervous breakdown. She woke one morning and found, she said, she 'simply hadn't the energy to move'. Doctor Graham Campbell prescribed a long holiday and a temporary Nanny, Mrs Broom, took over.

Realising her moment had come, Miss Vigers struck. She saw her best plan of ousting Nanny was to establish Mrs Broom as a preferable alternative. She formed, therefore, a close alliance with her . . . Miss Vigers now began to hint openly to Lord and Lady Weymouth that they would be wise to take this opportunity of getting rid of Nanny Marks.

Her chances were further improved because the whole family was about to go to France when, provided Nanny Marks stayed away, Mrs Broom could become even more deeply entrenched.

However, Miss Vigers failed. Mrs Broom was disliked by the children so Miss Vigers' plan was weakest at its most fundamental point. And Nanny Marks knew precisely what was going on. She returned well before the French holiday – and in fighting trim. On the holiday she re-established her control and position with the children and, especially since Valentine was still a very small baby, became once more indispensable.

'On their return, Alexander moved down from the nursery to a room near Miss Vigers and Caroline. The family was now split into schoolroom children and nursery children. In the holidays, Miss Vigers went away and the schoolroom children returned to the nursery, to be spoilt by Nanny and commiserated with for having to be with Miss Vigers. But in fact both antagonists now realised that each was firmly fixed in her respective position. They had arrived at a balance of power. Hostilities continued, but were confined to pin-prick scheming and bitchy remarks – continued indeed for years. While at his prep school, Alexander used to write to his mother and ask if Nanny Marks and Miss Vigers were still having their rows.

It could have gone on to the end, when time would have brought the children one by one under Miss Vigers' control as she had long ago prophesied. Then suddenly the true source of a Nanny's power delivered Miss Vigers into Nanny Marks' hands and enabled her to annihilate her and her kind for ever.

The instrument of her triumph was Christopher. He continued to love Nanny Marks and resisted all Miss Vigers' attempts to wean him. She therefore loathed him, castigated him as a nursery boy and used to terrify him – shouting at him and beating him with a ruler. Her presence paralysed him and he became totally unable to concentrate, particularly on reading. For a while he obtained relief by noticing that if he looked at her lips he could see her unconsciously mouthing the words that she was expecting him to say. However, she discovered this and thereafter hit his hands with a ruler if he so much as raised an eye from the page. The next ruse he employed was to hide all the reading books before the lesson but this too was found out and led to further beatings.[5]

The boy's unhappiness eventually led to the sacking of Miss Vigers, triumph for Nanny Marks and day school for Christopher.

The other servants had less obvious reasons for objecting to the governess, but it was rare for some alienation not to exist. They saw that she was not fully accepted into the family circle, and so, as gentry *manqué*, was not worthy of the respect that they accorded or feigned to accord to their employers and their employers' friends. Nevertheless, she had access to the dining room, and moved freely in other parts of the house; she went on picnics and expeditions with the family; she was often suspected of acting as an informer, whether she was guilty of this or not. The staff were obliged to wait upon her, to clean her room and wash her sheets, and yet she was not 'family'. The family demanded that the servants respect her, and yet denied her their own respect. She dressed like 'family', and yet was often paid less than the cook, and would be dismissed with much less fuss or upset to the household than the loss of the cook would occasion. The governess had no cause to 'act grand' and yet she appeared to do so. Poor woman. Her sin was that she did not fit into the clearly defined hierarchy on either side of the green baize door.

· 15 ·

The gracious vision

Since the 1860s, gales of change had been blowing through women's ideas of education, sweeping away the centuries of musty stagnation. One result was a new college set up not only to train women as governesses but to teach parents about the educational capabilities of their own children. It was the brainchild of Charlotte Mason (1842–1923,) the daughter of a Liverpool merchant, and best known as the progenitor of the Parents' National Educational Union. This started in 1887 as the PEU – the N was added later – and arose from the interest engendered by her lectures and her book on 'Home Education'.

In 1890 she established her 'House of Education', later known as the Charlotte Mason College, at Ambleside in Cumbria, amid the beautiful scenery of the Lake district. Her purpose was to run courses to train women – parents, potential parents, and governesses – in the revolutionary system of children's education that she had evolved from her own long years of teaching experience in Sussex and in Yorkshire. Her philosophy was based on the understanding of the child 'as a person' whose intellect and interest must be engaged if education was to be effective. The long treasured principle of learning by heart was abandoned, and its place was taken by the practice of reading aloud to children, after which they would narrate in their own words what they had understood. They were taught how to listen and absorb knowledge without taking notes.

A wide and far more stretching curriculum was to be followed than was usual for children. Their understanding was to be awakened initially by directing their interest to the beauties of the physical world around them. Their natural habit of inquiry was to be guided into becoming a structured search for knowledge. As one of Miss Mason's pupils said, describing the Mason principle, 'Teaching is not a technique exercised by the skilled on behalf of the unskilled. It is a sharing of the effort to know.'

Charlotte Mason had very great respect for the intellectual ability of the very young, and considered that, if this could be stimulated and fed with knowledge, their power for learning was almost limitless. She coined some trenchant aphorisms: 'Learning is convenient, but knowledge is vital'; 'Education is the science of relations'. But her sensible ideas were often cloaked in the cloying phrases typical of women writing in her time. In her monthly *Parents' Review*, through which she communicated with parents, she described her 'gracious vision' of a governess. The aim of the House of Education was to bring this romantic figure to life:

> Her face is kind, sincere and full of purpose. She is devoted to children and understands all nursery duties in health and sickness. She can sing and draw and tell a great store of tales. She has a quiet eye and a warm heart with the firmness of one who speaks with authority. She knows the names and songs of birds, can tell the names of some of the flowers, some of the stars. She speaks pure English undefiled. She does not teach the children science but she trains in them the seeing eye. The 'gracious vision' understands the laws of habit, knowing that habits make for character and character rules destiny. She knows the laws of a child's well-being and development; seeing him as a person, one and indivisible, she prefers to have entire charge of him under his mother.

It is no wonder that, even before the House of Education was properly functioning, there were already applications from parents who wanted to employ these paragons of governesses, and who were willing to pay any salary that Miss Mason thought appropriate.

By 1898 two-year courses, culminating in an examination and a certificate, were popular and fully subscribed. Potential young governesses were met at Windermere station by an elderly coach drawn by four horses. Their luggage was put inside, and the new girls sat on top beside the driver, who wore a scarlet coat and a grey hat. The footman who rode behind would let them try to blow his horn as they drove for five miles along the side of the lake to Ambleside.

The House of Education was a grey stone Georgian mansion, set in a large garden full of fine trees and, in spring, drifts of wild daffodils. The students' accommodation was simple, and the rules were strict and apparently arbitrary, but each had a salutary purpose: there was to be no more than one vase of wild flowers in each bedroom, for instance. This, it was said, taught the value of space, and of a few flowers and twigs rightly placed in a room. Only one letter might be written on a Sunday, and that must be to home, so that it could be a day of leisure. No one was allowed to go for a walk alone; this was intended to develop the ability to enjoy outdoor things despite distracting companions. (A vision comes to mind of a governess striding ahead while children trail beind wailing 'Wait for me . . .')

A student who was there in 1918 and 1919 wrote that she was trained to become 'an active and acceptable member of the household, one who demanded little but could cheerfully co-operate in daily living'. This was encapsulated in the phrase 'the art of living in other people's houses', an art that governesses were to be called to practise all their working lives.

As students, the young governesses came to respect 'the rules that saved labour for the domestic staff, accepting the limitations of hot water supply or lighting'. Requests for the comfort of armchairs and sofas were rejected, and in reply to a request from the students for some modification in the household rules Miss Mason said, 'Perfect arrangements and conditions do not produce the best preparation for future work', words to be remembered later by governesses in posts in large, cold, uncomfortable country houses.

A wide range of subjects was studied, for the Charlotte Mason philosophy dictated that the governesses' future pupils should not be limited in the scope of their knowledge by adherence to the normal childish curriculum. So they learnt languages, ancient and modern, history, geography, geology, and botany. A very strong emphasis was placed on nature study. The students were taken on organised walks for one and a half hours every afternoon, rain or fine, in the lanes and hills around Ambleside, searching for and learning the names of flowers, mosses and birds. This was another habit which later in life their pupils were to remember with mixed feelings.

The potential governesses would rehearse their teaching skills one day a week at the Practising School in Fairfield House which had been set up for this purpose. No charge was made to the parents of the children of Ambleside village who were their guinea-pigs.

The main thrust of Charlotte Mason's work was to train teachers, for children of all backgrounds, to similar standards in a new and far more liberal method of teaching. Her principles drew wide attention and respect, and by 1917 were being introduced into elementary schools.

Side by side with this ran a service to parents and governesses at home and abroad, known as the Parents' Union School. This service was used until well after the Second World War, both in Britain and among families working abroad. Full educational 'programmes' could be followed, the relevant books and instructions being posted to 'home schoolrooms'.

One sensible and well educated governess, interviewed in 1990, gave an excellent testimonial to the system. She had been asked in 1948 to take on the education of a girl who was living with her grandparents, after her own home life had fallen apart, leaving her 'rather mixed-up'.

'We decided,' said the governess,

> to join the PNEU and follow the full syllabus, which was ideal for her, with its wide range, scope for imagination and yet insistence on neatness, orderliness and attention to detail. Also, the regular termly exams were an impartial check on progress and standard for her age. Their choice of text-books was excellent and their lending library invaluable, as she was an insatiable reader.

This framwork for education was helpful to many governesses whether or not they had been trained at the Charlotte Mason College, since they could find out on arrival in a new post exactly what a child knew and from where to continue its work. It was even more helpful to those parents who felt that they could not make head or tale of what their children were or were not learning. It gave them a certain confidence that their children were following a planned curriculum which did not have to change with each change of governess, for continuity in education was a feature in only the best organised families; a rapid turnover in governesses was more usual, as families tried and discarded inadequate women in their search for one who suited them. If parents had always insisted on teaching qualifications, diplomas, or certificates as well as character references, this haphazard system, cruel to governesses and damaging to children, would not have persisted. More training centres would perforce have appeared if there had been enough demand for their product. Meanwhile the limited number of PNEU or otherwise trained governesses were matched by an equally limited number of parents who cared about giving their daughters a good education. The remainder continued to be satisfied with the second rate.

The Cunard family had a particularly large number of governesses, not surprisingly, as there were seven daughters: Laura, Veronica, Priscilla, Barbara, Penelope, and Virginia, with a half-sister, Grania, at the end.

A mixed bunch of teachers presided in turn over the Cunard school-room, mainly at Britwell in Oxfordshire, but also in London, during and after the First World War. One of the most memorable was Miss Marris, who was a person of imagination; when her pupils, who were all quite musical, hummed the tunes from *The Beggar's Opera*, Miss Marris impressed them by saying that she had met John Gay, its composer. She was an attractive young women, always beautifully dressed, in clothes from expensive shops like Marshall & Snelgrove and Debenham & Freebody. Virginia, the sixth daughter, was considerably upset when, on a journey to Oxford by train with her governess, they were met at the station by policemen who arrested Miss Marris on a charge of shoplifting.

A request had been made by her parents, when they were told that this was going to happen, that their young daughter should not be alarmed:

> The constable bowed to me, first, as we got out of the train, but when she saw him Miss Marris began to cry. It made me feel quite fond of her, and rather protective. He asked me whether she was strict with me, and I said 'No, very kind'. Then he said, 'Well, she'll sleep on a hard bed tonight.' Before they took her away she hugged me and asked me to forward her letters to a male friend, which I promised to do.

In the event, Virginia was not allowed to keep her promise, since the friend was presumed to be an accomplice; but she was consoled by being told that, though Miss Marris got six months in prison, there was no 'hard labour' because her pupil had said that she was very kind.

Another of their governesses, Miss Rolfe, whose perkiness inspired the children to nickname her 'Perks', had for that time an unusually broad sense of humour. She was in no way displeased by the limerick composed by Penelope, the fifth daughter:

> There was a young lady called Perks,
> Who always was making loud gurks;
> Once out in the garden
> She didn't say 'Pardon',
> So I told her she'd wind in her works.

Like all children, the Cunard girls were heartless in their attention to anything unfortunate in an adult. Another governess, Miss Boughey, tried to teach them Greek and Latin, but they were unable to concentrate on the lesson because some defect of her teeth caused her to spit a great deal when she spoke. Consequently, the paper on which she wrote was showered with little blobs of spittle, and they watched in fascination as her pencil travelled among them. It wrote in pale mauve, but each time the point got wet the writing turned dark purple.

Miss Boughey didn't last long, and neither did Miss Hyde or Miss Dicker or various others. 'I suppose they left out of exhaustion', says one of their pupils now. 'We were very mischievous.' In order to annoy one that they particularly disliked they dropped all their knickers out of the window. 'They floated down like a lot of little parachutes into the garden.'

The best by far of all their governesses was Miss Winifred Price, who was everything that Miss Charlotte Mason of Ambleside had planned in her 'gracious vision', with perhaps a touch of spice added. She was not especially gracious to look at, in fact she was very plain, small and round, always dressed in a long, baggy tweed shirt and cardigan, with her hair rolled in a bun behind her head and a rather red nose. It was not her hairstyle that gave rise to the affectionate name, Bun, that the girls gave her; it was more a reflection on her general appearance.

Mrs Cunard had engaged her on the recommendation of the PNEU, since Miss Price had done one of their non-resident training courses; she used all their books. She was well educated, though with certain gaps, but more importantly she was a person to whom teaching came naturally.

She came in 1918 when Penelope and Virginia were aged nine and six, and from the start they enjoyed their lessons with her. Their mother's impatient and unsuccessful efforts to teach Virginia to read were forgotten as Bun gently coaxed her into literacy. The governess was, of course, no good at maths, and did not venture beyond very elementary arithmetic. But history, scripture, French, some Latin, geography, and botany she taught well and imaginatively, and she was a good pianist.

> She had a huge map of the world, and we played what she called 'Dodging on the map'. She called out the name of a place, a river, a range of mountains, and we tried to be the first to hit it with the end of a ruler. The map was pitted with marks of our jabs. It certainly taught us where things were in the world.

The governess was particularly strong on religious history. She was an ardent High Churchwoman, and easily wooed the children away from the Anglican services that had always bored them; they much preferred the glamour and colour of her Anglo-Catholic church. They look on her in retrospect as 'a saint, really', but maintain that she never forced her religion on anybody. She just made it appealing.

Bun had an intelligent sense of priority: The first her pupils knew of the end of the 1914–1918 war was when through the schoolroom windows of their house in Portman Square came the cries of the newspaper boys calling 'Armistice signed! Armistice signed!' Bun made them drop everything immediately and, pausing only to put on their hats and coats, they walked out together to join the crowds moving towards Buckingham Palace; they saw wounded soldiers, dressed in their blue uniforms, being mobbed and kissed by all the girls who passed; they climbed on the palace railings, they sang and chanted with the crowd and delighted a nearby Frenchman with their knowledge of the words of *La Marseillaise*; they waved and cheered when King George and Queen Mary appeared on the balcony. Through Miss Price's good sense they had an Armistice Day worth remembering.

Bun had no trouble at all in keeping order. 'She was sharp, and firm, and entirely consistent. She never raised her voice, and never failed to punish if she said she would.' Her most frequent punishment, and the most effective, was so mild that in itself it is as much a measure of her pleasantness as a person as of her disciplinary ability. She was a genius at reading out aloud – Charlotte M. Young, Scott, Dickens – the children learned to love them all through her, as she read to them every evening. But if they trangressed in any way, the next reading aloud session was in jeopardy.

> We had to have our books out on the schoolroom table and be sitting ready for work at nine o'clock in the morning exactly. If we were even a minute late, she would look very sad, and say, 'That is five minutes less reading this evening, I am afraid.' She seemed to mind as much as we did.

This story might suggest that the Cunard children became not just disciplined but rather feeble under her rule, but this was not so. When she left them for a gap of eighteen months in about 1920, they reverted very rapidly to type under the governess who took her place and whom they much disliked. She was English, though called Miss Pfund, and was remarkable for a huge pile of plaited hair on top of her head.

'We were beastly to her and she was beastly to us,' says Virginia now.

> She locked me in a cupboard once, when I had done something wrong. After a while I called out, 'Miss Pfund, I want to spend a penny.' She called back, 'You can just stay where you are.' I called again, a little later, and got the same reply. So I wet my knickers, in revenge. She was furious, but I had won.

Penelope recalls how she dared to 'answer back' on an occasion when

Miss Pfund went too far. The children were obliged to clean the bath after they had used it, 'with a sort of sauce-pan scrubber on a stick'.

> She looked at the bath and decided I hadn't done it properly. She said, 'Penelope, you are plain, dirty and mean.'
>
> I couldn't stand that, and I answered angrily, 'I know I am plain, and I may be dirty, but I am not mean.'

This was courageous behaviour, for Miss Pfund's favourite punishment was to lift a child's arm and bring the elbow down hard on the edge of a table, aiming for the funny bone.[1]

It was a considerable relief when Miss Price, the adored 'Bun', returned, after a period with the Mitford family. Her benign and far more affective rule continued, and was carried on into the next generation. Twenty years later, in 1941, she came back to the family to teach the twelve-year-old Veldis Charrington, daughter of Barbara Cunard, in Surrey. She taught her for four years, much the same subjects as before, still 'hopeless at maths', still passionate about church history. She still dressed in reddy-brown Harris tweed and still read aloud wonderfully. 'Bun's voice,' said Mrs Charrington, 'never gets tired of reading.'

As in the earlier household, she got on well with everybody, even the nanny. 'They didn't actually sit together in the evening,' says Veldis, 'but they would meet to listen together to things on the wireless, like "Much Binding in the Marsh".'[2]

Miss Price, this most unusual governess, was cared for in the way she deserved. At Britwell she was housed in a very pleasant bedroom, on the nursery floor, near the girls' bedrooms, and the girls ate supper with her in the schoolrom. In the holidays she went home to Ealing where Amy, May and Muriel Price – always referred to as 'Me sisters' – all lived together, unmarried, in the family home. The Cunard girls remembered visiting them; Muriel had been the beauty of the family, and in a deep, rich alto she sang sentimental Victorian songs that they found a trifle embarrassing; 'Drink deep, drink deep of the waters, Melisande . . .'

Years later, in the spring, Veldis and Bun picked primroses together to send to Ealing where 'Me sisters' were still living.

The Cunard family went on visiting their old governess after she retired, and after she died they went to the sale of her effects. Their close attachment to her shows in the way that, seventy odd years later, one of her pupils reels off her address without pausing to think: Eleven Birch Grove Ealing Acton.

Schoolroom education between the wars was slowly undergoing a transformation for the better, partly because the general level of education for women was rising, and partly because parents were expecting more for their daughters. But it was an uneven process, and work in many schoolrooms carried on in the usual haphazard, unstructured way.

Although Jonathan Gathorne-Hardy's retelling of the saga of Miss Vigers versus Nanny Marks is a factual account of an episode in the life of a 1930s household, it is apparent that neither the saga nor the household should be regarded as typical. Life for most governesses was now much less exciting, and their activities and behaviour were seldom more than mundane. It is a strange fact that anecdotes about these women, whether recorded in memoirs or remembered in interviews, are in the main either dramatic or funny, as if people find it necessary to make memories of governesses entertaining. They fall into the same category as mothers-in-law, politicians and Irishmen. When the word 'governess' appears in the first sentence of a story the listeners relax and prepare to laugh. It is hard to know quite what governesses have done to deserve this, but it is certain that there are few tales told of them that are not either horrific or humorous, and they are almost always told at the governesses' expense. When not being laughted at, they are denigrated, in the same way as schoolteachers often are, perhaps as a kind of subconscious revenge taken by people who still resent the restrictions of their schooldays.

In the early chapters of Jessica Mitford's autobiography *Hons and Rebels*, governesses are frequently mentioned, generally in offhand and derisive terms.

There are six girls in the Mitford family, and they all in turn joined the schoolroom from the age of nine. Their only brother went away to school at eight.

> My mother felt that school for girls was unnecessary, probably harmful, and certainly too expensive. She prided herself that she was able to finance our entire education out of the proceeds of her chicken farm, which, after paying all expenses, netted something like £120 a year, about the right amount for a governess's annual wage in those days.' [This was in the 1920s.]
>
> Our schoolroom at Swinbrook, big and airy, with bay windows, a small coal fireplace and chintz-covered furniture, was on the second floor, next to the governess's bedroom. It was separated from the visitors' rooms and my parents' rooms by a green baize door. Here we spent most of our time. We had lunch, and sometimes dinner,

downstairs with the grown-ups except when there were visitors, in which case meals were sent up and we ate in the unenthralling company of the governess, fretfully wondering what delicious things they were having downstairs.

The schoolroom was 'presided over by a fast-moving series of governesses'. The fourth daughter, Unity, was 'the bane of governesses, few of whom could stand up for long to her relentless misbehaviour, and as a result we never had the same one for any length of time. They came and left in bewildering succession.' Diana Mosley later claimed that they had 'about fifteen in all'.

One left after the children discovered that she was terrified of snakes. They left a pet grass snake hanging on her lavatory chain.

> We breathlessly awaited the result, which was not long in coming. Miss Whitey locked herself in, there was shortly an ear-splitting shriek, followed by a thud. The unconscious woman was ultimately released with the aid of crowbars . . .

and left.

Another, Miss Broadmoor, was driven away by Nancy Mitford's imitating her refined speech. Her successor, Miss McMurray 'grew beans on bits of wet flannel and taught the names of different parts of these growing beans – Plumule, Radical, Embryo'.

The only one of their governesses that the children really liked was Miss Bunting, who taught them how to shop-lift.

> We made occasional trips to Oxford.. 'Like to try a little jiggery pokery, children?' Miss Bunting suggested. There were two main methods: the shopping bag method, in which an accomplice was needed, was used for the larger items. The accomplice undertook to distract the shop-lady while the lifter, or Jiggery-poker in Miss Bunting's idiom, stuffed her bag with books, underclothes or boxes of chocolates, depending on the wares of the particular store . . . The dropped-hanky method was suitable for lipsticks or small pieces of jewellery. Miss Bunting in her governessy beige coat and gloves, Boud [Unity] and I in matching panama straw hats, would strut haughtily past the deferential sales people to seek the safety of Fuller's Tea Room, where we would gleefully take stock of the day's haul over cups of steaming hot chocolate.
>
> Miss Bunting was very relaxed about lessons. Only when we heard my mother's distinctive tread approaching the schoolroom did she signal to us to buckle down to work. She knew nothing and cared less about algebra, Latin, or parts of the bean, and needless to say we liked her much better than any of her predecessors. We did all we could to make

life tolerably attractive for her, with the result that she stayed on for some years.[3]

Diana Mitford, writing later about her youth, describes their schoolroom life as 'humdrum'; the only governess who left an enduring mark on her was Miss Price, 'Bun', during her break from the Cunards. The Mitford children had long been bored by compulsory attendance at the local Anglican church, listening to scolding sermons from an uninspiring vicar. However, said Diana, when she was eleven,

> under the influence of an Anglo-Catholic governess I became for a year a subject of religious mania . . . A service a week was not half enough for me; I considered that one should go to church every single day, or, better still, several times a day . . . I was terribly concerned about Muv and Farve, and what might happen to their immortal souls . . . The thought of converting Muv occupied me for months.

The only geography Diana claims to have learnt from Miss Price was a study of the Holy Land.

> She stayed with us for four terms, about the limit of time any governess could abide us for. Then she packed up her shrine – crucifix, brass candlesticks, brass vases always kept bright and full of flowers – and went away. After she left I drifted back to a mild agnosticism, but I shall always be grateful to Miss Price because she made me understand, from inside as it were, what religion can mean to a person.[4]

The Cunard girls claimed that the Mitfords were 'furious' when Miss Price left to go back to her preferred family. 'They never forgave us.'

Most women remembering the governesses who taught them before the 1920s speak of hating them or of being bored by them. Those who were taught in the 1920s and 1930s tend to react differently. The boredom of lessons with the governess is still mentioned, but expressions like 'I was really quite fond of her' regularly occur. This seems to reflect the responsibility by now being taken by parents for their children's happiness as well as for their education. An unkind governess was soon exposed and no longer tolerated, and strong disciplinarians were considered to be trespassing on parents' preserves. Governesses were easily engaged and as easily disposed of.

This did not mean that every employer necessarily wanted to find a governess who was an exceptional person; it was not necessarily a fault in a governess that she should fail to be outstanding in any way. It was quite desirable, indeed, that she should fade into the background in a gathering – the more insignificant she was, the more easily she could be absorbed into the household. Too much intelligence might mean too great a wish to join in mealtime conversation, or a tendency to dominate household activities. In short, it was now the perfect governess who should be seen and not heard.

One mother, choosing governesses to teach her children in their large family castle in the Highlands of Scotland not long after the First World War, made a point of choosing women who could not possibly attract her husband. He had never shown a tendency to flirt with the governess, or anyone else in the castle for that matter, but there was no point in putting temptation in his way. So all the governesses engaged were plain. This mother also had a theory that only unintelligent people could understand how hard it was for children to learn, and so she deliberately chose governesses whom she considered to be stupid, in the hope that they would be sympathetic to her children's problems. This was the extent, however, of her maternal love. One of her daughters commented wryly many years later that there had been three people in the household (governess, nanny and, presumably, nursery-maid) who were employed so that the parents need have 'as little as possible to do with us'. This was so even during holiday time. The two youngest children were sent in the summer for two weeks' holiday at a resort on the East coast. Their governess alone accompanied them, to give them lessons in the mornings, and in the afternoons she sat knitting by the breakwater while they played on the shore. One of them commented in later life, but with little suggestion of sympathy, 'Governesses are lonely people . . .'[5]

At a time when women were overthrowing the final barriers to parity in education, when the goal of admission to full membership of Oxford university had just been attained, (Cambridge delayed until 1948), when the educational world was finally open to all, the private schoolroom remained obstinately in the nineteenth century. In the home, the ability of a governess to keep the children quiet, happy, and occupied was the paramount requirement. Her teaching abilities were still often considered of secondary importance. The comment 'My mother engaged her as being a disciplinarian, and was not interested in her educational standards, which were low', comes from another pupil of a 1920s governess. 'She knew no more than a little history and English.' This governess, Miss Farrow, left behind her the impression of being 'only interested in otter-hunting', a sport that was not practised locally, on Epsom Downs.[6]

Daphne Finch-Hatton, the small daughter of the Earl of Winchilsea, learnt no maths at all from her governess, Miss Plank, who came to her in 1925. This did not matter, because Daphne's parents did not think that maths were necessary for girls.

I don't think I learnt any history either. One only learnt what governesses could teach. They had their own books – my parents did not buy any. . .

Miss Plank was quite good looking, with dark hair in two long plaits which were wound into 'earphones' on either side of her face. But she was dull.

They *were* dull people, governesses. My main memory of Miss Plank is not of anything she taught me but of being taken for long, boring walks, dragging the dogs on leads.[7]

· 16 ·

Miss Paraman becomes Mrs Hobble-Gobble

Between the two World Wars, parents continued to be willing to supplement the governess's lessons with outside help. Singing teachers and music teachers would pay weekly visits, and the schoolroom piano would be used for practice in the evening after lessons. Masters from nearby prep. schools would earn extra cash coaching the girls in mathematics and, if the governess was deficient in languages, French or German teachers might come in too. In some families a French or German governess had been employed when the children were small, so the British governess who succeeded her might find her accent being corrected by a child more proficient than herself.

Few governesses were now capable of teaching dancing, and many parents sent their daughters to dancing classes if there were any within reach. The governess would usually accompany them, and would sit round the edges of large halls chatting to other governesses and nannies.

It was not an unpleasant life. In fact, if the parents were friendly and the children reasonably well behaved, it could be quite a pleasant one for a woman not consumed by ambition. This was the case with Miss Elkins. She was governess to the Lawrence family in the early 1930s and took over the education of the two elder girls, Libby and Robby, when they were eight and ten years old. Their younger brother, John, joined in their lessons until he went to prep. school. Lady Lawrence had been at a boarding school in Eastbourne during the First World War, and had so loathed it that she had sworn that her daughters would never be subjected to such a life. Hence the governess.

The girls did not ever become especially fond of Miss Elkins, but they were certainly not in awe of her, and would have had no hesitation in complaining to their parents had she made them unhappy. They hated the 'ghastly walks, the endless, dreary, wet walks' that they had to take with her. 'They almost put me off English countryside for life . . .' However, these were an essential part of life with a governess, and in the summer Miss Elkins would unbend so far as to play 'Bumble Puppy' with them on the lawn.

'She was barrel-shaped,' remembers one of her pupils, 'and always wore a ginger coloured wrap-around skirt and hideous lacey sweaters.'

Miss Elkins subscribed to the Women's League of Health and Beauty. She would attire herself in a suit of dark blue beach pyjamas and, with the help of League handbooks and the records they provided, she and the girls pranced and swayed in time to the music on the schoolroom wind-up gramophone.

Governess and girls had breakfast together in the schoolroom, but lunch was eaten in the dining-room with their parents. John fed upstairs in the nursery with his nanny. Their father considered that talking with interesting guests was an essential part of his daughters' education, so they and Miss Elkins were encouraged to join in the general conversation, Miss Elkins occasionally dropping the names of previous aristocratic employers.[1]

Miss Elkins had a tendency to show favouritism, and was inclined to 'pick on' the youngest daughter, Jenny, who was only partially in her charge. But had she been really unkind she would not have been able to get away with it for long. By now, most parents spotted ill-treatment fairly fast. When a young girl called Peggy Maitland did something naughty at breakfast, her governess, Miss Francis, leapt at her and scratched her face. The child was 'too scared' of the governess to tell tales, but her mother noticed the scratch, asked questions, and sacked the governess at once.[2] But Miss Wace, governess in the 1930s in Scotland to little Mary Gamell, had particularly unobservant employers. Smoking was not normally tolerated in any indoor employee, but Miss Wace was a heavy smoker, and Mary remembers her smelling strongly of tobacco. She was a throw-back to an earlier, crueller era: she would beat her small pupil's hand with a ruler, and shake her by the hair when she was angry with her. Mary was too frightened of Miss Wace to report her to her mother, although she knew 'she would have been horrified'. Eventually the child developed alopecia, a stress-related disease, in which her hair started to fall out. A specialist examined her and questioned her parents as to whether anything could be making her unhappy or frightened. Mary realised at once that if her symptoms got worse the governess might be made to leave. So she started pulling out her own hair at night and spreading it about her pillow. Miss Wace was eventually sacked.[3]

On the whole extremes of discipline and harsh punishment had by now died out of schoolroom life, but parents were still wary of it; the cruel governess was a figure of still recent memory. Mr and Mrs Harry Johnstone, bringing up their two children at The Myretoun in Clackmannanshire in the 1930s, first employed a German governess for Raymond and Kirsty. She was so unpleasant that they soon got rid of her and engaged a French governess instead, little realising that they were going from bad to worse. The French woman was particularly unkind and made both the children miserable. Kirsty, aged twelve, became crushed and inhibited, and Raymond, six years younger, grew noisy and naughty. It took their parents a year to realise what was going on, and then they were saved from the unpleasantness of sacking the governess by her developing appendicitis and leaving of her own accord.

The Johnstones then found a Scottish governess, who was known in the family as 'Sandy'. Before long there was a marked change. Raymond became very quiet and well behaved, quite unlike his previous rumbustious self. The parents again became worried, and wondered whether Sandy, who they knew to be strong on discipline, might be bullying the little boy in private. Before long, his mother heard Sandy raising her voice to Raymond, and took the opportunity to conceal herself and listen to what was going on.

'Hurry up, Raymond,' shouted the governess angrily, 'Put your boots on immediately!'

'It's all right, Mrs Hobble-gobble,' replied the victimised child, 'I'm coming, in my own good time . . .'[4]

If the problem of governesses abusing children had now been solved, the problem of neglect of governesses by their employers was only modified. In many respects life was much more pleasant than it had been: the governess went on family outings and picnics, and in the 1920s a lucky one might be sent abroad for a year with her pupil between her schooling and 'coming out' to do the London débutante season. The governess acted as chaperone and guide, and sometimes, for the first time, in Germany, France or Italy, would find herself using in real life the language that she had taught for so long in the arid atmosphere of the schoolroom. She went with the family on expeditions to the cinema, sometimes to the theatre. She was taken to the elder brother's school sports day. In many ways, if in an agreeable post, she could now have more fun. But somehow she never achieved the relationship that a nanny could develop with the family she cared for, and as a human being she still suffered a numbing neglect: if not wanted on an expedition, she was simply left behind without comment. But even when not needed by the family she was not expected to conduct a private life of her own. One governess remembers, in the 1920s, being seen by her employer with a male friend on her day off.

> She looked very much askance. We were just walking harmlessly along a road, but I could tell her by her manner that she was not at all pleased.

Often a governess's pupils had no idea where she spent her holidays, or even whether she had relations to welcome her home. 'I don't really know what her background was,' they now say vaguely, and often with some embarrassment, 'Governesses just disappeared during the holidays.'

This applied even to governesses who were a notable success: Miss Gough, governess to the Earl of Eglinton's family in the 1920s, was an intelligent, educated woman and is described as a superb teacher. She was firm and fair, and the children liked her. Even so, her youngest pupil, Janet Montgomerie, was quite unaware of the governess's existence after the term had ended. 'She went somewhere, I suppose, perhaps to a brother?' Janet did to some extent keep in touch with her governess in later years, making this a happier story than some. But Miss Gough herself had no illusions about how a governess was perceived:

> To the children she just means work. So they are glad when she leaves at the end of the term. And the nanny dislikes her. Nobody loves a governess . . .[5]

Although the governess had played a major role in their family life, after she had left a family it was rare that they would keep up with her or know what became of her later in life. There are of course notable exceptions to this, but by far the most usual comment is, 'I have no idea what happened to her afterwards . . .'

A nanny would sometimes be sent with younger children to the seaside – Frinton was a favourite resort – for a summer holiday, while parents enjoyed themselves on foreign beaches or on the grouse moors of Yorkshire and Scotland; but in the main a nanny's life was spent indoors and at home. Yet most nannies had far more far-reaching influence on the later lives of 'her children' than did their governesses. When a good nanny left after the youngest child had reached schoolroom age, she usually went to close friends or cousins of the family, and so contact was not lost. Or she might stay, in semi-retirement, in the family home, very often filling a 'grandmother/housekeeper' role in the now childless house. She remained to her charges, after they had grown beyond her care, a warm, living childhood memory, cherished by mother and children alike, tray-bearer in time of illness, sympathetic receiver of family news, adviser on emotional problems, ever understanding and loyal to 'her' children. Sometimes she would move on with a married girl to look after the next generation of babies, and she could show far more familiarity with the family than any other employee. Counterparts of the ageing nannies living their lives out in corners of Boot Magna Hall in Evelyn Waugh's *Scoop* can be found in country houses in Britain right up to the present day.

Jonathan Gathorne-Hardy suggests that it was because nannies came when the children were very young, assuming a quasi-parental role, that the love they earned never died and that, unlike governesses, they were never neglected after leaving. The argument can be taken further. The governess came very often at the end of the innocent years, at the age when the rebellious instincts of children begin to develop; if she lasted, she took them through what is now considered the difficult teenage phase. She became a buffer between them and their parents, attracting the resentment and callousness that adolescents often show people in charge of their discipline. When education was finished, and they reached theoretical adulthood, at seventeen, the governess was discarded with other childish things, a dispensable relic of the boring years.

A governess's career could become set in a pattern as the result of good or bad luck in the first engagement. A young woman, whose teaching skills and general pleasantness around the house were valued in her first job, would on completing it be recommended and passed on to friends or relatives of the family who were liable to appreciate the same qualities. Conversely, if the first situation went badly, the governess's future job-hunting could be blighted by half-hearted references, and she could progress from one unhappy position to another. As always, she was dependent on the 'character' she was given.

Not all governess stories are either funny or derogatory; the relationship of a large number of families with their governess was both pleasant and productive. A governess who speaks happily of her own successful career is Miss Evelyn Coward, now living in retirement on the Isle of Wight. She was educated as a day girl at Westwing College, Ryde, under a young and progressive headmistress. By the age of sixteen, Evelyn had obtained the Junior and Senior Cambridge School Certificates.

> I stayed on to continue some VI form studies, and to gain, under qualified staff, experience in teaching, eventually taking full charge of a junior form. Possibly I was being slightly exploited, but I loved the work and teaching was what I wanted to do.

Soon a longing to see the world beyond the Isle of Wight decided Evelyn to become a private governess. In 1928 she took the plunge. There were different agencies to be considered; she knew of the Ladies' League and Miss Locke-Stevens' as respectable ones. But informed help was at hand: hearing that she wanted to become a governess, 'a family friend advised that *the* agency for that would be Miss Lennox-Carr in Bond Street and that she would come to London and introduce me personally'.

> Armed with my former Principal's testimonial I duly met Miss Lennox-Carr, which seemed a more daunting process than was ever any future interview with a prospective employer. She must have thought me very unsophisticated and unwordly-wise.

Evelyn Coward made a good impression, and soon she was in her first post, looking after the young son of an army officer stationed at Woolwich. After her first two posts she never again had to use an agency. 'I continued by personal recommendation.'

> Nigel was a delightful little boy who had been born and spent the first years of his life in India. He was small for his age, and inclined to be delicate, which caused his mother some anxiety, and we spent as much time as possible out of doors in the not-too-salubrious air of that garrison town. He was quick and intelligent, forged his way through the three Rs and soon showed a desire to learn.
>
> When military duties forced his parents to move around we went to stay with his grandfather who was the head of an Oxford College. We were made very welcome, and in the house was an old family Nanny who helped with the household and adored Nigel – their feeling was mutual – so I had a certain amount of time to explore and get to know the city really well. We had a comfortable study to work in, lined with books, which thrilled me, as did the scholastic atmosphere. My pupil, of course, had his own preoccupations, rather less academic. He eventually went on to become head-boy of his preparatory school and win laurels in work, games, and leadership qualities at his public school.

Salaries in the 1920s and 30s seemed low even then, from £80 to £150 a year, and could be paid, Miss Coward remembers, monthly, termly or annually. There were, at least, no living expenses in term time, but 'a day out could make a large hole in a cheque'.

She felt that she was lucky to have her family in the Isle of Wight to go home to in the holidays. 'I have often wondered how people managed who had no home. Some preferred to forego holidays, or take temporary work.'

As she progressed from family to family her ambition to see more of the world was at least partially realised. Between 1928 and 1939 she had posts that took her to Sussex, Berkshire and Nairn on the Moray Firth, with five years based in London. In 1940 she was interviewed in Portsmouth by Lady Lawrence, mother of Miss Elkins' two pupils who were now out of the schoolroom. The eldest, having been schooled entirely at home, was, as she puts it, 'learning about living with other girls the hard way, in the ATS, having never been in a dormitory before'. Lady Lawrence herself had a job high in ATS Southern Command and needed a good governess for her youngest daughter at Oaksey, the family home. Jenny, aged fourteen, was to be taken through to School Certificate level. This requirement was new to Miss Coward, but she decided that, having taken the exam herself years before, with the help of specimen papers she could get any intelligent and interested girl through it again. She still treasures the telegram sent to her by Jenny two years later, 'You have succeeded, in spite of me!', but Miss Coward says modestly, 'I thought the boot was on the other foot.'

Miss Coward spent the years from 1942 to 1946 in the ATS, and was commissioned in 1944. Then, taking up her career again in 1948, she went back to being a governess. Although she was without formal teaching qualifications she could have found a position in a private school, but she still found that the freelance aspect of governessing appealed more to her than being tied to an establishment.

Her post-war posts took her to Gloucestershire, Inverness and London. While working in London she met a number of other governesses and made some good friends among them with whom she travelled abroad during the holidays. 'Travel was cheap, pay had improved, and we did not mind a certain amount of roughing it.'

Evelyn Coward retired from governessing in the early 1960s. She went back home to the Isle of Wight and taught in an independent school, where her sister was also a teacher, until she retired fully in 1972 'to devote more time to personal interests and hobbies'. In retrospect, she feels that she has had a rewarding career and an interesting life. She and her friends took their work seriously and 'tried to combine lasting educational values with modern conditions and requirements'. Living for a great deal of the time in country houses, she had ample opportunity to indulge her love of animals and of wild flowers. The latter was a special interest. During her time in Gloucestershire, inspired by the Wild Flower Society, she and her pupils and their grandmother hunted rare species by bicycle down the winding country lanes. When in 1952 she moved on to a new situation in Scotland, in a house on the shores of Loch Ness, she took this interest with her. Her own enthusiasm and her capacity to enthuse others were such that a few months later she was able to claim in a letter that 'the stalkers now came back with wild flowers in their pockets!' She had the amusement later of seeing this story in print in the *Wild Flower Magazine*.[6]

Photographs of former pupils, and fondly-kept letters from families she worked for, are evidence of the great affection and respect that Miss Coward inspired. This was a governess who left a strong and happy mark on the lives she touched, as one of her pupils warmly confirms. She repays the love she earned with the loyalty and discretion she shows when speaking of those in whose households she spent her working life.

A governess who was less fortunate in her career than Miss Coward could still find caring charities to help her in times of trouble. In 1930 the Jubilee Memorial Fund, dating from 1887, gave as its object 'to assist Aged and Destitute Governesses, by yearly grants of not more than £52'. (This fund was merged later with the GBI.) The Jackson Roeckel Teachers' Provident Association granted pensions to governesses when they became disabled. There were other charities to which they could apply; the requirement of being a spinster, destitute and of good character was usual. Florence Nightingale had not forgotten the governesses who had called her 'our sunshine'. At 19 Lisson Grove in central London her eponymous Hospital for Gentlewomen still gave free medical care to wives and daughters of professional men, to governesses and to artists.

But the organisation that provided most was the Governesses Benevolent Institution. By 1934 it offices had moved to Victoria Street, and in Maddox Street its Free Employment Bureau was still running. The GBI continued to provide financial relief to governesses in temporary difficulty, as well as annuities for their old age. Until 1937 it ran a seaside holiday house at Shanklin on the Isle of Wight, and it still administered the individual retirement homes at Chislehurst and at Beckenham. There was still a Ladies' Committee to decide which 'governesses in distress' were worthy of temporary assistance; decisions on the awarding of annuities were made 'by election of subscribers and appointment of the board of management'. To be considered, governesses had to be British, over fifty-five years, relatively poor, and either single or widowed. They had to have been governesses in private families for at least fourteen years and, most importantly, they had to be approved by the board: character was still a consideration. Another special benefit was that anyone dependent on a governess might apply to the GBI for some or all of their fees to be paid at Queen's College, with which it still had links.

In 1930, 2999 governesses benefited from the funds of the Institution: 475 were awarded free annuities, 317 had been granted temporary assistance, and 532 had used the employment bureau. One hundred and forty-five had enjoyed holidays in Furneaux Holiday House, and twenty-two were resident in the homes for the aged. Two hundred and fifty-five other grants had been made and ninety-seven governesses had received parcels of clothing.

At about this time the GBI was using new methods of raising funds. The needs of destitute governesses were not among the most pressing issues of the day, and so to attract attention the Institution became one of the first charities to use illustrations – pictures of sad looking governesses – to soften the hearts of potential donors.

· 17 ·

The post-war schoolroom

The outbreak of the Second World War might have been expected to dispose once and for all of the governess system, but initially it gave it a boost. Parents in Scotland and the north of England, who would normally have sent their daughters to boarding school, became chary of sending them south where most of the good girls' schools were to be found. Parents in the south were willing to accept invitations to 'share a governess' with friends and relations who lived far from the bombs and Doodlebugs. The large country house of the host parent would become in term-time a miniature school, with up to six or seven children all being taught by the governess, their parents dividing the governess's salary between them and paying their share of the household expenses. The governess would no longer expect to stay during the holidays, though she would be paid by the year.

With this influx of young outsiders into the house, and often with the absence of the father, the governess and the mother had a closer working relationship than before; but generally the traditional relationship between employer and employee persisted, and the barriers remained unbreached despite the different circumstances of wartime. Some things changed, however. In certain households governesses began to dine downstairs in the evening with the family, assuming the pupils were old enough to do so. Otherwise, the children still had supper with her in the schoolroom, but now she would fetch the tray herself from the kitchen. Because of the lack of servants, she would play a fuller role in the runnng of the house, and it was rare for a governess to be too proud to help with the washing up, as long as the family was doing it as well. Her employer was slowly being forced into a more companionable position.

Rules were relaxed that a mere decade earlier would have been inviolable. Governesses could now get away with smoking, after the working day was over, and it was no longer frowned upon for her to have a male friend and to go out with him at weekends.

Miss Martin, commonly known as 'Teenie', was about thirty when she came to look after the Renwick children in Warwickshire at the start of the war. Sue, the eldest daughter, remembers,

> She looked like a perky little robin, with a very prominent and apparently undivided bosom; she always wore a brown crocheted jumper, through which shone a pale pink celanese vest. The jumper's neckline exposed a mottled red V of skin – a type of skin that seems to have gone out now – perhaps it was the effect of the weather. Sometimes she would wear a beige wool cardigan, and always a brown tweed skirt with box pleats.

The four children kept happy memories of Miss Martin. She was an excellent pianist, and had a taste for the romantic. On a golden evening in late May, Sue was placed by Teenie at the open schoolroom window, drinking cocoa and eating Marmite sandwiches before bedtime. The governess then played a Chopin nocturne on the piano while a solitary blackbird poured out liquid notes from the top of a lilac bush. 'I still can't smell cocoa without thinking of it.'

Miss Martin also indulged in more practical romance. She had a Polish 'young man', who had been displaced by the war and was working locally. He was tall and good looking, she was tiny and plump, and they went off on long bicycle rides. Their bicycles were similarly paired off; they named his 'Supervius' and hers 'Supervia'. On a certain occasion they had hidden their bicycles in a ditch while 'they misbehaved together with the help of a five-barred gate, because the Pole was so much taller than Teenie'. Unfortunately someone stole one of the bicycles while they were engaged in this height adjustment, and in the investigation that followed their activities were revealed.[1]

The Renwick family treated the episode of Teenie and her Pole as hilarious though the details were not revealed to the children until they were older. In this they were ahead of their time, but not much; both World Wars speeded up the process of women's emancipation, and governesses benefited too, in that they were now being treated as fully fledged human beings, with the same rights and needs as others had.

They were even allowed to have private lives, though within certain limits. They had to learn for themselves what those limits were. One daily governess in 1946 felt so frightened of what her employer might do if it were discovered that she lived with a man to whom she was not married that she went to her voluntarily and 'confessed'.

> I didn't give a hoot. The children didn't know, and it didn't affect her work.

This parent was much more interested in the fact that the governess was a brilliant teacher, and did not want to be bothered with the details of her private life.

A governess was still not expected to argue with her employers, or to express views that might embarrass them in front of their friends. A Miss Wilkie, who had been taken on a family visit to stay with cousins in a large Scottish country house, overstepped the mark when she dared to express her views on the cruelty of keeping hens in batteries, a farming innovation in the 1950s. The party had been shown the newly established hen-batteries on the home farm during the morning. Miss Wilkie said nothing until lunchtime, when all the party were seated at the long dining room table, and then, her face taut and pale, told her host in a high, shaking voice that the system was inhumane and that he should be ashamed of himself. Her pupil remembers a ghastly pause. 'I don't think I had ever felt so shocked in my life, but I hardly knew whether it was because of what she had said, or because it was she, the governess, who had said it.' The governess looked down at her plate, and so did everyone else. Then the conversation started again, and the awkward moment passed away. The pupil, who had also hated seeing the hens in their cramped wire quarters, felt a respect for the governess that she had never known before.

> Up till then I had just thought she was ridiculous. She was skeletally thin, and always had a drop on the end of her nose. She wore long knitted khaki woollen knickers, for the cold, I suppose; the house was bitterly cold in winter and we all had chilblains; anyhow, we used to drop our rubbers under the schoolroom table so that we could dive down and look up her skirt to see if she had them on. Then we would giggle like anything, and she wouldn't know why. I know my mother was furious with her about the battery-hen business, and there was an awful row after we got home. My mother said whatever she thought she shouldn't have said it, because she was a guest: it was bad manners. But Miss Wilkie was right, of course, and tremendously brave. I don't think she was ever allowed to come on a visit again.

This was a family in which respect for good manners was intense. Another child was asked by her grandfather at lunchtime one day what lesson she had done with her governess that morning. 'Oh, only horrid old arithmetic,' she replied. No comment was made at the time, but she was summoned later to the book-lined study to be carpetted by her grandfather for five minutes on the subject of respect and good manners to anyone in her family's employ. She was then told to go and apologise to the governess for being rude.

The Second World War produced a new difficulty for governesses. Early in 1942 the Ministry of Labour prohibited women between the age of twenty and thirty-one from applying for domestic posts advertised in newspapers and journals unless they had a child under fourteen living at home. This was extended almost at once to women up to forty-one. A further modification came later, and the following wording prefaced each weekly employment column in *The Lady*:

> Caution: Except by permission of the Ministry of Labour, no man aged from 18–50, and no woman aged from 18–40, inclusive, may apply for a post through these advertisements unless the woman has a child of her own aged under 15 living with her, or unless the post applied for is part-time employment of less than 30 hours weekly.

For the time being this put almost any serious governess job out of reach for a young woman: governesses are normally childless and need full employment. One employer got round the restrictions by registering the woman who taught his children as the manager of his home farm on the Sussex Downs. For Hilda Payne this was no sinecure: as well as teaching the children, (who describe her now as 'a very, very nice person indeed',) she found herself looking after a variety of animals and farm-yard fowl, chickens, turkey, geese, guinea fowl and Muskovy duck, birds she had barely met before except in the pages of books. She took to it with enthusiasm, and was always referred to affectionately in the family as 'The Duck'. She remembers bidding for piglets, about which she knew nothing, in Chichester market, and persuading some soldiers (surely with no difficulty, as she is said to have been extremely pretty) to drive them back to the farm in an army lorry. She was helped in her work by two Italian prisoners of war, who found it difficult to take orders from a woman. 'They were very lazy,' she says. When their place was taken by Germans, one an officer of the Panzer Division, as he never failed to remind her, she found them much easier to control. In fact they became so attached to her that when she was badly stung while attending to the farm bees, and had to retire to bed with a temperature, they came over from their camp one evening.

The housemaid came to my room, and said, 'The Germans have come to
see you'. And there they were and they had brought flowers for me. The
younger one had brought a little Victorian posy, and the Panzer officer
had brought a huge bunch.

Later, he made her 'a really wonderful, beautifully carved wooden
jewel case'.

I never had any bother with him though, not anything like that. I gave it
to a friend, much later, poor Willi's jewel case . . .[2]

By 1950, when the Ministry of Labour's employment restrictions
were lifted, the trade in governesses had passed almost entirely into the
hands of the agencies. In March of that year the column in *The Lady* that
had for so long been headed GOVERNESSES, COMPANIONS AND LADY HELPS
was retitled simply SITUATIONS VACANT. Thereafter, only the odd appeal
for a nursery governess appeared, and that was usually for work
abroad.

A volume of the Gabbitas and Thring files of Employer's Requirements in 1953 shows a greatly diminished demand for governesses. In
the seven months covered, eighty-nine posts are offered to governesses,
of which 15% are abroad, all but one in Europe. Only 24% are resident
posts in Britain, mostly at £3 to £5 per week, spread fairly evenly
through Scotland and England, with one in Ireland. There is more call
for daily governesses, at 7/6 to 10/- per hour – 43% of the jobs offered –
but even so nearly half of these are listed as 'temporary' only. Sixteen
per cent are holiday jobs and, as Miss Coward suggested, these were
much sought after.

The age of the children to be taught is almost always given in the job
descriptions. Whereas before the war many girls would have been
taken by their governess up to the age of sixteen, now in only one fifth of
the eighty-nine posts are girls over eleven years mentioned. Governessing in the 1950s was becoming a function mainly for primary education.

But, though it appeared that the writing was on the wall for the
governess, she was not gone yet. The job still provided a useful way of
life to a number of women. For some it satisfied the urge for total and
intellectual involvement in the life of children, having for one reason or
another none of their own, and not wanting to work in an institution. It
was also still a useful way of life to women who had no training for
anything else. Teaching qualifications were not needed by most
agencies or parents; experience and good references were considered
more important. Some families were still not even very fussy about
those.

Doreen Beaumont was born about 1910, and came south with her family from the north of England. For some reason she was not proud of this fact, and tried in vain to discard the accent that betrayed her origin. She left her mother's home in Tunbridge Wells in 1941 to join the staff of a Sussex boys' preparatory school as art teacher. She had no teaching qualifications, but in wartime this was less important than being willing to turn a hand to anything that was required. Her art teaching was remarkable for its 'dash, lash and splash', which won her boys prizes in local competitions. She was known by all, boys and fellow teachers, as 'Monty', and is remembered as a strong character who could speak her mind powerfully on occasion and who was not prepared to be 'pushed around' by the equally strong-minded head-master of the time. He was not of a generous turn of mind when it came to financing her dramatic productions, for she also taught drama to the younger boys. This was not done, an ex-pupil avers, with much imagination, though at the time he enjoyed her classes. When she left, the headmaster wrote in appreciation, 'Never in the field of Art and Drama can one person have provided so much out of so little at so little cost in so short a time.' She stayed for ten years, and then the need to spend more time with her mother persuaded her to start work nearer home as a visiting daily governess.

In 1953 she took a position in Lord de L'Isle's family at Penshurst Place, taking over the schoolroom from an excellent governess, Miss Homewood. She had been old-fashioned and strict, but was much liked by her pupils, who kept in touch with her after she had left them. (Miss Homewood finished her career running the modern equivalent of a 'Dame school' in Penhurst Village Hall, living in a cottage nearby, and giving up teaching only in her eighties.)

In a house as large as Penshurst, the same that was described so eloquently in Mrs Markham's *History of England*, (see Chapter 5), it is surprising that a resident governess was not engaged; there was no shortage of rooms. One of Lord de L'Isle's daughters speculates that, though the greater economy in employing a daily governess may have been a minor consideration, he was probably more motivated by his feeling about the ambiguous position of a governess in the household. He did not like the traditional upstairs loneliness of a resident governess, and at the same time he was not prepared to have her share in his family life in the evenings.

Monty now became Miss Beaumont, and remained so for the next seven years. Anne, the youngest Sidney daughter, joined her elder sisters and other girls in the schoolroom in 1953 when she was aged seven, moving down from the nursery where the family nanny still ruled. She remembers Miss Beaumont, by then in her mid-forties, as grey haired, red-nosed, (she suffered from hay-fever) with a large bosom encased in various shades of botany wool.

> She would stand in front of the school-room stove with her legs wide apart, her skirt well pulled up, warming her bottom as she swayed slightly from side to side.

An elder sister, with that cruelly selective memory of childhood, recalls her habit of sticking her finger in her ear and wiggling it around 'with an appalling squelching sound'.

Miss Beaumont liked to place a large cushion on top of the logs in the log basket by the stove, on which she would then perch herself. One of the girls one day removed all the logs and balanced the cushion across the rim; they all greatly enjoyed the downfall of their governess as she slid ignominiously to the bottom of the basket.

A picture emerges of a governess who was not much respected or even liked by her puplils. We know from her record at the preparatory school that she had a good sense of humour, and that the boys were quite fond of her, so one suspects that the reason for her lack of personal success in private teaching was that she could not command the respect given to a good teacher. She was untrained and, in accepting the appointment, she may have misrepresented her abilities and bitten off more than she could chew. Nevertheless, she stayed for seven years.

The only subject at which Miss Beaumont excelled was 'handicraft', which she taught with enthusiasm and skill, and the girls enjoyed the lessons. Other subjects were harder going. The children were taught from Miss Beaumont's own copy of Arthur Marshall's *Our Island Story*, known more for its attractive presentation and simplification of historical issues than for any great accuracy. She supplemented it with mnemonic verse composed by herself:

> William 1, 1066,
> Ended up burnt on a bundle of sticks.
> William 11, 1087,
> An arrow sent him up to heaven
> 1100, Henry 1st,
> Received bad news of the very worst
> Stephen the Weak, 1135,
> The barons buzzed round like a great bee-hive . . .

It was not a work of genius, but Anne can still quote from it, so it was not entirely useless. They learnt Shakespeare from her copy of *Lamb's*

Tales and other subjects from books provided by the PNEU She had only a vague grasp of how the PNEU programmes were meant to be used, but attempted to follow their principle of reading and narration. Instead of reading aloud, however, and then encouraging the girls to 'narrate' in their own words what they had grasped of the meaning of the story or extract, she made them read the extracts to themselves and then write down as far as possible all they could remember. They were neither expected nor encouraged to discuss what they had read or advance any arguments. It was a negation of the objects of the PNEU system.

Miss Beaumont did not know enough about arithmetic to teach it in any way effectively. Holding up a book in her left hand, peering at it with raised chin through her reading glasses, she would often write the sums down wrongly on to the blackboard, so that the results did not work out as they did in the book, with resulting confusion.

Eventually Anne, who expressed at an early age a wish to become a scientist, was sent to Tonbridge to be tutored in maths on Monday and Thursday mornings. Miss Beaumont, incensed at what she saw as an insult, avenged herself by altering the handicraft lessons to those mornings, so that Anne could no longer take part in them.

There was not much, in fact, that Miss Beaumont was able to teach. The girls went out for gym and for dancing lessons, and one teacher came in for singing and piano lessons as well as another to teach them French.

The parents tried to make sure the children were reaching reasonable standards in most subjects by arranging for them to sit the examinations set by the PNEU at the end of each term. Miss Beaumont would take the papers home the day that they arrived, and the next morning her pupils would suddenly find themselves reading up historical episodes and geographical subjects that bore no relation to what they had been doing previously. Sudden emphasis was placed on long division or particular types of sums that they had recently neglected. 'If a bowl hold three pints of milk and a dog drinks half its contents in two minutes, how long would it take. . . ?'

Astonishingly, the following day, when the exam papers were set, there would be a problem starting, 'If a jug holds five pints of water, and three quarters of its contents leak through a crack in one hour, how long. . . ? Their other revision would prove to have been equally inspired, and the Sidney children's exam results, as judged when the papers were returned for correction by the PNEU, were always superb. Eventually the parents guessed that all was not entirely what it seemed, and the exam papers were thereafter sent to the father's secretary, who issued them only on the designated examination day. The results from then on became less startling.

Miss Beaumont was forgiven for so urgently desiring her pupils' success, and for her wish that they should not let her down. She was able to claim her share of glory when Anne was selected by the PNEU as a 'home pupil' (perhaps because of her splendid scholastic achievements) to read a lesson in a carol service in Holy Trinity, Brompton Road, London. Miss Beaumont rehearsed her tirelessly, making her read the lesson over and over again down the length of a long passage in Penshurst to where the governess stood in the library.

Miss Beaumont tried to persuade the girls to greater effort in the manner used by many governesses before her, frequently quoting the names of previous pupils as examples of perfection in work and behaviour. Noel, Mira and Sheila Winterbottom were three girls whom the Sidney children came to loathe and despise without ever meeting them.

That they did not much like Miss Beaumont either has a legitimate explanation. She showed favouritism, always a mistake in a teacher. Also, one of their number was dyslexic (admittedly a condition little recognised at that time, when children suffering from it were considered simply 'backward') but the governess was neither patient nor sympathetic and punished her slowness by slapping with a ruler.

'Poor old Miss Beaumont; I really had no feelings for her,' says Anne, years later. 'I don't remember wanting to please her; no-one cared much what she thought.'

Nanny, still busy in the nursery with the youngest child, dealt also with the older children's daily needs, caring for their clothing and their health. True to form, she disliked the governess, and nothing gave her more pleasure than to inform her that one of her pupils had a chill and so could not come to lessons. Otherwise she hardly communicated with her. The nanny had an ally in the housekeeper, who had been at Penshurst since before the war. Neither could understand why Miss Beaumont was allowed to stay.

The housekeeper had a daughter, and because she matched one of the Sidney girls in age Lady de L'Isle asked her whether she would like her daughter to join in the governess lessons. Total condemnation of both the governess and the schoolroom system came in the courageous reply:

It is very kind of you, m'lady, but when Angela grows up she will have to earn her living and we think it would be better if she went to the convent.

The only soul at Penshurst who liked the governess was Micky, the fox-terrier who, perversely, adored her. He would follow her hopefully as she walked down the drive at four o'clock each afternoon, returning sadly and alone when she caught the bus home to Tunbridge Wells; there she lived in a grey and gloomy house with her mother, a matching, rather grey figure. On an occasion when their parents were away, two of the Sidney girls were invited to stay in the Beaumont home for a weekend. They observed that the clocks had been moved forward in order that they could be made to go to bed early.[3]

After leaving Penshurst, Miss Beaumont did some more private teaching, and in 1964 she went back to the preparatory school 'on condition that she was not asked to play football with the little boys', as the headmaster recorded; teaching them to paint was what she enjoyed most. She stayed there until she retired in 1971, and is remembered with some affection. An erstwhile colleague described her as 'in a lot of ways a very remarkable person.'

As a governess, she is remembered only as 'Poor old Miss B.'

·18·

The governess comes home

E ven in the second half of the twentieth century, households with governesses still produced situations that seem extraordinarily incongruous. It was still not unusual in the 1960s and later for the governess to find herself eating alone, in the evenings, from a tray in the schoolroom, communicating neither with household staff nor with family until the following morning. 'You held a very in-between position in the house, not part of kitchen life or of the family life, and yet it was difficult to maintain friendships outside the household.' Although after hours the schoolroom became her private sitting-room, she would not be expected to have a visitor or to ask anyone in for a meal. Even had guests been allowed, the governess had no access to a kitchen, and could not do more than boil a kettle and make a cup of tea without infringing household rules.

The traditional bad relationship between governess and indoor staff tended to persist, as the following account shows. Miss Payne, she who was warned of problems by the rector when she entered the governess profession, was in one of her happiest posts in the early 1960s, in the Manor House, Hambleden, in Oxfordshire. She was devoted to the family, and her feelings were reciprocated.

But the butler's attitude was strange, and the cook's. The cook slept above me; I always got very tired, and she used to come in at night very late and stamp about in her room overhead, quite deliberately, so that I could not sleep. We really did not get on at all.

When they had dinner parties downstairs, and I felt they would not want me, I did not want to embarrass the Dowager, and so I would ask if

I might have the car to go to the cinema. But on one occasion when there was to be a dinner I was there, and I was to have a tray in the schoolroom. I suppose the cook was busy, with the dinner to prepare, but when the tray came up all that was on it was a boiled egg in an egg-cup. Well, I cracked it open, and inside it there was a whole little chicken, boiled! So I took it downstairs to the cook.

'Look at this,' I said, 'I can't eat this!'

And the cook said,

'Yes, you can, It's all right – you can just swallow it whole, like an oyster!'

And the butler. He could be very unpleasant. But on one occasion I got my own back. There was going to be a dinner party, and he said to me in the morning, 'They have got important guests tonight – royalty – so they certainly won't want *you*.' So later when I met Harry [the elder son] on the stairs, I said to him, 'Harry, may I come down to dinner tonight?' And he said, 'Of course you can.' So the butler had to serve me sitting there at dinner!

They used to speak very well of the butler, because he was in the church choir and that kind of thing. But I used to think, 'Little do you know . . .' Of course, he was only unpleasant when we were alone.[1]

These stories, told with humour by Miss Payne, would seem more in context in the nineteenth than the twentieth century. So would the situation in another large country house, where the governess was given a complete wing to run. She had a dining room, sitting-room, schoolroom and nursery in her care, with the bedrooms for herself, the children and the staff of nanny and nursery maid. She chose the menus for meals, and ordered the food herself from the kitchen of the main house. It was brought along to her wing on heated trollies. She was in entire charge of the children's life, and since, as one of her governess friends comments, 'she couldn't exactly have been called cosy!', for the children it must have seemed like living in a Victorian time capsule. A similar situation is recorded in the 1920s, when Lord and Lady Wimborne's younger daughter lived with her governess and staff in a small Lutyens house commissioned and built for their use in the grounds of her parent's manor house. When they wanted to see her, they would send down one of several Rolls Royces to bring her up with her governess to visit them. When they were away from home, the governess and her charge were free to enjoy the beautiful gardens round the main house. 'I lived,' says the daughter, 'the most solitary and remote life imaginable. I was alone with the governess from the age of 13½ to 18.'[2]

The governess, too, must have felt the loneliness. As one said sadly, considering her life recently from a retirement home in Surrey,

> You were left to yourself a great deal. I am a modest person, and don't expect too much. But I would rather have had less money, and have had a family to work for who were real friends.

Despite these echoes of earlier times, the position of a governess was changing. By the time the twenty-one-year-old Charlotte Mitchell became a governess in 1968, the way of life was one that a straightforward, young, middle-class woman could find pleasant and acceptable. Charlotte had a teaching certificate from the Froebel Educational Institute at Roehampton, but when she applied to Gabbitas and Thring for a teaching job abroad she was told that this was impossible without experience. 'But you could become a governess,' they said. She was engaged to teach the small daughter of an Anglo-French couple, while the mother was engaged in researching and writing a book. Although twenty-six years younger than the English mother she felt that there was no restraint between them; they were on first name terms, and Charlotte says that she was treated more as a friend than as an employee. So she had no objection to doing odd jobs to help her employer, such as the weekly shopping. She was paid £10 a week and all living expenses. To the French husband, however, she was definitely an employee: 'With him women were either servants or lovers, but not equals!'[3]

One of the last of the 'real' governesses, perhaps a representation of the ideal governess of the second half of the twentieth century, is Miss Anne Ross. She is not very far from the 'gracious image' that Charlotte Mason described some sixty years earlier but she is more human; she is not at all like the severe and melancholy figure described by St Jerome fifteen centuries before that, but she is a worthy product of 1600 years of governess evolution.

Anne Ross is attractive and active, and it is a surprise to discover that she is retired; she does not look nearly old enough for that. She lives in a small village near Salisbury, surrounded by mementoes of her career, and tending her immaculate terraced garden, with its productive fruit trees, vegetable patch and weedless flower borders. When asked how she came to be a governess, she thinks back to her education as a day girl at the Godolphin & Latymer school in London in the 1930s, just before the Second World War.

> The school wanted me to go on to university, but I said no. The war was obviously coming, and I thought, if I don't get a job now, before it comes,

I shall have spent all my life in institutions. I shall never have experienced 'life before the War'.

She persuaded the school to let her do a Froebel teaching course before she left, testing her teaching on their pre-prep pupils. Then she applied to an employment agency in London. She was given a job as a governess in Chesham.

Compared with friends who were working as secretaries I didn't earn much. But it was much more interesting, and I enjoyed the 'perks' of living in a family.

A year later she was called up, and joined the WAF, doing meteorology, which she greatly enjoyed.

As soon as the war was over and it was again permitted, she advertised in *The Lady* and went for an interview in a large house where she was to be governess to a small boy. 'The mother told me that other members of the household normally referred to him as "His little lordship",' she says, smiling, 'So I decided against that one.'

The job she took was with the Waldegrave family who lived in the Mendip hills near Bath. Almost all her career thereafter was with the same large family, teaching children of the next generation after the first lot married. She went away once to teach in South Africa for two years, but returned to teach the youngest Waldegrave. After five years she left again, to spend eighteen months working as secretary and general dogsbody to her aunt, Mrs Topham, at Aintree racecourse. 'But I missed my pupils, and left. She was very cross with me.'

One of her pupils of the second generation recalls meeting her for the first time:

My mother took me to the station. And there she was, wearing a hat, and she looked very solemn, very serious. In fact I thought she looked formidable. But she started smiling, and her gentleness came over at once. She really knew how to talk to children.

Anne Ross moved with members of the Waldegrave family between Somerset and the Hebrides, imparting her knowledge of wild flowers and of the names of shells on the seashore, loving it all as much as they loved her. She became an indispensable member of their extended household, and even when she was employed elsewhere she would always come willingly in the holidays to help in emergencies, house-keeping and nursing and once even cooking. 'I knew nothing at all about cooking. I had to telephone my mother for advice.' She is remembered as being 'totally adaptable, always mucking in. I have a memory of her mending every sheet in the house on a hand sewing machine.'

But essentially she was a teacher, and proved her ability by coping with up to ten or twelve children at a time, with ages ranging from eleven down to four years. They all called her 'Bo' or 'Val', not Miss Ross, but the friendly names belie the respect which they still show when speaking of her. She had a natural gift for teaching. One of her pupils of the first generation said 'I hate Sunday.' Asked why, he said it was because there were no lessons that day. Another child, years later, dreaded Monday, the governess's day off: 'What on earth are we going to *do*?'

Lessons with Val were fun, there was no doubt.

> She was not an academic, but she conveyed the pleasure of learning – she made it a hugely enjoyable process. Started off like that, you have it for life.

She also taught the essentials of civilised behaviour: You didn't tell tales, you were kind to people smaller or weaker than yourself, you were polite, considerate, honest. 'She taught it all without lecturing.' When a mother replied to a child who moaned 'It's not fair' with the words, 'Well, the world isn't fair,' Val riposted, 'Of course the world isn't fair, but we must try to make it as fair as we can.'

One pupil, who claims to have been a difficult child, remembers with gratitude the consistency of Miss Ross's approach:

> She was always *there*. And she was always firm. She was never angry, and she never raised her voice. She compelled discipline without apparent effort, not by punishing, but by saying, 'If you don't do this, you won't get that.' She always stuck to what she had said, and never broke her own rules. You knew where you were with her, you knew what the limits were. And you always had her unfailing affection, however irritating you were being. I would have ended up in an approved school, but for Val.

Another said, 'She held our family together.'

When all the children had finally gone to school, and there was no further need for a governess, Miss Ross felt that she did not want to start again with another family. She worked for four years in a preparatory school, 'teaching everything to five and six years olds'. In 1976 she retired, to live with her mother in their pleasant Wiltshire bungalow.

Miss Ross's feelings about her career are summed up in her own words:

I would never regret having been a governess. I really thoroughly enjoyed it. But I wouldn't say governessing was inevitably a happy occupation; it depends on who your employers are. I was fortunate in having employers who appreciated me, as I was not highly qualified in any way. And I was lucky in that both generations of the family were passionately interested in their children; it is important that parents and governess should work together as a team.

The children were intelligent, and she had no difficulty in motivating them.

I have great respect for teachers in schools, especially inner city schools, having to cope with the problems of keeping enthusiasm up. A governess doesn't have this trouble. It is a very great privilege to teach as a governess.

When asked how she feels about the lack of a private life of her own, she says that it would be very difficult to have a successful marriage and a successful career as a governess. She has no regrets that she took the governess option.

I was both stimulated and cosily looked after. I blame myself, really, that I didn't keep up a fund of friends outside my working life. It was laziness on my part. I took my social life from the social life of the family, and got pleasure from their friends.

Now, apart from one or two old school friends with whom she is still in touch, she feels that her social life is rather restricted. 'But that is my own fault. And it is just part of the job.'

She continues to see the family she was with for so many years. In talking to her, it is tempting to compare her to a popular unmarried aunt, though she would deny the simile. She is invited to Waldegrave family occasions – weddings, christenings, anniversaries – but wouldn't expect them to be continually dropping in, any more than she would her own nieces. 'They are all grown-up; they have their own lives, and I have mine.'[4]

What made Miss Ross such a successful governess may have been this independence of spirit. It was demonstrated after she retired when she informed everyone who knew her that from now on she would no longer be Bo, or Val, but wished to be called by her first name of Anne.

Perhaps it was that, after being with us all for so long, she needed to re-assert her own personality with a different name.

Hilda Payne shares Anne Ross's satisfaction in her choice of profession, and in the way she has led her life. Miss Payne was engaged to be married once, after she became a governess.

> But I felt I could not leave the children. It was my vocation; it was part of me. I know it was sometimes detrimental to me to become so fond of them, because it meant that I had very little private life. But I would never let the children down; I felt an even stronger loyalty to them than to the parents.

How would she advise a young woman now, considering a similar career?

> I would say it was a life full of pitfalls, and you have to take trouble vetting the people you are going to. You must do it tactfully, but the right kind of people will not object. After all, you are giving a piece of your life to them.

When a profession goes into decline, because the public no longer needs its services, though its members disappear from the public eye they do not actually vanish. There are retired governesses all over Britain, some in their own private accommodation, a few housed by the families they once taught, some in retirement homes run by charities.

The Governesses' Benevolent Institution, faced with the decline in numbers of governesses, expanded its scope and modified its name in 1952 to include the word Schoolmistresses, so becoming the SGBI. It still maintains its founders' aims in providing, for aged and infirm governesses and now also to other women connected with the teaching profession, free annuities, grants for relief of temporary need and help in obtaining accommodation.

Judicious selling of outdated property and re-investment in modern buildings has been a recurrent feature of the history of the Institution. Its offices are now at Chislehurst, in Kent, where the twelve cottages of the 1870s were replaced in 1967 by a purpose-built home of pleasant bed-sitting rooms and small flats. It is called Queen Mary House, for royal interest has been continuous; Queen Elizabeth, the Queen Mother became patron of the SGBI in 1936. There is enough ground surrounding the building to give wide areas of mown grass and space for the large trees that shield it from the road. The residents' flower gardens, carefully tended and each different in plan and planting, make a glowing strip of colour in front of a long southfacing wall. In an Activities Room in the grounds, adapted from a redundant garage, residents have facilities for dress-making, pottery or protecting their indoor plants in winter.

All the governesses on the SGBI books, wherever in Britain they are living, are considered to be members of the SGBI 'family'. This word is used with intent, and emphasizes the family attributes of independence against a background of security that the members enjoy. All members of the 'family', whether living in their own accommodation or in other 'Homes', are visited at regular intervals by 'the Visitor', one of the Chislehurst staff, who travels long distances to keep this contact alive and to see at first hand that no hardship is being endured unnecessarily. There are at present forty-four members of the SGBI 'family', two of whom live abroad, who have been governesses for a part or all of their working lives.

The Board of the SGBI are very eager to discover cases of need in retired governesses. All with whom the Institution can get in touch are made aware that in time of need there is assistance available in their own home, or 'a home for life' at Chislehurst should they ever want it. The only requirement is that on arrival they should still be physically able to cope for themselves. Should they become incapacitated later, there is a nursing section in a wing of the Queen Mary House: they will never have to leave the heart of 'the family'.

There is no sense of stagnation at the Chislehurst home; residents mix freely in the local community, coming and going as they wish; activities at home include recently introduced music appreciation classes, which are open also to friends in the neighbourhood. As I sat in the dining room at lunchtime, I was struck by the noise and liveliness of the conversation, which is not usual in a home for elderly people. It came as a surprise to hear that the youngest resident is seventy- seven and that one upright and active lady was about to celebrate her hundredth birthday. She was only one of three members of the 'family' who were born in 1890.

· 19 ·

Miss Weeton lives on

A great injustice is being done to the image of the governess: she is
being recreated in fiction in a totally unrealistic form. She is such
an unknown figure now, the reality of her existence so far removed from
daily life, that authors feel free to use her and change her to make her fit
the character they need for a book.

Since 1960, four books have been published entitled *The Governess*;
they are all fiction. One is in the Mills & Boon mould, set in the present
time. A young holiday governess meets her romantic destiny before the
end of the second chapter, though there will be some steamy scenes
before that destiny is fulfilled. In the second book, the governess is
deliberately engaged by an aristocratic employer with a sexual role,
indeed a child-bearing role, in mind, and she performs this role to the
satisfaction of at least some of the other characters; it is 'period' story,
and it would be interesting if it were true. The third is an intriguing
mid-twentieth century tale in which the governess dispenses her
favours, sexual and otherwise, in a novel attempt to keep together a
family whose unity appears to have been fragmented only by her
presence. The last is a gentle who-dun-it tale, set in the 1870s, and is an
excellent depiction of the life of a Victorian household; despite having
to play the unusual role of a murder suspect, the heroine is a good
portrayal of a governess of that time.

The first three stories have in common the attempt to exploit the
apparently sexually titillating effect of the prim, tight-laced, repressed

image conjured up by the word 'governess'. It has been done before. The possiblities were first explored in *Jane Eyre*, but it seems that they are limitless. If the reality of the British governess were nearer to fiction, mine would be a different book, and perhaps more fun to read. No doubt there are some good, sexy, true governess stories, but no-one I interviewed for this book has volunteered any. An element of lesbianism has been suggested once or twice, but nothing that would imply a great underswell of frustrated women who chose the private home in which either to develop or to repress their sexuality.

There is a danger that fiction may overlay reality, and that the true image of the governess will get lost. This has changed very little through the centuries: she has always been a hard-worked, under-paid, seldom appreciated person; very rarely academically qualified for her job, but often a good teacher; undemanding, but aware of her exploitation by others; remembered sometimes with pain sometimes with affection, and nowadays with a sense of nostalgia for the past.

The past, it seems, is where the governess belongs in most people's minds. The GBI no longer saw the need to continue acting as an employment agency for governesses after 1961, and Gabbitas and Thring say that demand for 'real' governesses dropped away in the 1970s. But there is still some call on agencies for governesses to go abroad, to work in diplomatic households and in the families of actors or musicians who are travelling; and in Britain they are still wanted for tutoring, holiday work, or for 'cramming' to get children through exams. However the problem that Ruskin identified still exists: a male tutor is treated with the respect accorded to a visitor and a professional; a governess, even if she is only in a post for a few weeks, still has to guard against the exploitation that has always gone with the job. Though employed only to teach, she finds that she is expected to help about the house. For this reason, women offering themselves for holiday coaching are scarce, and they tend not to describe themselves as governesses; they prefer to be called tutors.

The real governess, the woman who acts as companion and teacher to girls in the private home for years at a time, what of her? There is an irony in the fact that, after so many painful years, just when the British governess (*vide* Miss Payne, Miss Coward, Miss Ross and others) has found how to make herself appreciated and how to carve out a worthwhile life from the potential of governessing; just when the British private family has learnt to value the privilege of this form of education, and to treat its exponents with the respect they deserve; when the SGBI provides a true safety net for the elderly; just when all this is happily settled, the whole business has become an anachronism.

Yet it is still legal for children in Britain to be educated by a person without formal teacher training. It is the responsibility of the local education authority to make sure that children educated at home are being properly taught, whether by their parents or anyone else, but they are rarely called upon now to inspect a private schoolroom. Women teachers wanting permanent posts prefer teaching in a school environment, in the independent or in the public sector. Indeed, if a woman wishes to take a position as a resident or daily governess now, in a family home, she will not find one easily. She is met by a unanimously unfavourable reaction from British women who were educated by governesses themselves, and who might be considered potential employers; this is despite the fact that they almost all seem to feel themselves to have been exceptionally privileged in having this kind of education, and they are willing to express it:

> What could be better than having lessons all morning and running free all afternoon? No team games, no crocodile walks, no ghastly school-girl crushes on the sports' mistress.

> I had one exceptionally intelligent and able woman concentrating on just me and one cousin for four years – no wonder I was well educated.

> I think I can say that I never had a moment of real unhappiness all through my learning years; I was never teased, never bullied.

> That governess started me off on a lifelong love and appreciation, not only of English poetry but of French and German as well. This I feel I would never have had if I had gone to school.

> My governess was very critical; when she put 'excellent' on something, one's life was made. When it was 'fair', or 'poor' one really minded.

> I didn't like my governess, but, my goodness, she taught me well.

The reason why governess schooling is no longer a viable option becomes apparent, however, when these women are asked why they did not, or would not, educate their own daughters in the same way. The financial aspect is not mentioned; sharing a governess between families could still compare very favourably with girls' public school fees. The reasons are more various:

> You miss so much by not going to school; we had no organised games, no companionship, a very, very narrow life.

I completely missed out on any sort of science.

It took me some years, after my governess education, to discover that grown-ups were fallible. I had to get rid of my unnatural respect for authority. You learn that at school, and it is a much better preparation for life.

It led to one of the worst experiences of my childhood, sitting the School Certificate exam at the local grammar school. I was made to sit apart from the other children, because I didn't belong there, and I was stared at.

It took me years to learn how to talk to people of my own age. And I was terribly innocent.

For years after, when I was asked where I went to school, I just used to say 'abroad'. I was too embarrassed to admit that I had never been.

I used to pretend to people that I had been ill as a child, which was why I had a governess.

The trouble with not being exposed to other people of your own age is that you don't learn to be laughed at.

One thing is very difficult if you have never been to school: you don't know where you stand, whether you are stupid, whether you are clever; you don't know anything about your abilities; you have nothing to compare yourself with. It is a great drawback. And you mind, when you are older, when you don't win at games, or if you don't succeed at things. You don't know how to cope with it, because you haven't gone through all that at school.

I just don't think you could get away with it now . . .

An elderly, retired governess, when asked much the same question replied, rather sadly,

People get rid of their children now; they send them to school – it's less trouble; they just don't want to be bothered.

So, the reader may say, the *real* governess no longer exists – the real, old-fashioned governess?

The reader would be wrong. She does exist. She is alive and well and living in Gloucestershire. Her name is Maureen Cunliffe, and at the moment she is resting between posts. Listening to her talk, it would seem that little has changed in the governess's life since the beginning of the nineteenth century. Just as Nellie Weeton, ill-used by her relations, set out to earn her living in 1809 with no qualifications but an ability to teach, so did Maureen Cunliffe in the 1980s. If she had wished to travel she might have found an agreeable post; but she wished to stay in England and, like Nellie, she needed a home as well as a job. She found that in order to have both, she had to put up with the modern equivalent of Victorian conditions of service. In fact, her whole story bears a striking similarity to that of the governess who wrote those poignant letters and diaries nearly two centuries ago.

Maureen Cunliffe was born in Lancashire in 1934 into a middle-class family, and has one elder brother. Her mother worked as a secretary. Her father worked with an insurance company. When Maureen was young he dominated the household with his strong personality. 'He was a very difficult, self-centred man.'

She was educated at a Roman Catholic convent school; although it was a day school she was miserably unhappy there and cried every night at home.

> The nuns themselves were all Reverend Mothers, many of them from titled backgrounds. They were not sisters. The sisters were the ancillary ones, the ones who did all the laundry and the polishing of the floors. They were old fashioned, and a lot of it rubbed off on me.

She left in 1952, with five O-levels, having spent only one year in sixth form. She had studied English, language and literature, biology, scripture, French, art and needlework. 'The strongest girls went on to Oxford or Cambridge – the nuns did not believe in any other universities – and the weakest went to teacher training college.' But Maureen went straight to the Royal College of Music, for she had developed her one great talent, and she was an excellent pianist. After she had gained diplomas in teaching and performance, and the initials ARCM and GRSM, she left, and moved with her family down to Devon. Based at home, she taught English, music and general subjects for ten years, becoming Head of Music in three different schools, both state and independent. She was much in demand as an accompanist.

At twenty-nine she married, and had two sons.

It was a dutiful marriage. I had worked faithfully for my parents, living at home, and now I devoted myself to being a most loving wife and a good mother. It was not long before I discovered that my husband was a man whose character was very like my father's.

They travelled, following her husband's work, to Singapore, and to Cyprus, and then Maureen Cunliffe came back to England by herself to look after their sons while they went through school.

My husband is not known for his generosity. He was working for a long time in Saudi Arabia, earning a large, tax-free salary. But he only sent home enough money for one person to live on; and I had to feed three of us. I felt that he was using my expertise in financial management to protect his savings. He would not allow me any access to them.

Her sons eventually left school and started their own independent lives. Her husband came home, and her mother died. Maureen's now very elderly and difficult father came to live with them. He had torn up his wife's will and, in order to find out what was in it, she was obliged to ask the family lawyer for a copy, from which she found that all her mother's money had been left to her. It was not a huge amount, but for the first time in her life she could afford to take a holiday.

She took her two sons to Lanzerote, and on their return they persuaded her to stay on in London for a while – 'for a breathing space'. She dreaded going home, where 'the atmosphere had become very difficult'. With her sons' encouragement she decided to stay away and find a job to keep herself going. The only position for which she felt she had any qualifications was that of a governess. Now she came up against the problem that 'no agency wants to take you on their books as a governess unless you are a qualified teacher. Experience and ability to teach is not enough.'

Advertising in *The Lady*, Maureen Cunliffe had only three replies, all addressed to 'Dear Nanny'. One was from America, one from a Contessa in Italy, and one from a Convent school in Greece. To all of them she sent photographs and photocopies of her references and certificates, which her younger son had obtained for her from home. 'It was quite expensive, with the postage as well. But only the nuns bothered even to reply.'

Eventually she managed to persuade an employment agency to help her. She was exhaustively vetted, and then offered an interview with the family of a rich Arab diplomat. She had asked for £150 a week, considerably less than the £200 to £250 that a governess would normally expect, but in the end was grateful for the £100 a week she was offered, all living expenses to be paid by her employer.

At the interview she was told that she would care for and teach four girls, but when she arrived in the very sumptuous two-level flat off the Edgware Road to take up her post she found that there were after all five, aged respectively fifteen, thirteen, eleven, seven and four years.

As the governess Maureen Cunliffe lived on the upper floor and never in all her time there visited the family quarters on the floor below. She rose at six every day and was considered to be on duty until ten o'clock at night. Each morning, in term-time, she had to take the four elder girls by taxi to their Iraqi school in North London; after leaving them she came home again by bus. The procedure was reversed in the afternoon.

Between these two expeditions she was in charge of the youngest child. She attempted to follow the Montessori system of 'Learning by playing' with the little girl.

> But the mother was jealous; she seemed to resent her daughter enjoying herself with me, I felt, and she made it quite clear that she didn't trust me at all. She was often quite vindictive.

During the holidays, Maureen's duties were to teach all the girls English, taking them in turn one after the other all day long. She had to care for them indoors and chaperone them out of doors, teaching them at their parents' request 'manners and decorum'.

She found it impossible to establish a normal working relationship with the mother, and describes her as 'quiet and cunning, wearing a great deal of colourful clothing and jewellery, with rings on every finger; she used to drape herself all over the place like a beautiful meringue.' The mother and the governess must have contrasted strangely, the one so exotic in appearance, the other neat and trim, in the simple dark clothes that she felt suitable for her position. 'And I always wore white gloves when we went out.'

All orders in the home were given by the husband. He treated the governess with great politeness, always calling her 'Madam', which is what the governess called his wife. He appeared, however, not to have understood the terms of her employment, and she had the greatest difficulty in persuading him to allow her the agreed half day off each week. She liked to take this on a Sunday, when she would meet her sons and go with them to the Brompton Oratory; the frequent rather noisy parties on the floor below made it hard for her to wake after a sleepless night and get to the Oratory on time. She had to press very hard indeed to get the occasional week-end off, and it was only allowed with extreme reluctance.

The two great problems, always, were to do with money and with the overwork. I had to fight and argue each week to get my wages – almost to bargain for them, and he would only give them to me with a great show of unwillingness. I always had extra bills to claim for as well, that I had paid out of my own pocket, because the women of the family never carried any money. This was for things like the two taxis that took us all to Harrods. The mother and the elder girls went in the first one, and I came in the second one with the youngest, and I had to pay both drivers. But I would only be refunded for these fares after much argument and in an atmosphere of deep suspicion. I found it very difficult. For some reason I was expected to provide my own coffee and lavatory paper, too, but all the family used them.

The teaching and the chaperoning work she did not mind, though the elder girl was disobedient and the youngest very spoilt. What she found exhausting were the extras. She was continually carrying heavy crates of bottles of mineral water and groceries, when deliveries were made each week to the block of flats. It made her nervous to be sent out on errands late at night, usually to buy newspapers or huge orders from Macdonald's. She carried enormous loads of laundry to and from the local launderette, sometimes washing five machine-loads at a time. 'People used to see me there so often, tending the machines, that they thought I was the manageress!' She had to deal with the household and personal washing of the whole family and iron it all when she took it home.

Unlike Nellie Weeton or Charlotte Brontë she was not expected to mend the family's clothes: this was, after all, the twentieth century. From her own life experience she had brought more modern skills than stitching; she often sat in the evening surrounded by the component parts of transistor radios or the vacuum cleaner, repairing them as best she could.

She did not make any objection to all this.

I am accustomed to it, as my own family has used me all my life, I suppose. I am old-fashioned, and naturally submissive. In any case, it is not easy to refuse to do things when you are living in a family.

But slowly the feeling of being in total servitude got her down, and she felt her freedom threatened.

The father once kept my driving licence for several days, and I had difficulty in getting it back. They talked of taking me on holiday with them to Kuwait, but I wondered what might happen if I let him have my passport.

Her employer used to keep the front door key in his room; to get out on her Sunday mornings off she had to send a child to him to ask for it. It made her uncomfortable to feel so locked in at night.

'I wondered what would happen if there were a fire. You can't tie duvets together to escape out of the windows!'

It was not a 'culture clash' that made her leave; she accepted that her employers lived in a different way than she had been used to, and she was willing to adapt.

I had become very fond of the children, but I was being exploited. It was rather clever, really. If you bring an intelligent, educated woman into your home, she will have the ability to do more than the things you engaged her for, more than is written on paper. I discovered that I was running the family, while the mother . . . well . . . They were not using me just as a governess, which in itself is a full time job. I was a chauffeuse and laundry-maid and general dogsbody as well. *What they wanted was three people for the price of one . . .*

There is no date on this complaint. It has been the cry of governesses as long as there have been governesses to cry.

Notes

Introduction
Elfgifu and after

1 Quoted Dorothy Gardiner, *English Girlhood at School*, 1929, pp 6, 8
2 Mrs Jameson, Essay 'On the Relative Social Position of Mothers and Governesses', from *Memoirs and Essays*, 1846, p252
3 Gardiner, p22
4 Josephine Kamm, *Hope Deferred, Girls' education in English History*, 1965, p9
5 Gardiner, p23
6 Ibid., p24
7 Mary Cathcart Borer, *Willingly to School, A history of women's education*, 1976, p23
8 Alice Zimmern, *The Renaissance of Girls' Education*, 1898, p3
9 Gardiner, p4
10 Ibid., p31
11 Borer, p34
12 Kamm, p16
13 Ibid., pp24, 25
14 Nicholas Orme, *English Schools in the Middle Ages*, 1983, pp 52, 53
15 Borer, p35
16 Gardiner, p63

17 Bea Howe, *A Galaxy of Governesses*, 1954, p18
18 Kamm, pp17–18
19 Gardiner, p99 and *Encyclopaedia Britannica*, 1911 edn.
20 Kamm, p25
21 Gardiner, p99
22 Mrs Irene Taylor, housekeeper at Mrs Fife's in the 1930s, to author, June 1989

Chapter 1
'Without any cherishing'

1 Paston Letters, No 65
2 From *Early Chancery Proceedings*, ii, pp167, 188, quoted Gardiner, pp119, 120
3 Paston Letters, No 256
4 Zimmern, p5
5 Ibid., p5
6 Foster Watson, *Vives and the Renascence of Education for Women'*, 1912, pp182, 183, quoted Gardiner, p165
7 Ibid., quoted Kamm p36
8 Harold Nicolson, *Good Behaviour*, 1955, pp148–149, 153–154
9 W. H. G. Armytage *Four Hundred Years of English Education*, 1964, p6

10 *State Trials*, Vol 1 p736, quoted
Gardiner, p176
11 Kamm, p37
12 Anne Chambers, *Eleanor, Countess
of Desmond*, 1986, p25
13 Gardiner, pp181, 182
14 Ibid., pp186, 191
15 Ibid., p193

Chapter 2
'Kiss me and be quiet'

1 Fanshawe, *The Memoirs of Lady
Fanshawe*, (1676), 1907 edn. p22
2 Gardiner, p258
3 Antonia Fraser, *The Weaker Vessel*,
Methuen edn., 1985, p151
4 C. V. Wedgewood, *The Trial of
Charles I*, p101
5 Quoted Gardiner, p235
6 Quoted Kamm, p56
7 Gardiner, p211
8 Hannah Woolley, *The
Gentlewoman's Companion*, (1675)
quoted Borer, p109
9 Woolley, quoted Gardiner, pp218,
219
10 Woolley, quoted Kamm, p59
11 Borer, pp100, 101
12 Quoted Kamm, p74
13 Gardiner, p224
14 Lady Masham's *Occasional thoughts,
in reference to a vertuous or Christian
Life*, (1795) quoted Gardiner, p381
15 Lady Mary Wortley Montagu, *The
Letters and Works of Lady Mary
Wortley Montagu*, ed. Lord
Wharncliffe, 1877, pp4–5, &
pp235–245
16 Ibid., p511

Chapter 3
'The custom of knowing nothing'

1 *Lord Hervey's Memoirs* ed.
Sidgewick, 1952, pp498, 745–748
2 Jean de la Bruyère, *Caractères, Des
Femmes*, (1688) Firmin-Didot edn.
1879, p160
3 *St Simon at Versailles*, tr. and ed. by
Lucy Norton, 1980 edn. p239
4 Gardiner, p270
5 Kamm, p117
6 Ibid., p118
7 Ibid., p121
8 Maria Edgeworth, 'Female
Accomplishments' in *Essays on
Practical Education*, (1798) 1822 edn.,
Vol 2, pp387, 388
9 Kamm, p113
10 Gardiner, p353
11 Kamm, p114
12 William Law, *A Serious Call to a
Devout and Holy Life*, (1728),
Chapter XIX, p348
13 Jean-Jaques Rousseau, *Emile, ou
De l'Education*, (1762), Vol 1V,
pp44–50
14 Gardiner, p460
15 Frances Power Cobbe, *Life, as told
by herself by Herself*, (1894), pp58–60
16 Charlotte Papandiek, *Court and
Private Life in the Time of Queen
Charlotte*, (1886) Vol 1, pp47–96

Chapter 4
'This phrenzy of accomplishments'

1 Edgeworth, pp370–421
2 Quoted Gardiner, p370
3 Quoted Gardiner, p394
4 Mary Wollstonecraft, *A Vindication
of the Rights of Woman*, 1792, pp38–
84
5 Mary Somerville, *The Personal
Recollections of Mary Somerville*, 1873,
p22–25
6 Papandiek, Vol 1, p113
7 Hannah More, *Strictures on the
Modern System of Female Education*,
(1799), pp66, 69, 100–105

8 *Female Tuition, An Address to Mothers on the Education of Daughters*, Anon, (1785) quoted Gardiner p353
9 Armytage, p131
10 Somerville, p22
11 Alice Thornton, *The Autobiography of Mrs Alice Thornton*, 1875 edn. p10
12 Wollstonecraft, *Vindication*, p378
13 More, quoted Gardiner p357
14 Papandiek, Vol 1, pp111, 112, 116
15 Edgeworth, p390
16 Somerville, p41

Chapter 5
Lessons with the governess

1 Jane Austen, *Pride and Prejudice*, (1813) Chap 49
2 Ibid., Chap 22
3 Ibid., Chap 51
4 Janet Dunbar, *The Early Victorian Woman*, 1953, p74
5 Quoted Kamm, p142
6 E. Lynn Linton, *The Girl of the Period and other essays*, (1883) Vol 2, p103
7 Mrs Ellis, *The Daughters of England*, (1845), Chap 3 pp69–70
8 From *The Leader* (1850) quoted Dunbar, p131
9 Quoted Borer, p200
10 Questions quoted in *The English Miss, today and yesterday*, Percival, Alicia C., (1939), pp106–108
11 Felicia Lamb and Helen Pickthorn *Locked up Daughters*, (1968), p29
12 Agatha Christie, *Agatha Christie, an autobiography*, 1977
13 The Revd. Dr Ebenezer Brewer, *My first Book of History* (1864), quoted P.H.J.H. Gosden, *How they were taught*, (1969), pp51, 52
14 Gosden, p521
15 Mrs Markham, *A History of England*, (1823) 1875 edn., p198

16 Gosden, p117

Chapter 6
The market place

1 Jameson, *On the Relative Social Position of Mothers and Governesses*, in *Memoirs and Essays*, (1846), pp253–255
2 Ibid., p295, 296
3 Ibid., p255
4 Papandiek, Vol 1, p105
5 Sarah Trimmer, *Some Account of the Life and Writings of Mrs Trimmer*, (1814), Vol 1 pp198–201
6 Bea Howe, *A Galaxy of Governesses*, 1954, p59
7 Papandiek, *Journals*, Vol 1, p106
8 Dinah Maria Craik, *A Woman's thoughts about Women*, (1858) pp5–6, 41–64
9 Barry Turner, *Equality for Some, The Story of Girls' Education*, 1974, pp76–7

Chapter 7
'The dullest life ever dragged on by mortal. . .'

1 Mary Wollstonecraft, *Thoughts on the Education of Daughters*, (1787), Cadell 2nd edn.
2 Ellen Weeton, *Miss Weeton – Journal of a governess*, 1807- 1811, ed. Edward Hall, 1936
3 Jameson, p271, 272
4 Mrs Fresson to author, April 1990, and from *Anne Brontë at Blake Hall* by Susan Brooke, Brontë Society Transactions 1958, Vol 13, part 68, pp239–250
5 Margaret Lane, *The Brontë Story*, 1953, pp122, 123

Chapter 8
'The despotism of fashion'

1 Cobbe, p60
2 From *Report of Royal Commission on Secondary Education* Vol VI, 1895, quoted by Gosden, p160
3 Cobbe, p58
4 Ibid., pp62, 64–65
5 *Royal Commission Report*, 1895, quoted by Gosden, pp158, 162
6 Cobbe, p63
7 *Report of the Schools Enquiry Commission* Vol. 1X, 1868, quoted by Gosden, pp154–163
8 Betty Askwith, *The Lyttletons, A Family Chronicle of the Nineteenth Century*, 1975
9 M. J. McManus, 'Shaw's Irish Boyhood' in *G.B.S. 90, Aspects of Bernard Shaw's Life and Work*, ed. S. Winsten, 1946, p37
10 Margaret Lane, *The Tale of Beatrix Potter*, 1946, p32
11 Kamm, p170

Chapter 9
Charity begins in hostels

1 Kamm, p173
2 Orme, p55
3 Askwith
4 Louisa, Lady Antrim, *Some Children in the Sixties* in 'Little Innocents', ed. Alan Pryce-Jones, 1932, p81
5 Margaret Lane, *The Brontë Story*, 1953, pp122
6 Quoted Kamm, p133
7 Lady Frances Balfour, *Lady Victoria Campbell*, 1910, pp33–40
8 Gosden, p164
9 Cecil Woodham Smith, *Florence Nightingale*, 1950, pp110, 117–124
10 Patricia Clarke, *The Governesses,*

Letters from the Colonies 1862-1882, Introduction, p1–2, 4
11 John Burnett, *A History of the Cost of Living*, Pelican, 1969

Chapter 10
Fighting for respect

1 William Makepeace Thackeray, *The book of Snobs*, 1846, pp88–91
2 Borer, p263
3 Turner, p68
4 Gerardine MacPherson, *Memoirs of the Life of Anna Jameson*, (1878) pp37–38, 155
5 Balfour, pp33–40
6 Frances, Lady Fergusson of Kilkerran, to author, 1980
7 John Ruskin, *Sesame and Lilies*, (1871)
8 Jameson, pp276–277
9 Ibid., pp281–283, 290–296
10 Edgeworth, 'Female Accomplishments' in *Essays on Practical Education*, (1822), Vol 2, pp412–414

Chapter 11
The Lady joins the fray

1 Emily Davies, *Thoughts on some Questions relating to Women, 1860–1908*, (1910), pp11, 12, 15–18

Chapter 12
'I'll deal with you later'

1 Winifred Gerin, *Charlotte Brontë The Evolution of a Genius*, 1967, p12
2 Princess Stephanie of Belgium, *I was to be Empress*, 1937, pp55–59
3 Antrim, *Little Innocents*, ed. Pryce Jones, p81.
4 Kenneth Rose, *Curzon, A Most Superior Person*, (1969), p20

5 Letter in possession of Viscount
Scarsdale
6 Askwith, pp98–100

Chapter 13
The governess in war and peace

1 Baroness Elliot of Harewood to
author, June 21 1989, and from *In
a lifetime full . . .* by Peggy
Wakehurst, 1989
2 Lady Alexandra Metcalfe to
author, June 1989, and from
chapter by Baroness Ravensdale
in *Little Innocents*, ed. Pryce-Jones,
pp27–28
3 Agatha Christie
4 Alice Baird, ed.' *I was there'*,
*Reminiscences of St James', West
Malvern*, 1956
5 Lady Heald to author, June 1989
6 Lady Mary Clive, *Brought up and
Brought out*, 1938, pp23, 72– 75.
7 The Dowager Viscountess
Hambledon to author, March 1990
8 Mrs Scrope Egerton to author,
March 1990
9 Miss Hilda Payne to author,
March 1990

Chapter 14
The sweetbread eaters

1 Miss A. Bulley, & Miss M.
Whitley, *Women's Work*, 1894, p8
2 Burnett, p301
3 Juliette Huxley, *Leaves of the Tulip
Tree*, 1986, pp30, 31
4 Mr Kenneth Rose to author, July
1989
5 Jonathan Gathorne-Hardy, *The
Rise and Fall of the British Nanny*
(1972), Arrow edn., pp194–196

Chapter 15
The gracious vision

1 Mrs Virginia Barrington and Mrs
Penelope Loveday to author,
March 1990
2 Mrs Timothy Raisin to author,
March 1990
3 Jessica Mitford *Hons and Rebels*
1960, pp16–18
4 Diana Mosley, *A Life of Contrasts*,
(1977) 1984 edn. pp29, 30
5 Christian Miller, *A childhood in
Scotland* 1981, pp36–37, pp88–89
6 Mr Cecil Gould to author,
November 1989
7 Lady Daphne Straight to author,
November 1989

Chapter 16
**Miss Paraman becomes Mrs
Hobble-Gobble**

1 The Hon. Lady Adams and the
Hon. Mrs Dundas to author,
November 1989
2 Mrs Scrope Egerton to author,
March 1990
3 Lady Stormonth-Darling to
author, November 1989
4 Mr Raymond Johnstone to author,
January 1990
5 Lady Robert Crichton-Stuart to
author, August 1989
6 Miss E. Coward to author, March
1990

Chapter 17
The post-war schoolroom

1 The Hon. Mrs Susan Baring to
author, December 1989
2 Miss Hilda Payne to author,
March 1990
3 The Hon. Mrs Harries to author,
December 1989

Chapter 18
Miss Weeton lives on

1 Miss Hilda Payne to author,
March 1990
2 The Hon. Mrs Talbot to author,
April 1990

3 Miss Charlotte Mitchell to author,
1989
4 Miss Anne Ross to author, April
1990

Bibliography

ARMYTAGE, W. H. G., *Four Hundred Years of English Education*, C.U.P., 1964

ASHLEY, Maurice, *England in the 17th century*, Penguin, 1952

ASKWITH, Betty, *The Lyttletons, a Family Chronicle*, Chatto & Windus, 1975

ASTELL, Mary (Mrs Drake), *An Essay in Defence of the Female Sex*, Anon 1697

AUSTEN, Jane, *Pride and Prejudice*, 1813

BAIRD, Alice, *I was there – Reminiscences by girls and teachers of St James', West Malvern*, Littlebury & Co, Ltd, The Worcester Press, 1956

BALFOUR, Lady Frances, *Lady Victoria Campbell, a Memoir*, Hodder & Stoughton, 1910

BARNARD, H. C., *Girls at School under the Ancien Régime*, 3 Lectures delivered at the University of London, Burns and Oates, 1954

BEATTIE, J. W., *The Story of the Governesses' Benevolent Institution*, Private Circulation, 1962

BELL, Quentin. *Virginia Woolf*, Hogarth Press, 1972

BORER, Mary Cathcart, *Willingly to School, A history of women's education*, Lutterworth Press, 1976

BULLEY, Miss A. & WHITLEY, Miss M., *Women's work*, 1894

BURNETT, J., *A History of the Cost of Living*, Penguin, 1969

BURNEY, Fanny, *Diaries*, 1842

CHAMBERS, Anne, *Eleanor, Countess of Desmond, 1545–1638*, Wolfhound Press, 1986

CHOLMONDELEY, Mrs Essex, *The Story of Charlotte Mason*, J. M. Dent, 1960

CHRISTIE, Agatha, *Agatha Christie, an Autobiography*, Collins, 1977

CLARKE, Patricia, *The Governesses, Letters from the Colonies, 1862–1882*, Hutchinson, 1985

CLIVE, Lady Mary, *Brought up and Brought out*, Cobden Sanderson, 1938

COBBE, Frances Power, *Life – as told by herself*, 1894

CRAIK, Dinah Maria, *A Woman's thoughts about Women*, 1858

CRESPIGNY, Mrs Philip Champion de, *The Mind of a Woman*, Edward Arnold, 1922

CURTIS, S. J. and BOULTWOOD, M. E., *An Introductory History of English Education since 1800*, University Tutorial Press, 1970 Edition

DAVIES, Emily, *Thoughts on some Questions relating to Women, 1860–1898*, Bowes & Bowes, 1910

DICTIONARY OF NATIONAL BIOGRAPHY, edition of 1909

DUNBAR, Janet, *The early Victorian Woman, Some Aspects of Her Life*, George G. Harrap & Co. Ltd., 1953

EDGEWORTH, Maria. *Essays on Practical Education. 1798. The Parent's Assistant*, 1796–1800

ELLIS, Mrs, *The Daughters of England*, Fisher & Son, 1845

ENCYCLOPAEDIA BRITANNICA, edition of 1911

FANSHAWE, Anne, Lady, *The Memoirs of Anne, Lady Fanshawe*, John Lane, Bodley Head, 1907

FIELDING, Sarah, *The Governess or The Little Female Academy*, 1749

FITZGERALD, Brian, *Daniel Defoe*, Secker & Warburg, 1954

FOSTER, Watson, *Vives and the Renascence of Education for Women*, Arnold, 1912

FRASER, Antonia, *The Weaker Vessel* Weidenfeld & Nicolson, 1984

GARDINER, Dorothy, *English Girlhood at School, A study of women's education through twelve centuries*, OUP, 1929

GATHORNE-HARDY, Jonathan, *The Rise and Fall of the British Nanny.* Hodder & Stoughton, 1972

GERIN, Winifred, *Charlotte Brontë, The Evolution of Genius*, OUP, 1967

GIBBS, Lewis, *The Admirable Lady Mary*, J. M. Dent, 1949

GOSDEN, P. H. J. H., *How they were taught*, Blackwell, 1969

HERVEY, Lord, *Lord Hervey's Memoirs*, ed. Romney Sedgewick, William Kimber, 1952

HOULBROOKE, Ralph, (ed.) *English Family Life, 1576–1716.* An anthology from diaries, Blackwell, 1988

HOWE, Bea, *A Galaxy of Governesses*, Derek Verschoyle, 1954

HUXLEY, Juliette, *Leaves of the Tulip Tree*, John Murray, 1986

JAMESON, Mrs Anna, *Memoirs and Essays illustrative of Art, Literature and Social Morals*, 1846, (Essay No VI on the Relative Social Position of Mothers and Governesses)

KAMM, Josephine, *Hope Deferred, Girl's education in English History*, Methuen, 1965. *Indicative Past, 100 Years of the Girl's Public Day School Trust*, Allen and Unwin, 1971

LA BRUYERE, Jean de, *Caractères*, Des Femmes, 1688

LANE, Margaret, *The Tale of Beatrix Potter, a Biography*, Frederick Warner & Co. 1946. *The Brontë Story*, Heinemann, 1953

LANGLAND, Elizabeth, *Anne Brontë, The Other One*, Macmillan, 1989

LAMB, Felicia and PICKTHORN, Helen, *Locked up Daughters*, Hodder and Stoughton, 1968

LAW, William, *A Serious Call to a Devout and Holy life*, 1728

LINTON, E. Lynn, *The Girl of the Period and other essays*, 1883

MACPHERSON, Gerardine, *Memoirs of the Life of Anna Jameson*, 1878

MARKHAM, Mrs (PENROSE), *A History of England*, 1823, John Murray, 1857 edition

MARTINEAU, Harriet, *Biographical Sketches*, 1869

MILLER, Christian, *A Childhood in Scotland*, John Murray, 1981

MITFORD, Jessica, *Hons and Rebels*, Gollancz, 1960

MITFORD, Nancy, *The Sun King*, Hamish Hamilton, 1966

MONTAGU, Lady Mary W., *The Letters and Works of Lady Mary Wortley Montagu*, edited by Lord Wharncliffe, 1887

MORE, Hannah, *Strictures on the Modern System of Female Education,* 1799

MOSLEY, Diana, *A Life of Contrasts,* Hamish Hamilton, 1977

NICOLSON, Harold, *Good Behaviour,* Constable, 1955

NORTON, Lucy, *Saint-Simon at Versailles,* Hamish Hamilton, 1958

ORME, Nicholas, *English Schools in the Middle Ages,* Methuen, 1983

PAPANDIEK, Charlotte, *Court and Private Life in the Time of Queen Charlotte,* ed. 1886 by Mrs Vernon Delves Broughton

PASTON LETTERS, J. M. Dent, 1924

PERCIVAL, Alicia C., *The English Miss, today and yesterday,* Harrap, 1939

PETERS, Margot, *Unquiet Soul, A Biography of Charlotte Brontë,* Hodder & Stoughton, 1975

PRYCE-JONES, Alan, (ed.) *Little Innocents (a collection of essays about Childhood),* Cobden Sanderson, 1932

REANEY, Mrs G. S., *English Girls, their Place and Power,* Kegan Paul, 1879

ROUSSEAU, Jean-Jaques, *Emile, ou De l'Education,* 1762

ROSE, Kenneth, *Curzon, A Most Superior Person,* Weidenfeld & Nicolson, 1969

RUSK, Robert R., *The Doctrines of the Great Educators,* Macmillan, 1969, (4th Edn.)

RUSKIN, John, *Sesame and Lilies,* (Lecture at Manchester Town Hall, 1864) 1871

SEWELL, Mrs, *Mother's Last Words,* 1860

SIDGEWICK, Mrs Alfred, *The Grasshoppers,* Hodder and Stoughton, 1913

SINCLAIR, Catherine, *Modern Accomplishments,* 1836

SOMERVILLE, Mary, *The personal recollections of Mary Somerville,* 1873

STEPHANIE, Princess, of Belgium, *I was to be Empress,* Ivor Nicholson & Watson, 1937

THACKERAY, William Makepeace, *Book of Snobs,* 1846–7

THORNTON, Alice, *The Autobiography of Mrs Alice Thornton,* Surtees Society, 1875

TRIMMER, Mrs Sarah, *Some Account of the Life and Writings of Mrs Trimmer,* 1814

TURNER, Barry, *Equality for Some – The Story of Girls' Education,* Ward Lock Educational, 1974

WAKEHURST, Peggy, *In a lifetime full . . .* Biography, Privately printed, 1989

WATERSON, Merlin, *The Country House Remembered,* Routledge & Kegan Paul, 1985

WEDGEWOOD, C. V., *The Trial of Charles I,* Collins, 1964

WEETON, Ellen, *Miss Weeton – Journal of a Governess,* edited by Edward Hall, OUP, 1936

WINNIFRITH, Tom, *A New Life of Charlotte Brontë,* Macmillan, 1988

WINSTEN, S., (ed.) *G.B.S. 90. Aspects of Bernard Shaw's life and work,* Hutchinson, 1946

WOLLSTONECRAFT, Mary, *Thoughts on the Education of Daughters.* 1787. *A Vindication of the Rights of Woman,* 1792

WOMEN'S INSTITUTE: Mrs Phillips, *A Dictionary of Employments open to Women,* 1898

WOODHAM-SMITH, Cecil, *Florence Nightingale,* Constable, 1950

ZIMMERN, Alice, *The Renaissance of Girls' Education,* 1898

Index

Index by Christine Shuttleworth